Fishing for Men

*A Practical and Biblical Guide to
Sharing the Gospel with Others
and Winning them to Christ*

Richard A. Seymour

Integrity Press
LaGrange, Wyoming 82221
www.ClarityMinistries.org

Unless otherwise indicated, all Scripture quotations are from the Bible, New King James Version. Copyright 1979, 1980, 1982 by Thomas Nelson, Inc. Publishers, and are used by permission

Beginning with chapter five, quotes or short accounts of actual incidents are placed *in italics* before chapters or sections of the book. Names of individuals and occasional specifics are changed in some accounts, 1) to respect the concerns and wishes of those involved, 2) because the incident recorded represents a number of similar experiences and so I simply chose a name as representative of the many, or 3) because I simply could not remember the names of the individuals, though the incidents recorded were real and actually happened.

ISBN 0-9760620-0-3

Cover Design/Photography and Book Layout by Scott Keenum
DesigNet Advertising & Marketing, LLC, Southaven, MS 38672

Printed in the United States of America
Integrity Press, Post Office Box 10, LaGrange, WY 82221
www.ClarityMinistries.org

Dedicated to the One to Whom I owe everything,
my Savior, the Lord Jesus Christ

and

To my Kathy,
accomplished homemaker and home school teacher,
wonderful mother and sweetheart,
and most importantly,
an incredibly godly woman.
With all my love and gratitude
for making our lives so rich.

My Heartfelt Appreciation

I was influenced *early* in my Christian walk to make "fishing for men" and faithfulness to the Gospel major priorities. I have been touched by some of the most effective, faithful, and zealous ambassadors for Christ this world has ever known. In many cases their influence upon my life has been through their writings, long after they had gone to Heaven. In other instances it has been my privilege to have learned firsthand from some whom God has used greatly to win others to Himself. Whether it was the clarity of their message, their knowledge, or their zeal and devotion, I've gained so much from each of them.

These men have been pastors, missionaries, educators, authors, editors, founders of great ministries and movements, thinkers, philosophers, evangelists, business and professional men, Bible teachers, musicians, and radio personalities, but they all have had one thing in common: they are or were actively involved as witnesses for Christ and His Gospel. Though some failed noticeably at times, yet for the most part and to the man, they have been practitioners in the art of sharing the Gospel, discipling other believers, and teaching sound doctrine. I thank the God of our "so great salvation" for these who have been highly effective in their witness for the Lord Jesus Christ.

Sir Robert Anderson	George Muller
Lewis Sperry Chafer	William R. Newell
Percy Crawford	J. Irwin Overholtzer
M. R. DeHaan	William Pettingill
Charles E. Fuller	John R. Rice
Arno C. Gaebelein	Harry Rimmer
Jonathan Goforth	Charles C. Ryrie
Barney Holland	C. I. Scofield
John "Praying" Hyde	Charles Spurgeon
Harry A. Ironside	A. Ray Stanford
William Kelly	J. F. Strombeck
Lance Latham	J. Hudson Taylor
Martin Luther	R. A. Torrey
J. Vernon McGee	Dawson Trotman
J. Gresham Machen	Henry Clay Trumbull
C. H. McIntosh	C. Sumner Wemp
George Miles	Benjamin B. Warfield
D. L. Moody	Walter L. Wilson

May the Lord of the harvest raise up a new army of clear witnesses of the Gospel of God's grace in our needy generation.

IF

IF to be a Christian is worthwhile, then the most ordinary interest in those with whom we come in contact should prompt us to speak to them of Christ.

IF the New Testament be true—and we know that it is—who has given us the right to place the responsibility for soulwinning on other shoulders than our own?

IF they who reject Christ are in danger, is it not strange that we, who are so sympathetic when the difficulties are physical or temporal, should apparently be so devoid of interest as to allow our friends and neighbors and kindred to come into our lives and pass out again without a word of invitation to accept Christ, to say nothing of sounding a note of warning because of their peril?

IF today is the day of salvation, if tomorrow may never come and if life is equally uncertain, how can we eat, drink and be merry when those who live with us, work with us, walk with us and love us are unprepared for eternity because they are unprepared for time?

IF Jesus called His disciples to be fishers of men, who gave us the right to be satisfied with making fishing tackle or pointing the way to the fishing banks instead of going ourselves to cast out the net until it be filled?

IF Jesus Himself went seeking the lost, if Paul the Apostle was in agony because of his kinsmen, according to the flesh, who knew not Christ, why should we not consider it worthwhile to go out after the lost until they are found?

IF I am to stand at the Judgment Seat of Christ to render an account for the deeds done in the body, what shall I say to Him if my children are missing, if my friends are not saved or if my employer or employee should miss the way because I have been faithless?

IF I wish to be approved at the last, then let me remember that no intellectual superiority, no eloquence in preaching, no absorption in business, no shrinking temperament or no spirit of timidity can take the place of or be an excuse for my not making an honest, sincere, prayerful effort to win others to Christ.

J. Wilbur Chapman

CONTENTS

My Heartfelt Appreciation
IF by J. Wilbur Chapman

THE GOSPEL PRIORITY

THE GOSPEL MESSAGE

THE GOSPEL PRESENTATION

THE GOSPEL MESSENGER

THE

GOSPEL

PRIORITY

Every follower of Jesus
should make fishing
for men and winning
others to the Lord
the business of life;
the thought of the
Saviour's words is
that fishing for men
is not to be an
incident of life but
the business of life,
that for which we live
and which we are
constantly carrying on.

R. A. Torrey

1

A Lifelong, Life-Changing Resolve

*And He said to them, Follow Me, and I will
make you fishers of men.*
Jesus speaking to His disciples in Matthew 4:19

To be the "fisher of men" the Lord wants you to be demands
no small commitment. It is a serious matter to devote one's life
to the task of winning others to Christ, but it is what God expects
each of His children to do.

When I speak of devoting your life "to the task of winning
others to Christ" I am not thinking in terms of your becoming
what is commonly called a "full time Christian worker," a
Christian professional. I am referring to a heart attitude that
recognizes the primary reason God leaves His children on earth is
to bear witness of Christ and His Gospel, to be ambassadors for
Christ. It is the attitude of Mr. Armour of Armour Meats. When
asked what he did for a living I understand his reply was, *"I'm a
full time witness for Jesus Christ and I pack pork on the side to
pay my expenses!"* That is fishing for men in the Bible's sense
of the word. That is putting the eternal welfare of others before
our own agendas.

To put it a little differently, Biblically speaking a missionary
is not one who goes some place to preach the Gospel; a
missionary is one who preaches the Gospel *as* he goes some
place. By this definition all believers in Christ should be
missionaries.

I will have much more to say about this later on but for now
I want to share some testimonies of believers who are now in

Heaven with the Lord. Let their words speak to your own heart and ask yourself: **"Do I think they are happy *now* with the choices they made *then* to devote themselves to spreading the Gospel?"**

William McCarrell

Pastor, prominent in many Christian organizations

Fishing for men keeps you fresh, fragrant, and fruitful. . . When run down, fish for men. It will refresh you. To do personal soul-winning gives pulpit conviction, fire and effectiveness. . .You will dry up personally if you leave personal evangelism out of your life, even though you may draw crowds and be popular. Personal soul-winning makes truth felt-truth. It solves practically every church problem—giving, missions, attendance, spirituality. You will find new possibilities in yourself if you win souls.

Jonathan Goforth

Missionary to China

The following is recorded concerning the influence of the book, The Memoirs of Robert Murray M'Cheyne, *upon Jonathan Goforth. The thrilling story of M'Cheyne's spiritual struggles and victories, and his life-sacrifices for the salvation of God's chosen people, the Jews, sank deep into his very soul. All the petty, selfish ambitions in which he had indulged vanished forever, and in their place came the solemn and definite resolve to give his life to the ministry, which to him meant the sacred, holy calling of leading unsaved souls to his Savior.*

Henry Clay Trumbull

Sunday School missionary, Civil War chaplain, author of thirty-eight books, editor of *The Sunday School Times.*

I determined that as I loved Christ, and as Christ loved souls, I would press Christ on the individual soul, so that none who were in the proper sphere of my individual responsibility or influence should lack the opportunity of meeting the question whether or not they would individually trust and follow Christ. The resolve I made was, that whenever I was in such intimacy with a soul as to be justified in choosing my subject of conversation, the theme of themes should have prominence between us, so that I might learn his need and, if possible, meet it. That decision has largely shaped my Christian life-work in the half-century that has followed its making.

Dwight L. Moody
Sunday School worker, leader of the YMCA, pastor, educator, evangelist

While in England in 1867 Moody heard these words: "*The world has yet to see what God will do with and for and through and in and by the man who is fully and wholly consecrated to Him.*" Moody determined to be such a man!

Twenty five years later (1892) when asked by Peter Bilhorn, a Christian musician, what was the secret of his power, Moody replied: *I made a promise to God and it is the rule of my life that I would speak to at least one man every day about his soul's salvation.*

Will H. Houghton
Pastor, song writer, evangelistic song leader, educator
Dr. Houghton wrote this song in honor of D. L. Moody

Lead me to some soul today,
O teach me, Lord, just what to say;
Friends of mine are lost in sin,
And cannot find their way.
Few there are who seem to care,
And few there are who pray;
Melt my heart and fill my life,
Give me one soul today

William Booth
Founder and first General of the Salvation Army

He inscribed the following in the autograph album of King Edward VII, King of England, June 24, 1904:

Your Majesty,
Some men's ambition is art,
Some men's ambition is fame,
Some men's ambition is gold,
My ambition is the souls of men.

R. A. Torrey
Pastor, educator, city mission worker, evangelist, author

I would rather win souls than be the greatest king or emperor on earth; I would rather win souls than be the greatest general that ever commanded an army; I would rather win souls than be the greatest poet, or novelist, or literary man who ever walked the earth. My one ambition in life is to win as many as possible. Oh, it is the only thing worth doing, to save souls, and men and women, we can all do it.

L. R. Scarborough
Pastor, denominational leader, educator

If I have any power, it is in this: there is never an hour, day or night, but that I can close my eyes and weep over a lost world.

William Evans
Bible teacher, educator, author

Souls, souls, souls! I yearn for souls. This is the cry of the Savior—and to save souls He died upon the cross, and remains until eternity their intercessor.

Souls, souls, souls! This is the cry of Satan—and to obtain them he scatters gold to tempt them, multiplies their wants and pleasures, and gives them praise that only infatuates.

Souls, souls, souls! This must be our one cry and passion, Christian worker; and for the sake of one soul we must be willing to spend and be spent.

Charles M. Alexander
Evangelistic song leader and choir director

Be a soulwinner if you are never anything else. You will find very few who want to shine in winning souls all the time.

It was said of Charlie Alexander that he never urged others to do what he was neglecting himself, and everywhere he went he left the impression that he wished to introduce everyone to Christ.

Paul, the Apostle

Missionary, faithful witness for Christ, human instrument God used to record half of the books of the New Testament:

For though I am free from all men, I have made myself a servant to all, that I might win the more. I have become things to all men, that I might by all means save some. Now this I do for the gospel's sake. . . (First Corinthians 9:19, 22, 23).

Give no offense, either to the Jews or to the Greeks or to the church of God, just as I also please (adapt myself to) *all men in all things, not seeking my own profit, but the profit of many that they may be saved. Imitate me, just as I also imitate Christ* (First Corinthians 10:32-11:1).

I tell the truth in Christ, I am not lying, my conscience also bearing me witness in the Holy Spirit, that I have a great sorrow and continual grief in my heart. For I could wish that I myself were accursed from Christ for my brethren, my kinsmen according to the flesh (Romans 9:1-3).

Brethren, my heart's desire and prayer to God for Israel is that they may be saved (Romans 10:1).

For what is our hope, or joy, or crown of rejoicing? Is it not even you in the presence of our Lord Jesus Christ at His coming? For you (the ones he had led to Christ) *are our glory and joy* (First Thessalonians 2:19, 20).

For I am not ashamed of the gospel of Christ, for it is the power of God to salvation for everyone who believes, for the Jew first and also for the Greek (Romans 1:16).

But none of these things move me; nor do I count my life dear to myself, so that I may finish my race with joy, and the ministry which I have received from the Lord Jesus, to testify to the Gospel of the grace of God (Acts 20:24).

But I want you to know, brethren, that the things which happened to me have actually turned out for the furtherance of the Gospel (Philippians 1:12).

Only let your conduct be worthy of the Gospel of Christ, so that whether I come and see you or am absent, I may hear of your affairs, that you stand fast in one spirit, with one mind striving together for the faith of the Gospel (Philippians 1:27).

For Personal Reflection and Application

❖ How important do you think personal witnessing is to the Christian life? How does it compare in importance to other Christian virtues such as prayer? Studying God's Word? Moral purity? Personal holiness?

❖ If Christians *as a whole* are to see to it that the Gospel is spread throughout the whole world, may an *individual* believer be rightly considered a "fisher of men" whose primary ministry or responsibilities are not in direct aggressive evangelism, such as, mothers of small children, those who give or pray sacrificially toward reaching the world with the Gospel, the very elderly or bedridden?

❖ If one claims to be a fisherman but *never* does anything to help in catching fish, is he a fisherman? If you claim to be following Him but you never attempt to reach anyone or to influence anyone to come to Christ, are you really following Christ as the Bible describes?

❖ How important do you feel personal witnessing ought to be to *you*? How important *is* it in reality?

❖ If other Christians are only as faithful as you are in sharing the Gospel or sending it to others, would Christianity be growing, stagnating, or be dying?

❖ Will you resolve—without any reservations—to become the "fisher of men" God wants you to be, no matter what the cost?

❖ What steps can you take now to become a better, more faithful, and effective witness for Christ?

Jesus Christ is the only
One worthy of my
unconditional surrender
and allegiance, and His
purpose for me is the
only purpose worth
pouring my entire
life into.

RAS

2

My Own Spiritual Journey

My earliest memories of a religious nature consists of attending a small church in my home town of Washington, D. C. I had a couple of aunts who were fairly active in the denomination with which we were affiliated, and my Mom was pretty faithful in attending and taking the kids. This was back in the 1940s—the generation that lived in and through the Second World War.

I did the usual churchy things: attended services, participated in Vacation Bible school, and enjoyed some of the special events, like when Santa would appear at our Christmas party and have presents for all the children.

I recall responding to the "altar calls" from time to time although it was very difficult for me to do anything publicly. You see, I was born with a double harelip and cleft palate, and so my physical appearance and my severe speech impediment made me very self-conscious. I did not like crowds at all and I was extremely fearful of having to do anything in front of others. In school, for instance, the most dreaded experience I ever had to endure was the yearly ritual called the *oral* book report. It was always a heart-wrenching experience for me.

Similarly, urgent pleas of the pastor or evangelist to "come forward" to make public whatever type of decision they were advocating at the time, was nearly an impossible thing for me to respond to. However, there were times when I would work up enough courage to make the short trip to the altar. To my young, fearful mind that "short trip" sometimes seemed miles long.

A Teenage Drifter

As far back as I could remember (until I entered junior high school) we always lived at the same address: 104 Southeast 13

Street, between Ostrow's Delicatessen on the one side and People's Drug Store on the other. But soon after I graduated from Bryan Elementary School we moved to the Anacostia area across the Anacostia River. That fall I entered Kramer Junior High School. Church attendance had begun to be more sporadic than previously, and the move sort of cemented my pattern of nonattendance at church.

As a young teenager I began to drift, not just spiritually but in other ways as well. I was having a lot of reconstructive surgery during those years and it seemed I was constantly in Sibley Hospital undergoing surgery, or recuperating at home, healing and building up my blood, so that I could turn right around and go back into the hospital for more surgery. It was not an especially fun time in my life. Looking back, I'm certain I had no conception (nor did anyone else) of what emotional upheavals were occurring within me. What I experienced and felt back then is much clearer to me now.

The only times I recall ever praying was before each operation (*Lord, get me through the next two to four hours. Get me through safely.*), and when my Father was near death (*Lord, please don't let Daddy die!*). Other than those occurrences, I was a pretty godless young man; not especially wicked, mind you, but godless nevertheless. Mom would always say I was a "good" boy and that I never gave her "a moment's trouble." But mothers are not around all the time, nor can they read a child's mind.

I became very bitter and angry inside. I wouldn't have admitted it then, but I know now that I blamed God for my condition, and for the necessity of having so many operations, and for the meanness of people. I often thought about death and dying, and suicide. There were times I did not want to live another day. During my junior high days, I made three feeble attempts at ending my own life; that's how miserable I was deep inside. I did not like myself. I thought I was ugly and deformed, and I hated the fact that I had to repeat myself so often and it was embarrassing to have to write down what I wanted to communicate to others.

The only times I darkened the door of a church while in high school was either for an occasional visit with friends, a family wedding, or to attend a funeral. Church just didn't interest me. It wasn't relevant to anything I was interested in, and when I did attend, boredom was the only feeling I recall.

My Plans

My course selection for my senior year in high school was called Diversified Training. This was a special innovative (for that time) arrangement whereby those who were not intending to go on to college, and who wanted to get a jump start on a career, could elect to attend classes daily until noon; then, from 1-5 p.m., we worked a regular job as part of the requirements for graduation. I, along with my friend Gene, became an employee at the same bank. It was our intention to become career bankers.

Upon my graduation, my parents moved to Miami, Florida, and I lived with my grandparents for that first year of full time employment. This was the plan all along: that I would spend that first post-graduation year in my current job, learning the ropes, attending night classes sponsored by the American Banking Association, and then join my parents in Miami where I could latch onto a job there and begin my banking career in earnest.

God Had Other Plans

After that initial year at the Bank of Maryland, my sister Mary and her husband, Ted, drove me to my parents' house in Miami. We arrived on the last Saturday of May, 1953. After all the greetings and hugs, my Mother let me know that there was a "nice little church" a few blocks away that she just "knew" I would enjoy, and she urged me to go with her the next day. I wasn't interested, but for her sake I agreed to attend the evening youth meeting, if they had one. And did they ever have one!

I was expecting a small handful of other social rejects (like me) to be present, but I was in for the surprise of my life. I arrived for the meeting about five minutes early and to my amazement I walked into a room that was full with wall-to-wall teenagers and young college students. It was "standing room only." There must have been eighty or more there that night. A few teenagers greeted me; one even offered me his seat, which I refused, preferring to stand near the door just in case I wanted to get out fast.

There was life in that group! And as the meeting progressed, there was lively, energetic, and joyful singing; a couple of kids made some announcements concerning upcoming events, and then they had "Testimony Time." Little did I realize that the move to Florida, the visit to this youth group, and the next few weeks following that meeting, would be THE pivotal time of my entire life.

As the meeting moved forward I discerned one common thread as these teens shared their testimonies. Every one of them made it clear that, though they were unworthy, and though they were by no means perfect, yet they knew they had eternal life and were certain of going to Heaven when they died.

I first thought they were terribly mixed up and confused, or on a gigantic ego trip. "After all," I thought, "no one can be certain now that they will go to Heaven then. You have to wait until you die and stand before this big awesome God. At that time, and not until that time, He would let you know whether or not you were good enough to be allowed in." That was my first impression of what I was hearing and it turned me off to what they were saying.

However, the more I listened, the more it began to sink into my thick skull that they weren't saying anything about their own goodness. Instead, they were emphasizing God's goodness and grace in sending His Son, the Lord Jesus Christ, to pay the complete penalty for all of our sins on the Cross. And in explaining the Gospel—for that's what they were doing, using the vehicle of their own personal testimonies—they further emphasized that the salvation that Christ had paid for and that God offered to us, was His love gift, received only through faith in Christ, and not at all as the result of any good works or efforts on our part. Such a wonderful message was brand new to me.

Receiving Christ

I certainly did not understand or comprehend it all, but what a revelation it was to my blinded heart! I had a lot of questions, especially those of the *what if* and *you mean to tell me* variety, but I had heard enough that I wanted to hang around. Besides they treated me as just one of the gang. They didn't make me feel that I was different in any way. They persuaded me to stay for the evening service and even got me into the youth choir that night—

singing in front of people. Miracle of miracles!

But the real miracle came the third Sunday evening when I decided I would "walk the aisle" and get saved. I don't recall anything about the pastor's sermon that night, but when the invitation song began ("Just As I Am") down the aisle I went. The pastor greeted me, shaking my hand and asking, "Dick, are you coming forward to receive Christ as your Savior?" Answer: Yes. "And do you wish to follow Him in water baptism and become a member of the church?" Answer: Yes. "And do you plan to live for Him?" Answer: Yes. "Then have a seat here on the front pew and I'll pray with you in just a moment."

No one else responded that night so Pastor Bill had me stand, facing the congregation, and the good folks came by one-by-one, shaking my hand, congratulating me, rejoicing with me, thanking God for my "decision," and letting me know they would be praying for me. Once that "welcome line" had passed, I walked up the aisle to where the pastor and youth director were standing near the front door. Each greeted me warmly, said they would be praying for me, and wished me a "good night."

I walked home that night just as lost as when I had arrived at the church earlier in the evening. No one had opened their Bible and shown me how to be saved, how to be certain of having eternal life, how to know I was completely forgiven and Heaven-bound. I was like a slippery fish ready to slide right back into my ocean of uncertainty. But God was working.

Later that night, as I tossed and turned on my bed, the pastor's question kept running through my mind: "Dick, are you coming forward to receive Christ as your Savior?" I had answered yes, but I knew I hadn't received anything. So, after what seemed like a long struggle, I slipped out of bed, got on my knees, and prayed, "Lord, if all of this is true—that You love me just as I am and that Christ died for me, then the best I know how, I trust in Him right now as my Savior."

I waited for a feeling. It didn't come. I knew I should feel something. I was told from childhood that if I ever got "genuinely converted" I would know it by feeling the presence of God. My burdens would be lifted. Everything would become brand new. I'd be thrilled and excited.

At first I felt nothing. After a few moments I finally did feel something—disappointment. I thought, "It didn't take. I should have known better. It's never worked before; I should have known it wouldn't work this time either." I got back into bed, disgusted with myself for being duped once again, and went straight to sleep.

I hadn't found employment yet, so the following morning after my parents had gone to work, I got my mother's Bible and began reading it as I ate a bowl of cereal. I read the Bible all day long, almost nonstop. Before I laid it down that Monday evening I had discovered this verse: *"Believe on the Lord Jesus Christ and thou shalt be saved"* (Acts 16:31 KJV). I knew that was what I had done the night before so, I concluded, "I must be saved." It struck me that it didn't say anything about emotions or feelings. It just said to 'believe in Christ,' and I had done that. That was my first experience of taking God's Word at face value, and that's been the pattern of my walk with Him for over fifty years.

Surrendering to Christ's Lordship Over My Life

In July, a month after my conversion, I rode each evening with my pastor to revival services he was conducting in a "mission church" in the inner city. At the conclusion of the last meeting I made another momentous and life changing decision, and that was to turn my life over to Christ totally, to allow Him to take control of all of my life for all time, surrendering to His Lordship over me. Once I made that initial surrender (based on Romans 12:1, 2), I never looked back. I still worked in banks off and on, but never again did I live for banking or a career.

There have been times when I have gotten myself into trouble through wrong or stupid decisions; I've fallen flat on my face time after time. I've had my ups and downs, yes, and downright failures, but I've known since then that He is the only One worthy of my unconditional surrender and allegiance, that His purpose for me is the only purpose worth pouring my entire life into. From that evening on I have known experientially that "to live is Christ" (Philippians 1:21).

The Rank Amateur

Soon after I trusted Christ I began wanting to share the Gospel. I knew so little of the Bible at that time that I often had to refer to the Table of Contents when a speaker would say, "Turn in your Bibles to…" I would try to share what I knew of the Gospel but would often get bogged down in arguments and debates, or those I would witness to would have difficulty understanding me. Though I had most of my surgery behind me, I still had a speech impediment and it would be a while before I could carry on a running conversation with someone and be understood. I stumbled and fumbled my way through many witnessing situations. Most of these attempts to win others to Christ ended in frustration and failure.

I began to pray earnestly about reaching others. I longed for a true burden for souls like the apostle Paul described in Romans 9:1-3; 10:1. I longed for "fruit that remains" (John 15:16). I knew I needed to change my attitude from that of a debater to one who could tenderly lead others to Christ (Second Timothy 2:24-26). I grew painfully aware that my bitter spirit was driving others away from Christ rather than drawing them to Him. I begged God to give me a tender heart (Ephesians 4:29-32), and the change began to come—ever so gradually.

Learning to Share the Gospel

Becoming proficient in sharing the Gospel did not happen overnight, nor did that ability come to me as the result of memorizing some "canned" outline on how to share the Gospel (and I'm not against memorizing soul winning outlines). I am convinced that my own ability in sharing the Gospel is primarily the direct result of six things:

Exposure to a clear Biblically sound Gospel from the very beginning of my Christian life—having *grace* and *faith* and *gift* and *not of works* emphasized and clarified for me over and over again.

Memorizing Scripture—hundreds of them, especially those Bible verses relating to Christ's death and resurrection, salvation, and assurance. Power is in the Word itself, not necessarily in your explanation of the Word.

Having good strong examples. I was privileged to work with, to observe close-up, and to learn from some of the most gifted personal witnesses I've ever seen or known.

Reading, especially in the area of evangelism, including biographies of those men and women who devoted their lives to it: servants like R. A. Torrey, Dwight L. Moody, Dr. Walter L. Wilson, J. F. Strombeck, Harry A. Ironside, Lance Latham, M. R. DeHaan, John R. Rice, Jonathan Goforth, Sir Robert Anderson, J. Hudson Taylor, Henry Clay Trumbull, Charles E. Fuller, and the list goes on. Not that I fully agreed with all that I read, but I learned so much from these men of clarity, of zeal and fervency, of boldness, and of tact and patience in attempting to win the lost.

Prayer and reliance upon the Holy Spirit. My very first attempt at witnessing was to a black man sitting on a bus bench in Miami, Florida. I had prayed for days before going out "to find someone to witness to." You'd better believe I was depending on the Lord to lead me and to open up the way before me, and He did. That became my pattern for years: *pray* and *trust God's Spirit* to work through me.

I'm ashamed to say this very Biblical and God-honoring pattern was somewhat discarded once I became "good at what I did." By my senior year in Bible school fellow students were calling me "Mr. Soul Winner." Later, someone once introduced me to Peter "Dynamite" Deyneka as "the best personal witness for the Lord that I know." I was in my early twenties at the time and I'm afraid pride reared its ugly head and I fell into the same trap as King Uzziah, godly king of Judah who accomplished great things for God, but *"when he was strong his heart was lifted up, to his destruction... "* (Second Chronicles 26:1-16).

I learned that it is probably not a good practice to praise others too highly, especially when they are young. Unwise praise of others tends to turn their heads and hearts away from the Lord. Thankfully, my fate was not as severe as that of King Uzziah who became "a leper until the day of his death" (v. 21).

I've come to my senses in this matter, but it is vitally important to *"keep* (my) *heart with all diligence, for out of it spring the issues of life"* (Proverbs 4:23). Anyone of us is capable of falling, or leaving our First Love, of gradually, imperceptibly replacing praying with "saying prayers," and of relying upon our own experience, abilities and/or knowledge instead of trusting in the power and wisdom of the blessed Holy Spirit within us.

Doing it. There is no substitute for actually witnessing to lost folks. No sermon, no course or seminar, no book (including this one), can make you a fruitful witness for the Lord. According to Scripture, you will reap to the degree that you sow (Second Corinthians 9:6; Galatians 6:7). There are no shortcuts; there is no way to bypass actual witnessing. Reading thrilling stories of others' exploits, or writing a paper on the subject won't accomplish it. You must do it! Not until you get out where the lost are and begin to fish will you catch anything.

The *doing* gives life to the theories and principles about witnessing that you learn. *Doing* is putting flesh on the bones of knowledge. *Doing* sharpens the mind, quickens the spirit, excites the heart, and firms up the will.

It isn't enough to know the Gospel "backwards and forwards" while not actually doing anything of a concrete nature to spread the Gospel "to all the world." We desperately need to take Jesus' words to heart when He said of Himself, *I must work the works of Him who sent Me while it is day; the night is coming when no one can work* (John 9:4). The world's "night" is also coming— very soon, I think. During earth's darkest hour the Church will be gone. What we do we must do quickly!

Make it your aim to put into practice what you learn. Perhaps in no other area is it more necessary to learn by doing than in sharing the Gospel with those who are lost.

For Personal Reflection

❖ Are there possibly some people in your life who are not especially attractive or popular—those whom you should be reaching out to? Why not write their names down and begin praying for them regularly, and ask God to use *you* in their lives.

❖ When you *do* have personal contact with someone with an obvious physical, mental or emotional problem (or when someone like this attends your meetings), what are some practical ways you can make them feel accepted? How could over doing a good thing actually be counter productive with people like this?

❖ Are you memorizing Scripture, reading biographies that challenge you in the area of evangelism, forcing yourself to get out of your comfort zone in order to "catch men alive?"

George Muller felt the
value of souls, and
he formed habits of
approaching others as to
matters of salvation,
even in public conveyances.
By a word of witness,
a tract, a humble example,
he sought constantly to lead
someone to Christ.

Arthur T. Pierson in
George Muller of Bristol

3

What is the Gospel?

Moreover, brethren, I declare to you the gospel which I preached to you,...For I delivered to you first of all that which I also received: that Christ died for our sins according to the Scriptures, and that He was buried, and that He rose again the third day according to the Scriptures (First Corinthians 15:1,3-4).

Here is your first assignment. In the spaces provided below write the answer to the following question. Do not quote any Bible verses and do not consult anyone else's opinion. Answer the question in your own words based on your own knowledge. Here's the question: ***What are the things I must do to guarantee that I will eventually end up in Heaven?*** *After* you've written your answer, continue reading. Do not change anything about your answer as you read further. Keep it as a record of where you started in your understanding of the Gospel and compare it to what follows in the remaining pages and chapters.

My Answer to the Above Question:

_____

_____

_____

_____

What elements were contained in your answer? Faith? Good works? Faith and works? Turning from certain sins or habits? Observing church rituals, ordinances, or traditions? Sincerity? Prayer? Kneeling at the altar? Other public demonstrations of faith? Total surrender? Perseverance? Did you conclude that there is only one condition you must fulfill in order to "eventually end up in Heaven?" Or are there two? Several? Many? Did you, perhaps, find yourself having to admit that you really don't know what you must do to go to Heaven? Maybe that's the very reason you are reading this book, to find the answer to this all important question.

I won't attempt an analysis of your answer at this point. We will move on and come back to your response toward the end of the book. Meanwhile, there is more than enough Scriptural information and insights provided throughout the book to lead you to your own conclusion as to the accuracy of your reply to the question.

Now, to the subject of the chapter: What is the Gospel? It is vitally important to know exactly what the Gospel is, and to know it in no uncertain terms, for only as you have a proper understanding of the Gospel will you be able to effectively explain it to others.

Good News for All

To begin with, the Greek word translated gospel in your English translation of the Bible means "good news." Remember that the next time you hear a sermon or read a gospel tract. Is what you hear or read good news? Consider especially, is it good news to those for whom it is intended—the unbeliever? If what the speaker or the literature is telling the unbeliever to do in order to be saved is not good news to the unsaved person, then whatever else the message may be, it is not THE Good News of Jesus Christ! For instance, telling a nonbeliever to give up all their sins, get baptized, join the church, keep the commandments, and live a consistent Christian life for the rest of his life, is decidedly not good news. It is, in fact, very bad news for the unregenerate, spiritually dead nonbeliever. It is impossible for any amount of good works proceeding from an unbeliever to be pleasing to God. He needs to be rescued, not whitewashed or reformed.

The Angel Verified that the Coming of
the Savior was Good News for Everyone

The Bible portrays God's salvation message as truly good news for the ones who need it most—the entire world of unbelievers—*everyone.*

There is the beautiful account of Jesus' birth found in Luke 2:1-20. The shepherds were out in the fields at night tending their flocks when an angel appeared and made this amazing announcement: *Do not be afraid, for behold, I bring you good tidings of great joy which will be to all people. For there is born to you this day in the city of David a Savior, who is Christ the Lord* (2:10-11). Notice, without using the word gospel, how the angel described the event of the Lord's coming: *good tidings of great joy.*

Notice further, this message of "good tidings of great joy" is for *all*—"which will be to *all* people." You see, since *gospel* means *good news,* then by its very nature it must be good news for the unregenerate, unsaved, ungodly nonbeliever. Keep that uppermost in your mind when you analyze your own presentation of the Gospel. Is the message you proclaim good news to the unbeliever? If it isn't, it cannot be the Gospel of which the Bible speaks. It may be close. It may have elements of the Gospel in it. It may say glowing things about Christ. But when it comes down to the essential question of what one must do to be saved, if the condition or conditions given is really bad news to the nonbeliever, then the Gospel of the Lord Jesus Christ has not been given.

What Christ Accomplished on the Cross
Verifies that the Gospel is Good News for All

Consider the Scripture's account of what Jesus accomplished when He died. Second Corinthians 5:19: *That is, that God was in Christ reconciling the world to Himself, not imputing* (charging) *their trespasses to them and has committed to us the word of reconciliation.* What a statement! And what a contrast to so much of what we hear preached today! Has the world been reconciled to God? It says so, doesn't it. Reconciliation means basically to do away with a difference, to remove the obstacle or barrier.

When you get your monthly bank statement you attempt to get the balance in your check register to agree with the balance shown on the bank's statement. If you are able to accomplish that sometimes tricky feat, you say, "I've reconciled my check register to my bank statement." What does that mean? Well, if there is a difference when you begin the process, and you discover what the difference is and make the necessary adjustments, you have eliminated the difference and you've done it properly. That's reconciliation.

God reconciled the world to Himself at Calvary some 2,000 years ago by charging the world's sins to Christ. It is, in the popular vernacular, a done deal! Jesus cried out from Calvary's cross, "It is finished!"— and it was and is. Why then, should any of us attempt to get the unbeliever to do impossible things regarding his sins when all that should have been done, and could have been done concerning them, has been done by God Himself in the person of His dear Son.

The Scripture with which I began this chapter states clearly that the Gospel includes the fact *"that Christ died for our sins according to the Scriptures... "* That's good news to be sure. The only One who could do something permanent about our sins did it! The payment has been made and it was complete. There is nothing that needs to be added to it. The unbeliever may place his faith in the Savior who paid his penalty in full and know that he will receive forgiveness, will immediately become the possessor of eternal life, and be born into God's family.

The Resurrection of Christ Verifies that the Gospel is Good News for All

Another integral part of the Gospel according to First Corinthians 15:1-4 is that Christ *"rose again the third day according to the Scriptures."* How does His resurrection demonstrate that God's saving message is truly good news? The remainder of this fifteenth chapter of First Corinthians discusses the saving value of Christ's literal resurrection from the dead in detail.

For instance, from the negative side:

If Christ is not risen, then our preaching is vain and your faith is also vain (empty)...*your faith is futile; you are still in your sins! Then also those who have fallen asleep in Christ have perished. If in this life only we have hope in Christ, we are of all men the most pitiable* (First Corinthians 15:14, 17-19).

But thank God there is a positive side to this:

But now Christ is risen from the dead, and has become the first fruits of those who have fallen asleep...We shall not all sleep, but we shall all be changed—in a moment, in the twinkling of an eye, at the last trumpet. For the trumpet will sound, and the dead will be raised incorruptible, and we shall be changed...The sting of death is sin,...But thanks be to God, who gives us the victory through our Lord Jesus Christ (vs.20, 51, 52, 56, 57).

Yes, Jesus died for our sins but it doesn't stop there. He also rose from the dead, conquering death for us, thus guaranteeing that those who place their faith in Him do not put their faith in a dead god, or idol, or religious zealot, but in the living Savior. He is the One who alone has paid the penalty for sin and returned from the dead on His own power, proving once and for all that He is all He ever claimed to be and He accomplished all the Father sent Him to accomplish. He did pay the penalty for our sins and His resurrection from the dead proves it beyond any question! There is no better "good news" than the fact that we can know God personally through our Savior who died for our sins according to the Scriptures and rose again!

God Meeting us Where We Are in Our Lost Condition Demonstrates that the Gospel is Good News for All

Romans 5:6, 8-10 states: *For when we were still without strength, in due time* (at the right time) *Christ died for the ungodly...God demonstrates His own love toward us, in that while we were still sinners, Christ died for us. Much more then, having now been justified* (declared righteous) *by His blood, we shall be saved from wrath through Him. For if when we were enemies we were reconciled to God through the death of His Son, much more having been reconciled, we shall be saved by His life.*

Notice these important components of the Gospel:

The Lord initiated everything—*Christ* died for us, *God* demonstrated *His* love toward us before we made any move toward Him—when we were without strength, while we were still sinners, and when we were His enemies.

Our salvation is totally dependent upon Christ, His character and work on our behalf: Christ *died* for the ungodly...Christ *died* for us...we shall be saved from wrath through *Him*...we shall be saved by *His* life! No wonder the Bible calls it the good news. It truly is.

Turning the Good News into Bad News

There are those, however, who preach or teach from the Bible and who call their messages the gospel, but who actually turn the good news into bad news. "How could it be," you might ask, "that an apparent messenger of God would proclaim something called the gospel that would, in fact, be bad news?" The answer to this can be quite involved but I'll illustrate how it can happen by sharing three incidents that occurred in my early Christian life which left indelible impressions on me.

The Deeper Life Speaker

When I was young in the Lord I attended a week-long series of meetings on the deeper Christian life. The meetings were held in my home church and the speaker was an internationally famous Bible teacher.

Each night, beginning with the Sunday meeting, he strongly emphasized that if Jesus Christ was not the absolute Lord and Master of all areas and details of our lives, then we were not truly saved. I knew this was wrong. I knew it from Scripture and I knew it from my own life. It was all I could do to not jump up in the middle of the messages to correct this brother but I was too shy back then to do such a thing and, besides, it would not have been the proper thing to do. Several of us, however, did ask him questions after the meetings, but he didn't budge on his position.

On Wednesday he spoke at the local Christian Businessmen's Committee luncheon. Some of us went to hear him. Imagine our surprise bordering on shock when, as he shared his personal testimony, he revealed that he trusted Christ as his Savior at a certain age but then lived more wickedly after that than he ever had before. Finally, nine years later he surrendered to the Lordship of Christ over his life.

As soon as the luncheon was over we spoke with him. The obvious question was, "How could you be saying all week long that there is no salvation apart from making Christ the Lord and Master of your life, and yet today you confided in us that such was not your own experience?" I'll never forget his reply. In a very loving but firm tone he replied something like this: "The most miserable years of my life were those nine years when I ran from God, though I knew He was my Savior. I don't want what I went through to be the experience of others. So now I insist on others making Christ Lord of their lives right up front. That way they won't know the heartache I knew as a rebellious son."

I don't question the man's sincerity for a moment, but did he—do *any* of us—have the right to change the message in order to guarantee that a newborn child of God won't live in rebellion or disobedience to God? Does adding demands for obedience to the Gospel guarantee that the one responding to such a message will not become disobedient or rebellious along the way? Isn't the Holy Spirit who indwells each believer at the moment of salvation, capable of dealing with His own? Dare we ask the unbeliever to do the impossible? Think about it.

In this example *the speaker's past experiences dictated the kind of "gospel" he would preach.* And that "gospel" was anything but good news to the unsaved natural man!

The Missionary Evangelist

A number of years ago a denominational paper contained an interview with one of their better known evangelists who had recently returned from India. Apparently many thousands had "made decisions" for Christ. The interviewer asked how the evangelist explained such phenomenal results in a country which is almost totally non Christian. The evangelist explained: "When I went to India I determined that I would make the gospel as difficult as I could. I would tell the people that if they wanted to become Christians it would mean giving up their idols, turning from their sin, getting baptized, joining the church, devoting themselves to prayer and the reading of God's Word with the intent of obeying it. In spite of this, thousands committed their lives to Christ."

Note carefully what this man said: "*I* determined to make the gospel....difficult...in spite of this..." I wondered then as I wonder now, how many of those thousands who "made decisions for Christ" really understood the Gospel and truly put their trust fully in Christ alone for salvation. Is the Gospel of God's grace a message that we can reshape any which way we choose to fit whatever mold we determine is appropriate at the time? If the Gospel of Christ is carefully described, defined, and delineated in Scripture then it is not a message to be tampered with, to be restructured, or to be dressed up or down depending on the audience or our whims. This speaker must have known that the Bible message of salvation was simple; otherwise there would have been no reason for him to "make it difficult."

In this case the missionary-evangelist *decided to present a difficult message to test the genuineness of those making decisions*; a test which is of man's concoction and which, therefore, has no true validity in determining the genuineness of anyone's salvation.

The Televangelist

A relative was coming to visit me and my parents in Florida. She was religious but not saved. Leaving her church, or even admitting there were any flaws in her church, was out of the question. As a believer in Christ of less than a year, I felt totally inadequate to witness to her, much less to win her to the Lord. But just prior to her arrival I was scanning the TV section of the paper which listed the programs coming up for the week. I noticed that a certain evangelist was going to be on one night while this relative was visiting, so I devised the following plan.

I thought if I could engage her in a certain board game which she thoroughly enjoyed playing, I could set up the board on the coffee table with me sitting on the floor with my back toward the television and her sitting on the couch facing the TV. I would turn on the television before we began our game, making sure it was tuned to the proper channel, so that when the televangelist's program came on it wouldn't appear as if I had set her up.

Everything seemed to work out beautifully. At the scheduled time the program came on. There was good music by the choir, special solos, a testimony or two, and finally the speaker. He gave a pretty good salvation message—*until* he came to his invitation. My heart sank as he explained what the listeners would have to do if they wanted to be saved. He said, "First, you have to repent, which means to turn from your sins. You must quit your sinning. In fact, you cannot come to Christ with your sins. Then, you must receive Jesus Christ as your Savior and Lord, and finally you must confess Him publicly before the world."

I was crushed, angry, and terribly disappointed. I knew I had received Christ alone at my bedside some months before. The sin question was not even on my mind at the time of my conversion, and there was no one present before whom I could confess Him. All I knew was that God loved me as I was, Christ died in my place to be my Savior, and that He would save me if I trusted Him to do so, which I did. The goodness of God had led me to change my attitude toward Him and the salvation which He offered so freely (Acts 20:21; Romans 2:4).

I tried to apologize to her only to be told, "Don't worry about it, Dick. You don't need to feel badly. What he said is what I believe." In speaking with her further, it was quite apparent she was not saved and had no concept of the true Gospel of God's grace.

In this case the evangelist was *simply wrong as to what God requires of the unbeliever for salvation.*

An interesting side note about an inconsistency of which many televangelists are guilty: Have you ever noticed that in a televised meeting that the evangelist often tells the live audience to do several things in order to be saved—turn from sin, walk forward, believe in Christ, confess Him publicly; then he will turn to the television audience and say something like this: "If you will simply bow your head where you are and trust Christ to save you, He will do it right now where you sit." I'm not trying to nitpick but doesn't such an approach to the Gospel invitation convey that it is easier to be saved while watching television than it is to be in attendance at the meeting itself? It boils down to the condition or conditions that God requires for salvation. Is there only one thing to do or are there several things that must be done?

Whatever the answer, we need to be consistent with what the Bible reveals about this very important area of our Gospel presentation.

No Other Way of Salvation

Had there been another way by which a holy God could allow sinful man into His presence while still maintaining His holiness, other than through the offering of His Son, such a way would be available as an option. But there is no such way. God explains it this way: *Is the Law then against the promises of God? Certainly not! For if there had been a law given* (a principle, a rule to live by) *which could have given life, truly righteousness would have been by the law. But the Scripture has confined all under sin, that the promise by faith in Jesus Christ might be given to those who believe* (Galatians 3:21-22).

This one Gospel, the sole way of salvation, is available to all. God is more eager for man to hear of His gift of salvation and to receive it, than man is to respond to the light he has already been given. And just how is this righteousness, this gift, received by sinful man? The promise is *by faith in Jesus Christ* and given to those who *believe* in Him.

God has given only one condition by which man is able to obtain eternal salvation: belief in His Son, the Lord Jesus Christ. It is not believe plus something else. How does this compare to your answer to the question at the beginning of this chapter? Are you scratching your head? Are you angry that I would make such a claim? Do you think that there must be more to it than that? Well, there is more to it, but it may not be what you think. Stay with me as we cover this all-important subject in greater detail throughout the book and I think most or all of your questions or objections will be adequately covered from a thoroughly Biblical viewpoint.

Whose Gospel are we to Preach?

Paul the apostle wrote, *For I am not ashamed of the gospel of Christ, for it is the power of God to salvation for everyone who believes, for the Jew first and also for the Greek. For in it* (the Gospel) *is the righteousness of God revealed from faith to faith; as it is written, "The just shall live by faith"* (Romans 1:16-17).

There are many so-called gospels but there is only one Gospel of Christ, only one saving message. There is not the evangelical gospel, the Catholic gospel, the charismatic gospel, the denominational gospel, nor the Pauline gospel. There is only one good news message that saves and it is His. That one unique Gospel has power to save all who believe it. It also condemns all who do not believe it.

God is so serious about how we treat His one and only saving message that He warns of judgment to anyone who contaminates His Gospel. He led Paul to write one of the most sobering statements in all of Scripture: *I marvel that you are turning away so soon from Him who called you in the grace of Christ, to a different gospel, which is not another; and there are some who trouble you and want to pervert the gospel of Christ. But even if we, or an angel from heaven, preach any other gospel to you than what we have preached to you, let him be accursed. As we have said before, so now I say again, if anyone preaches any other gospel to you than what you have received, let him be accursed* (Galatians 1:6-9).

Genesis 41:32 indicates that God repeats something twice when it is firmly established, or when it will definitely happen. Twice in this passage God says those who preach a perverted or changed gospel are accursed! We dare not treat Christ's Gospel lightly or think that it does not matter if we give it in accurate terms. *In a very real sense, the way we treat the Good News concerning the Lord Jesus Christ is the way we actually treat Him.*

For Personal Reflection and Application

❖ How should the fact that there is only one way of salvation influence the way you treat The Great Commission (Matthew 28:18-20; Mark 16:15)? The way you view those who have never heard the Gospel? Think: if the heathen can be saved by their own sincere belief in their concepts of God, what would be the worse thing we as Christians could do to them? [You'll find the answer later in the book].

❖ Pastors sometimes think along the lines of *The Missionary Evangelist.* Many faithful pastors grow weary of seeing folks get saved, join the church, be involved for awhile, and then drift away. To correct the problem they may resort to making it more difficult to "get in" (that is, they begin demanding more up front at the point of salvation). The thought is if you make it more difficult up front the prospective convert will "count the cost" before becoming a Christian. Then, if they come to Christ under these new, more demanding conditions, they are more likely to become involved and be more loyal to the church. Does this necessarily work? Instead of changing or adding to the Gospel, what do you think would be a more sensible and Biblical approach to developing more faithful church members?

❖ Have you personally trusted in the Lord Jesus Christ for your own salvation; or have you, perhaps, simply gone through the outward motions of joining church, praying at the altar, giving public testimony, singing for the Lord, attending meetings—trying to convince yourself and others that your relationship with God is fine?

❖ Do you regularly thank the Lord for the good news, and for the great privilege of having had it come to you, and for having understood it for yourself? Why not stop and thank Him right now?

❖ How thoroughly do you relate to the truth that Christ died for you when you were "without strength" and while you were "still a sinner?" Does the truth of this tremendous demonstration of God's personal love for you move you as it should? If you are not personally moved by it perhaps there is a problem in your relationship with Him.

Lord, help me to so enter into the depths of Your love and sacrifice for me that your love will overwhelm me and bring about a deep and permanent change within.

Soul winning is the first duty of every Christian, the most important activity anybody can pursue, the one work with the greatest eternal rewards, the one Christian business that Heaven most rejoices over.

John R. Rice

4

What is "Fishing for Men?"

The phrase "fishers of men" appears only twice in the New Testament: Matthew 4:19 and Mark 1:17. However, in recording the same event, Luke says it like this: *Do not be afraid. From now on you will catch men* (Luke 5:10). And perhaps Luke's account gives the clearer meaning of what it means to fish for men. When we fish for fish we intend to catch a few, though that does not always happen. Even so, when we fish for men our intention should always be to catch a few, though that doesn't always happen either. But does a fisherman stop fishing just because he goes a few days or weeks without catching anything? Not hardly. Real fishermen do not give up that easily.

The analogy is clear enough. These men—Peter, Andrew, James and John—were commercial fishermen. They were professionals. They knew fishing, and they knew the waters in which they fished. In the account in Luke they had "toiled all night and caught nothing" (v. 5). That in itself seems pretty miraculous to me for they were not fishing with a fishing line on a pole, with a hook on the end of the line. That's the way I fish. No, they were using nets. And to toil all night with nets and to catch *nothing* would be virtually unheard of. They were bound to have at least caught some trash fish, but they caught not a single fish of any kind. No doubt God had set them up for what was about to occur.

As they were washing their nets Jesus passed by, got into Simon's boat and asked to "put out a little from the land," and from there He sat down and taught the people. Then the record says, *Now when He had stopped speaking, He said to Simon, "Launch out into the deep and let down your nets for a catch." But Simon answered and said to Him, "Master, we have toiled all night and caught nothing; nevertheless at Your word I will let down the net."* (vs. 4,5).

The result was astounding. Two boats nearly sank "because of the great number of fish" and their nets began to break. This so startled Simon Peter that he fell down at Jesus' knees, saying, *"Depart from me, for I am a sinful man, O Lord!"* (v. 8). In fact, they were all astonished at the great catch of fish. It was at this point when Jesus told them to not be afraid for "from now on you will catch men."

How Do We Catch Men?

First, we catch men for the Lord by telling them about Christ and His saving work, witnessing of Him. After His resurrection, but before He ascended back to the Father in Heaven, Jesus told His disciples, *You shall receive power when the Holy Spirit has come upon you; and you shall be witnesses to Me in Jerusalem, and in all Judea and Samaria, and to the end of the earth* (Acts 1:8).

Earlier, before His death and as He spoke to them in the upper room on the night in which He was betrayed, He gave these promises: *But when the Helper comes, whom I shall send to you from the Father, the Spirit of truth who proceeds from the Father, He will testify of Me. And you also will bear witness...When He, the Spirit of truth, has come...He will glorify Me* (John 15:26, 27; 16:13, 14).

The bait—if I can use that analogy without seeming flippant—is none other than the lovely Lord Jesus Christ Himself. He attracts people to Himself, and the Holy Spirit within us points men to Christ through our witness. Jesus Himself said, *And I, if I be lifted up from the earth, will draw all peoples to Myself* (John 12:32). The sad truth is that all too often Christians tend to emphasize their church, their upbeat services, their special speakers or performers; always trying to attract the nonbeliever to attend something, when all the time it would be far simpler and more profitable to simply tell them about the Lord Jesus Christ— Who He is, and what He has done for them.

You may need to sugar-coat your church, your pastor, or your special meetings, but you never have to sugar-coat Christ. He's plenty sweet enough as He is. People just need to know the true Lord because their concept of Him is so often warped and misguided. Folks are often turned off to religion or church, but

I've never met anyone who was repulsed by Jesus.

The Holy Spirit was given specifically to equip us to catch men by drawing them to Christ Himself. The Spirit was not given primarily to make us spiritual, or to impart spiritual gifts to us, or to enable us to perform, or to in any way draw attention to ourselves or our ministries. God's Spirit was given to empower us as witnesses of the Lord Jesus Christ!

Secondly, we catch men for the Lord by reasoning with them and persuading them from Scripture of the truthfulness of the Gospel. The apostle Paul was a master at doing this. When Paul and his company came to Thessalonica they went to the synagogue. *Then Paul, as his custom was, went in to them, and for three Sabbaths reasoned with them from the Scriptures, explaining and demonstrating that the Christ had to suffer and rise again from the dead, and saying, "This Jesus whom I preach to you is the Christ." And some of them were persuaded; and a great multitude of the devout Greeks, and not a few of the leading women, joined Paul and Silas* (Acts 17:2-4).

Paul let the Scriptures do the talking (cp. Isaiah 55:10, 11), and he knew the Scriptures well enough to walk these well-versed Jews and Greeks through God's Word to the point of decision— belief in Christ (carefully note Acts 18:4, 13, 19, 24-28; 19:8-10, 26). We see this method at work again a little later in this same seventeenth chapter of Acts: *Now while Paul waited for them at Athens, his spirit was provoked within him when he saw that the city was given over to idols. Therefore he reasoned in the synagogue with the Jews and with the Gentile worshippers, and in the marketplace daily with those who happended to be there* (vs. 16, 17).

REASONING FROM SCRIPTURE, PERSUADING THROUGH THE WORD, IS THE MOST EFFECTIVE WAY OF WINNING OTHERS TO CHRIST, and thus to "catch men" alive for Him!

It has been my observation over the years that those believers who do not seem very effective in winning others to Christ are too often weak in the reasoning/persuading department.

Thirdly, we are to catch men by being winsome ourselves. Now I'm aware that there are those who say we are not told in Scripture to "win" others to Christ, only to bear witness of Him. They tell us we are to simply present the message and then allow

God's Holy Spirit to do His work of winning the individual to Christ. Interestingly, I've never heard any advocates of this position admit that "we are never told in Scripture that the *Holy Spirit* wins souls."

Of course, the final authority on this issue is the Bible, and Proverbs 11:30 is a great verse concerning winning others to Christ. *The fruit of the righteous is a tree of life, and he who wins souls is wise.* To win souls in this verse means *to bring, to lead*, and that is exactly what we are asked to do as we witness. The more winsome we are as we present Christ, the more likely we are to bring or lead others to Him, and the less winsome we are personally the less likely we are to lead very many to the Savior.

Cold or argumentative Christians drive others from the Lord rather than drawing them to Him. The apostle Paul had the proper balance when he said, *For though I am free from all men, I have made myself a servant to all, that I might **win** the more* (First Corinthians 9:19).

Second Timothy 2:24-26 spells out pretty clearly how we are to relate to those who do not know Christ. *And a servant of the Lord must not quarrel but be gentle to all, able to teach, patient, in humility correcting those who are in opposition, if God perhaps will grant them repentance, so that they may know the truth, and that they may come to their senses and escape the snare of the devil, having been taken captive by him to do his will.* How we speak, how we communicate, how we relate to others does matter. We need to be the kind of witnesses for Christ whom the Spirit can use to *win* others, not just to inform them of certain facts.

What "Fishing for Men" is Not

It is not debating or arguing the Gospel. In fact, in light of the verses just quoted, it is never proper to argue the Gospel. Obviously, you will disagree with those to whom you are sharing Christ, but you never have the right to be disagreeable. A disagreeable spirit is a sign of immaturity and should be confessed to the Lord as the sin that it is.

Fishing for men is not the same as applying undue pressure upon others to receive Christ. I've been in meetings where the speaker would pull every trick imaginable out of his hat to "get people down the aisle." I recall one evangelist who invited folks to walk forward for salvation, for dedication of life, for rededication, for church membership, for baptism, for prayer, or as an example to others to make their decisions public, and finally he said, "If you love God and hate the devil, come forward." He wanted to make sure he got everyone down front. His photographer was snapping away and I'm sure his monthly report to his constituents (supporters) looked and sounded pretty impressive. Such shenanigans are a disgrace and should never be confused with the convicting, drawing work of the Holy Spirit in applying the proper pressure upon the unsaved to respond to the Gospel invitation.

Fishing for men is not just living a good Christian life devoid of sharing the message of salvation. Living a godly life is absolutely essential to honoring the Lord and in developing an audience with the unbelieving world, but we do not live a "truly godly life" if we keep silent about Christ's willingness and ability to save those who trust in Him. I'll elaborate upon this in a later chapter.

As Dr. Torrey's quote at the beginning of chapter one indicates, fishing for men *"is not to be an **incident** of life, but the **business** of life, that for which we live and which we are constantly carrying on. "* Biblically speaking, if catching men for Christ is not a part of your life, you are not a fisher of men. Reaching others, getting the Gospel to them, winning them to Christ, should be our heartbeat, the overriding reason for being alive, our passion. There is nothing more important, insofar as service is concerned, than leading people out of spiritual darkness and into God's eternal light. Nothing else God calls upon us to do has such staggering and eternal consequences.

Why Does God Leave Us Here?

Think about it: wouldn't it be far better for us if, once we placed our faith in Christ, we were immediately removed from planet earth and escorted into the presence of the Lord in Heaven? I think most everyone would agree that such an arrangement would be far better for us. However, it would not be better for the world. If we were immediately removed from here at the point of our salvation, there would be no "light" and no "salt" by which to attract unbelievers to Christ. God's method is that those who believe in Christ should bear witness to those who do not know Him and, in so doing, win as many of them as possible to the Savior. The entire Bible bears this out:

Let the redeemed of the LORD say so, whom He has redeemed from the hand of the enemy (Psalm 107:2).

But as we have been approved by God to be entrusted with the Gospel, even so we speak, not as pleasing men, but God who tests our hearts (First Thessalonians 2:4).

The prophet who has a dream, let him tell a dream; and he who has My word, let him speak My word faithfully. "What is the chaff (dreams) *to the wheat* (God's Word)*?" says the LORD. "Is not My word like a fire?" says the LORD, "And like a hammer that breaks the rock in pieces?"* (Jeremiah 23:28, 29).

And He said to them, "Go into all the world and preach (proclaim, tell) *the Gospel to every creature"* (Mark 16:15).

One of the clearest passages along this line is Second Corinthians 5:14-21. Several statements especially stand out. In verse 15 we are told that *those who live* (believers) *should live no longer for themselves, but for Him who died for them and rose again.* Then, in verses 18 and 19 we are reminded that we have been given the "ministry of reconciliation" and that to us has been "committed the word of reconciliation." It's difficult, if not impossible, to let someone know that reconciliation is offered to them without *telling* them. That's our "ministry" and that's the "word" we are to share.

The conclusion of the passage is that *we are ambassadors for Christ, as though God were **pleading through us**: we implore you on Christ's behalf, be reconciled to God* (v. 20). Let the emphasized words ring in your heart's ear: God *pleading through us!* What a concept. And that's the heart of what it means to fish for men, to catch them, for you see, we do this pleading "on Christ's behalf," that is, in His place, in His absence. The King James Bible says "in His stead." What we are to do now is what He did then, and what He would do now if He were here bodily. And what is that? I'll let Him answer for Himself: *For the Son of Man has come to seek and to save that which was lost* (Luke 19:10). Dare we do less? Can we honestly claim to be following Him if we are not functioning as His Ambassadors, pleading with others to trust in Him?

Though fishing for men does not necessarily mean that you spend all your waking hours reaching out to those who are lost, it certainly does mean you make yourself fully available to the Lord to do your part in reaching this world for Christ. What that part may be is between you and the Lord. He may want you in so-called fulltime Christian service, or He may desire that you enter the business or professional fields, or His place for you may be to be a godly homemaker who leads her children to the Lord and nourishes them in the things of God. What title or position you have is immaterial. What's important is your lifelong priority. If it's anything less than living for, serving, and sharing Christ, you are not where you should be spiritually before the Lord.

Examine your heart. If you see anything there that competes with your loyalty to Christ, confess it to God and ask Him for the inner strength to put it out of your life. Only as He is preeminent in your affections will you be able to forsake all else for Him and to follow Him—catching men for His kingdom.

For Personal Reflection and Application

❖ If "fishing for men" and "catching men" alive describes what is involved in *following* Christ, would you say you are following Christ?

❖ As a habit, do you find yourself inviting unsaved friends, neighbors and family members to Christian *events* instead of inviting them to come directly to Christ? If so, why do you think you do this?

❖ Have you convinced yourself that "serving the Lord" is all God expects even if you make no effort to see that the Gospel is spread throughout the world?

❖ Other than by direct personal witness, what other means could you use to reach the lost? (By *"direct personal witness"* I mean face–to–face).

THE

GOSPEL

MESSAGE

Every grand human
scheme or plan to save
oneself fails on one
essential pivot: that man
depends on his own
righteousness, when in
reality there is no
righteousness in man
that will fit him for
acceptance before an
absolutely holy God.

RAS

5

Understanding the Message:
God's Demand

Ginny and I were sitting cross-legged on the grass during afternoon free time, a stone's throw from the main meeting hall. We were at summer camp in Boca Raton, Florida. I was a speaker; she was a camper.

Sensing she may not know Christ as her Savior, I asked, "Ginny, how good do you think you have to be to go to Heaven?"

"Pretty good, I suppose," she replied. "Better than I am, that's for sure."

"Yeah, but how good?" I responded.

She thought a moment and then replied, "I guess so good that someone who knows you really well couldn't think of anything bad to say about you."

I told Ginny that she was getting pretty close to what the Bible says about it, and she indicated that she would like to know just how good she had to be to qualify for Heaven. I proceeded to show her that it is perfection God demands, and that's why no one qualifies. We could never meet that standard.

Once Ginny grasped this basic truth, it was only a few brief moments later that she trusted Christ and we bowed our heads and thanked Him together for her new found faith.

———◇———

There are certain key elements in the salvation message which, if you learn them well, will greatly assist you in giving the Gospel in a natural, fluid, and Biblical way. I usually emphasize five major points:

- **God's Demand**
- **Man's Condition**
- **God's Provision**
- **Man's Response**
- **God's Guarantee**

It will serve you well to memorize these points with supporting Scriptures. You will want to learn these main points so well that they will flow naturally as you share the Gospel. Let's discuss the first point: *God's Demand.*

Only the Perfect Need Apply

I call this "The Missing Ingredient" in most Gospel presentations. The common view among men is that in order to qualify for Heaven you must be good enough to enter. I believed this as a boy. It seemed logical enough, though I'm not certain I ever thought about it long enough to be logical about it. If God is good and Heaven is a good place, then it must be a place for good people.

This logic is not altogether flawed, but I would change one element of it to make it read like this: If God is perfect and Heaven is a perfect place, then it must be a place for *perfect* people. Yes, dear reader, you are reading it correctly. The plain Bible truth is that in order to live in God's presence forever you must be absolutely perfect—as perfect, in fact, as He is perfect! It is not goodness that God requires; it is perfection. You might be thinking, "I've never heard that before." That's why I call it *The Missing Ingredient* in most Gospel presentations. Even Christians are sometimes totally ignorant of this truth. But consider these Scriptures:

Psalm 5:4: *For You are not a God who takes pleasure in wickedness, Nor shall evil dwell* (abide, sojourn, live) *with You.*

Habakkuk 1:13a: *You* (God) *are of purer eyes than to behold evil, and cannot look* (approvingly) *on wickedness.*

Revelation 21:27: *But there shall by no means enter it* (New Jerusalem which will be part of the New Heaven) *anything that defiles, or causes an abomination or a lie, but only those who are written in the Lamb's Book of Life.*

Second Peter 3:13: *Nevertheless we, according to His promise, look for new heavens and a new earth in which righteousness dwells.*

Before proceeding any further, I want to impress upon you how very important it is to thoroughly grasp the truth that absolute perfection is required for entrance into Heaven. It will prove such an advantage when you are sharing the

Gospel with someone.

When I was first starting out in my Christian walk I found, to my utter amazement, that I was good at debating the Bible. So good, in fact, that I relished any and all verbal encounters I could muster. I would go out of my way to engage others in God-talk, as we called it. I did win many religious debates. I did not win many people to Christ. Fortunately, it didn't take too long for me to realize the error of my ways and I began praying, "Lord, give me a tender heart, give me the wisdom I need to win others to You."

In the debating mind-set that dominated me for awhile I did share the Gospel. It was so easy to show unbelievers how wrong they were in their thinking, especially concerning misconceptions about how "good" they thought they were, or how they could not earn or merit salvation. However, a predictable pattern emerged that had me completely stumped for months.

As my prayer for tenderness of heart and for wisdom began to be answered I still found that I often did not get very far in my presentations of the Gospel. In fact, I would normally cover two points and get stuck. The two points were what I learned in Bible school and what I often read in books on the subject of sharing the Gospel with those who are lost: 1) you are a sinner; 2) because you are a sinner you cannot save yourself. Unless I was witnessing to a very open person who was eager to know what the Bible said on the subject, I would often get bogged down right about here in verbal wrangling—not hard debating anymore, but just going around and around and getting nowhere fast.

In the Lord's good providence, two weeks after I trusted Christ as my Savior, I started attending a home Bible study a few blocks from my parent's house. The Bible teacher had an unusual ability of making difficult Bible passages and truths understandable. He was an excellent communicator of the Gospel. In fact, he was a master at it. I've never heard anyone who could convey the Gospel more clearly, nor get better results from his witnessing. His definition of a soul winner is one I've always remembered: *a soul winner is one who specializes in making the Gospel understandable to the lost.*

And that was exactly part of the problem I was wrestling with at that point in my life—I felt I wasn't making it clear to unbelievers because so often I couldn't get far enough along in my presentation for them to really know what Christ had done for them, and what they had to do in order to have eternal life.

I had trusted Christ as my Savior in June of 1953. I entered Miami Bible Institute in January, 1954. It was during that time, and on into that first semester of college, that I was going through this frustration. I was witnessing almost daily but could hardly think of anyone I had actually led to Christ. It seemed I never got far enough into sharing the Gospel for them to know how to receive Christ. Then I began to take careful note of what a few others were doing that allowed them to just flow into and through the Gospel. You know, it's one thing to hear someone teach; it's quite another thing to analyze the way they communicate, and why they do and say the things they do. I began to analyze. What a revelation.

It wasn't long before a major shift in my witnessing technique began to develop. No longer did I start with man—putting the emphasis on convincing the unbeliever that "you're a sinner and you can't save yourself." I had discovered a way to share the Gospel that I felt was more Biblical—placing the emphasis on *God*, who and what He is. It has proven to be one of the most important and effective truths I've ever learned. I'll give you a make-believe scenario. When I am actually into presenting the Gospel with someone the major point I attempt to make early in the conversation would normally go something like this:

You know, Jimmy, when I was younger I used to think that only good little boys would go to Heaven and all the bad little boys would go to hell. Imagine my surprise when I discovered in my late teens that it isn't goodness that God demands, it's perfection. In fact, we have to be as perfect as He is to qualify for Heaven. Now, if there's one thing I'm sure about myself it is that I am not perfect. How about you? Would you say you're perfect? [No]. *Do you know anyone who is?* [No]. *Neither do I.*

Analyze with me what has just taken place. Let it sink in that this one truth, if fully grasped by the unbeliever, becomes great leverage enabling him to understand the Gospel far more easily than would normally be so.

Follow this closely: You are speaking to Jimmy about the Gospel. You cover the point of perfection being necessary to live in God's presence forever and Jimmy agrees with you that no one is perfect. Later on in the conversation when you get around to discussing whether or not Jimmy is qualified for Heaven, he may want to draw attention to all of his good deeds. At that point all you've got to do is to remind Jimmy that, "We've already agreed, haven't we, that none of us is perfect; and that the Bible teaches we've got to be perfect to enter Heaven?"

Still later, when you may want to cover the fact that salvation is a gift which cannot be earned, Jimmy may want to question that. If he does, all you've got to do is to again refer back to what has already been agreed upon and that is: "Since it is perfection that God demands, none of us qualify for eternal life or salvation. We cannot merit it or earn it by our goodness. That is why it has to be a gift from Him. We wouldn't be able to get it any other way."

Can you envision the tremendous advantage that this approach can give you in establishing what God demands before He will allow anyone to enter Heaven? It gives you a true Biblical leverage that you can use effectively to reach others with the message of the Gospel.

"You are a Sinner" versus "You must be Perfect"

One of the obstacles created in just telling the unbeliever "you are a sinner" is found in the various conceptions the unsaved have of that word *sinner*. It creates a mental image ranging from not being all you should be, to being a horrible, vile, despicable, morally corrupt person. This was one of the reasons why it was sometimes so difficult for me to get beyond that point. Unless you are talking with someone who is philosophically bent, you'll find the vast majority of people will agree that they are not perfect, whereas many will argue whether or not they are sinners.

You may be reacting to the above by thinking, "But they are sinners. They're not just imperfect. They willfully sin." That is very true. However, the question remains: What keeps unsaved people from qualifying for salvation, sins committed, or not having God's perfection? In Second Corinthians 5:19 we are told that *"God was in Christ reconciling the world to Himself, not imputing* (charging, reckoning) *their trespasses to them."* If the transgressions of the world were not imputed or charged to the world, then to whom were the world's transgressions charged? To Christ, of course (verse 21). That being true, no one goes to hell on account of the sins they commit because *the full payment for all the sin of all people and for all time has already been paid.*

I deal with man's sinfulness in the next chapter, but for now I'll make this point: *the real issue is not the sin question but the Son question. What will you do with Christ?* People go to hell for one reason only—not having the righteousness of God imputed (credited) to them, which is only accomplished when the ungodly person places his or her faith in the Lord Jesus Christ. The apostle John stated it a little differently, but the end result is the same: *He who believes in Him is not condemned; but he who does not believe is condemned already,* **because** *he has not believed in the name of the only begotten Son of God* (John 3:18).

Condemnation before God, then, is not due to the sins one commits but rather to the failure to place one's faith in the Sin-Bearer, the Lord Jesus Christ. *Failure to grasp this truth is failure to understand the very foundational basis for the true Gospel of God's grace.*

Consider the following clear verses on this important aspect of your Gospel presentation.

Second Corinthians 5:21: *For He* (the Father) *made Him* (Christ) *who knew no sin to be sin for us, that we might become the righteousness of God in Him.*

In Christ alone we receive God's righteousness, the very thing which enables us to be in His presence. The negative obstacle to salvation, the sin question, was already taken out of the way when Christ "died for our sins" (compare Isaiah 53:6; First Corinthians 15:3,4; First Peter 2:24; 3:18). The positive aspect, having God's righteousness credited to our account, is taken care of when we trust in Christ, apart from our works. It is upon that single act of faith in Christ alone that imputes (credits) His righteousness to the believer. We qualify for Heaven, then, based upon a by-faith righteousness which is given to us, rather than by a by-works righteousness of our own making.

Romans 4:5: *Now to him who does not work but believes on Him who justifies the ungodly, his faith is accounted for righteousness.*

God only justifies (declares righteous) one kind of person:

the ungodly person who believes in Christ. It is not of our works; it is through faith alone. Why faith alone? Think through what these last two verses have said the believer receives through faith: God's very own righteousness! Can the righteousness of God possibly be improved upon? Of course not. Then if, as Romans 4:5 makes clear, your *faith* is accounted for righteousness where is there any room for any other conditions or steps in salvation? Once you have believed in Christ as your Savior you have been justified (declared absolutely righteous) by God. *As far as your eternal standing with Him is concerned, there is no room for improvement.*

However, there are those who insist that water baptism is essential for salvation; or that you must walk a church aisle to be saved; or give up certain sinful habits; or live a life of total obedience; or make impressive promises to God. But wait! The moment you trust in Christ to save you, you are made "the righteousness of God in Him." God's righteousness becomes yours through faith and in no other way. You can't improve upon the perfection of God! You don't need anything else to be assured of salvation. No other steps or conditions can possibly improve upon the righteousness of God which is by faith!

The story is told of a time when D. L. Moody was riding a trolley to where he was to speak that evening. The trolley was full so Moody had to stand. An infidel recognized him and arrogantly asked, "Tell me, Mr. Moody, how far is it from Chicago to Heaven?" Moody shot back, "Just one step: *'Believe on the Lord Jesus Christ and thou shalt be saved.'* Will you take that step?" The infidel backed away. Moody stepped forward. "Just one step, sir, from Chicago to Heaven. Believe on the Lord Jesus Christ. Will you take that step?"

The gentleman became so flustered he got off of the trolley at the next stop. Moody got off behind him, and as the man hurried away, Moody cupped his mouth with his two hands and yelled, "One step from Chicago to Heaven. Believe on the Lord Jesus Christ. Will you take that step?" He then got on the next trolley and proceeded to his meeting.

At the conclusion of his message that evening, Moody told of the incident and reminded those in the audience that there is only one step from Chicago to Heaven. When he invited those who were trusting in Christ that night to come forward for prayer, encouragement, and literature, among the seekers was the infidel!

Only one step, one condition. Upon the one act of faith in Christ as one's Savior—and only upon that one condition—the believer is declared righteous before a holy God. What a Savior! What a complete salvation!

Now, more verses.

Philippians 3:9: *And be found in Him* (Christ), *not having my own righteousness, which is from the law, but that which is through faith in Christ, the righteousness which is from God by faith.*

What's the key to having "the righteousness of God" as my own? Being found in Christ. It doesn't say anything about being found in the right church, or being found in the baptismal waters. Being "found in Christ" is it. And how is one placed "in Christ?" You are placed "in Him" the moment you receive the righteousness which is from God by faith in Christ. Could it be any clearer or more to the point? Once again we see that what is required for entrance into Heaven, God's righteousness, is received through faith in Christ, apart from our own righteousness.

Romans 9:30-32: *What shall we say then? That Gentiles, who did not pursue righteousness, have attained to righteousness, even the righteousness of faith; but Israel, pursuing the law of righteousness, has not attained to the law of righteousness. Why? Because they did not seek it by faith, but as it were, by the works of the law. For they stumbled at that stumbling stone* (meaning the requirement of faith in Jesus as their Messiah).

The Gentiles, not even trying to be righteous, received righteousness by faith. Israel, trying so hard to be righteous through their own efforts by observing the Mosaic Law, did not receive it. Why? The ONLY reason given: *Because they did not seek it by faith.*

It will help you so much in your witnessing if you will constantly remind yourself that there are only two kinds of righteousnesses: there is man's *by-works* righteousness which cannot save, and there is God's offer of a *by-faith* righteousness, which is the only kind that does save. Virtually everyone you witness to will be attempting to reach God or to please Him by their own efforts and works. Your assignment, then, will be to share with them God's tremendous alternative—His very own righteousness given to them as a gift when they place their faith in the Lord Jesus Christ, who is altogether righteous and, who became sin for them that they might become the righteousness of God in Him.

Romans 10:1-4: The apostle Paul continues: *Brethren, my heart's desire and prayer to God for Israel is that they may be saved. For I bear them witness that they have a zeal for God, but not according to knowledge. For they being ignorant of God's righteousness, and seeking to establish their own righteousness, have not submitted themselves to the righteousness of God. For Christ is the end of the law for righteousness to everyone who believes.*

When sincere people want to please God they do the normal, logical thing: they perform good deeds of one kind or another. They don't need to be criticized for that. They need to be educated from God's Word. Zealous Israel was ignorant of God's righteousness, so they did what seemed sensible—they worked more diligently to keep the Law. They were diligently *"seeking to establish their own righteousness"* but in doing so they were guilty of *"not submitting themselves to the righteousness of God."* How very sad. But this tendency of man to impress God with good intentions and deeds is certainly not unique to Israel. All men the world over, and throughout history, have been guilty of approaching God on the basis of their performance.

Ignorance is the culprit. Too often unsaved men don't know any better. It is as Jesus said as He was being crucified, *Father, forgive them, for they do not know what they do* (Luke 23:34). Paul made the same point in **First Corinthians 2:7, 8:** *But we speak the wisdom of God in a mystery, the hidden wisdom which God ordained before the ages for our glory, which none of the rulers of this age knew; for had they known, they would not have crucified the Lord of glory.*

How shall they know? How will the unsaved world become aware of the true Gospel of Christ in which "the righteousness of God is revealed" unless we who have received Christ learn the Gospel thoroughly and then take it to the world of men who are lost in their ignorance?

For Personal Reflection and Application

❖ What are some mistaken ideas you may have had in the past as to how to qualify for Heaven?

❖ Where do you suppose such ideas originated? From something you read? From your church's tradition and doctrine? From preaching you heard? From Sunday school classes? Or, perhaps from friends or family?

❖ Ask yourself, "Am I incorporating this Missing Ingredient into my presentation of the Gospel?" I cannot urge you strongly enough to incorporate the Missing Ingredient into all of your future presentations of the Gospel. I believe you will be astounded at the results.

❖ Why do you think some with whom you share the Gospel may say, "I've never heard that before." Do you think they really haven't heard it, or perhaps they did but didn't understand it? What can you do to assure that those who hear the Gospel from your lips will know they have indeed heard it?

The Gospel is offensive
because it strips people of
all room for pride in
human accomplishment.
There is a reproach associated
with the message of the
Cross because it removes
every possibility of
self-deliverance. No one
can give God anything in
exchange for salvation.
Nothing the sinner can
give is acceptable as a
substitute for sin.

Robert P. Lightner

6

Understanding the Message: Man's Condition

Man's Condition is the flip side of God's Demand. If God, on the one hand, requires perfection; and man, on the other hand, cannot deliver the goods, he definitely has a great, great need. In discussing man's condition it's important to give careful attention to three unchangeable truths:

First, Man is Not and Cannot Be Perfect

Jeremiah 17:9-10 states: *The heart is deceitful above all things, and desperately wicked; Who can know it? I, the LORD, search the heart, I test the mind, even to give every man according to his ways, according to the fruit of his doings.*

Nothing is as deceitful and wicked as the human heart—absolutely nothing. Therefore, we dare not trust in what we feel in our hearts. To trust in feelings, or in impressions, or in hunches, is a most dangerous and unreliable practice. God alone is able to properly and accurately read and interpret what comes out of our hearts.

A person is in a very precarious position who thinks, "I just know in my heart that my beliefs, my church, or my experience is right." *Above all things* in verse nine means that there is nothing more deceitful, and *desperately* means the heart is incurably wicked. So, there is nothing anywhere on earth more deceitful than the heart of man, and there is no earthly cure for the wickedness of the human heart. To trust in the sincerity of one's heart, then, is sheer folly.

Ecclesiastes 7:20 is an excellent verse to use with someone who is a more respectable sinner, one whose life is pretty consistent. He may be a just man. He may do good. But at some time or other he also sins, meaning he is not perfect. Here is what it says: *For there is not a just man on earth who does good and does not sin.*

The New Testament parallel to this verse is **James 2:10**: *For whoever shall keep the whole law, and yet stumble in one point, he is guilty of all.* So one slip, one sin, one mistake, and we are disqualified from entering God's perfect Heaven. That's the way it has to be since God's new Heaven will have no sin whatever in it. Even this "just man" does not measure up because at one time or another in his life he has sinned. He is not a murderer, he's not a thief, nor a rapist. He's simply an imperfect sinner who is incapable of changing what is already an established fact.

This is basically what **Jeremiah 13:23** tells us: *Can the Ethiopian change his skin or the leopard its spots? Then may you also do good who are accustomed to do evil?*

In **Isaiah 64:6** it says, *But we are all like an unclean thing, and all our righteousnesses* (the best things we do) *are like filthy rags; we all fade as a leaf, and our iniquities, like the wind, have taken us away.*

Here is a devastating indictment against man's righteousness as compared to God's perfect holiness. If all our righteousnesses —the very *best* we can do—are viewed as "filthy rags," what must our normal, average output be in God's eyes? If our best is filthy in His holy eyes we are hopelessly lost in and of ourselves. If God Himself does not provide a way out of our hopeless situation, there is no escape possible. Our best efforts are worthless in this regard.

Romans 3:10, 23 adds: *As it is written: There is none righteous, no not one... For there is no difference; for all have sinned and fall short of the glory* (perfection) *of God.*

None righteous, *all* have sinned, *all* fall short of God's perfection. That's the problem with man and his efforts to reach or to please an absolutely holy God—there are no exceptions to this rule. *All* includes every single one of us.

When verse twenty-two says "there is no difference" it is not speaking of degrees of sin but of the reality, the presence, of sin in each of us. A Hitler is obviously more wicked than a sincere, church-going grandmother who fills her life with good deeds. However, there is no difference in one respect between Hitler and the kindest, sweetest, most religious grandmother in the world:

both have sinned, both have fallen short of God's glory or perfection. Therefore, both have the same problem, the same need, and are in the same condition. Perhaps the grandmother hasn't murdered anyone or even cheated on a test when she was a little girl in school, but she has come short of God's glory and so needs a Savior just as every other sinner on earth.

Note: There *are* degrees of sin. Under the Mosaic Law some sins were worthy of death by stoning, while others were not. Obviously, therefore, there was a severity that some sins carried with them that others did not.

We sometimes misunderstand Jesus' statement in the Sermon on the Mount where He made it clear that to hate someone in your heart makes you a murderer in God's eyes, and to lust after a woman is equated to being guilty of adultery. However, wishing someone dead does not do the same damage as if you actually killed that person. If you killed someone you would end their life prematurely, you would bring much hurt to the family and loved ones of the victim, you would bring a great deal of grief to those who love you, plus you could possibly spend the rest of your life in prison or be executed for your crime. Christ's point was virtually the same as that found in this Romans passage—*that we are all sinners.* Even if you have never literally murdered anyone or committed adultery, your inner thoughts and desires reveal how you are viewed by God, and it is to God alone that we must give an account.

Secondly, There is Nothing Man Can Do—No Amount of Good Works—to Obtain or Merit this Perfection

Romans 8:7-8 nails it down pretty well when it says, *The carnal* (fleshly) *mind is enmity against God; for it is not subject to the law of God, nor indeed can be. So then, those who are in the flesh cannot please God.*

The natural man without Christ—described here as being "in the flesh"—has a mind that is not, nor can it be, subject to God's law; nor is it possible for the person without Christ to please God. This is a pretty strong indictment, isn't it? One may think, "You mean to tell me that my church attendance, my prayers, doing penance, being a good neighbor, being an honest employee—these good things do not please God?" *As far as salvation is concerned* there is nothing the natural man can do to cause God to act favorably toward him. God has and does act favorably toward the unbeliever but it is because of who and what *He* is, not because of what is in sinful man. Man of himself has nothing within himself that pleases God. In this matter of salvation, what pleases God is found in His Son and nowhere else. More about this later.

Ephesians 2:8, 9 is crystal clear: *For by grace you have been saved through faith, and that not of yourselves; it is the gift of God, not of works, lest anyone should boast.*

Grace is God's unmerited favor, undeserved, unearned, and it cannot be bought. Faith is simple trust or belief in Christ. The *gift* is the salvation referred to. Some say the "that" in the phrase "and *that* not of yourselves; it is the gift of God" refers to grace or to faith. Neither, however, can be the object of this phrase because grace and faith are both feminine gender in Greek, the original language of the New Testament. Whatever, therefore, modifies either word would normally agree in gender. "That not of yourselves" is neuter. So that which is the gift of God and not of ourselves is salvation—the whole concept, plus the actual miracle of salvation becoming our personal possession when we place our faith in Christ. This, of course, agrees with the rest of Scripture. For instance, Psalm 3:8 declares, *"Salvation belongs to the LORD..."* And Jonah 2:9 adds, *"Salvation is of the LORD."*

There are probably no better verses in Scripture than Ephesians 2:8, 9 to show the unsaved person the mechanics of salvation, that is, how God saves, the basis upon which He saves, what is required of man, and that being saved is "not of works" and "not of yourselves." All of that in two, easy-to-memorize verses, back-to-back. I will frequently return to Ephesians 2:8,9 in this book, as well as other similar verses that should be emphasized over and over again. Repetition is theological glue which makes truth stick so that it is not easily forgotten, so don't be surprised when I repeat some verses over and over again.

Another favorite of mine is **Titus 3:5-7:** *Not by works of righteousness which we have done, but according to His mercy He saved us, through the washing* (cleansing) *of regeneration* (new birth) *and renewing of the Holy Spirit, whom He poured out on us abundantly through Jesus Christ our Savior, that* *having been justified by His grace, we should become heirs according to the hope* (anticipation) *of eternal life.*

Notice it once again: we cannot be saved by any "works of righteousness which we have done." Why? I remind you of Isaiah 64:6: "our righteousnesses are as filthy rags" in God's eyes. It is "according to His mercy He saved us." Someone once said that in salvation mercy is God *not* giving us what we *do* deserve—Hell! Grace, on the other hand, is God *giving* us what we do *not* deserve — Heaven! We deserve much worse than God gives us.

Galatians 2:16 makes it clear that we are not saved by keeping the Law. *Knowing that a man is not justified by the works of the law, but by faith in Jesus Christ, even we have believed in Christ Jesus, that we might be justified by faith in Christ and not by the works of the law; for by the works of the law no flesh shall be justified.*

The meaning of "justified" is to be considered or declared righteous. It is not the same thing as *being* righteous. It is more of a legal term—how one is viewed by the Court of Heaven. If I committed a crime but the evidence was not sufficient to convict me I would be acquitted; that is, found not guilty, even though I had actually committed the crime. Justification, however, goes beyond pronouncing one not guilty. Justification states, "You are not only 'not guilty' but you are also declared absolutely righteous" by the Judge of the universe—as if you had never been guilty of sinning in the first place. Someone once put it this way: To be justified means just-as-if-I'd never sinned—a simple, convenient way to remember the gist of justification, though there is much more to it than that.

It is certainly clear enough from the above verse that keeping the Law, that is, obeying it, living by it, making it the foundation upon which you rest your hope of salvation, is not the way to become justified before God. Yet, there are thousands upon thousands of sincere, church-going folks who feel that if they just live by the Ten Commandments God will surely be satisfied. They completely miss the purpose of the Law, which is to reveal our sinfulness. The Law was never given to provide a means of salvation.

Regarding man's condition, you may also want to read again Romans 4:5, 9:30-32, and Philippians 3:9, all of which point out that man cannot make it by any works of his own.

The Third Truth Concerning Man's Condition
Before God is that God's Judgment Upon Sin is Death

Physical death is one appointment everyone will keep. **Hebrews 9:27** nails this truth down pretty firmly when it states that *it is appointed for men to die once, but after this the judgment.* But there is a greater, more fearful death that is the ultimate result of sin and that is the Second Death, where unbelievers are in an eternal state of separation from God and where there is no escape. Note carefully Revelation's description: *Then Death and Hades were cast into the lake of fire. This is the second death. And anyone not found written in the Book of Life was cast into the lake of fire. This is the seond death* (20:14, 15).

Here are additional verses indicating that death (of all kinds) is the result of sin.

Romans 6:23: *For the wages of sin is death, but the gift of God is eternal life in Christ Jesus our Lord.*

Sin has a consequence: it is death, or separation from God. Adam suffered it when he sinned. We suffer it when we sin. Whether we speak of physical death, spiritual death, or the Second Death, all forms of death are the direct or indirect result of sin. The usual meaning of the New Testament word translated "death" is *separation*, and it is the only divinely designated payment for sin found in Scripture. The ultimate penalty for sin was fully paid when Christ was separated from God the Father 2,000 years ago. That being true, *there cannot, first of all, be anything else that pays for sin.* The wages of sin is not a good life, it is not water baptism, it is not man's sincerity, or doing one's best, it is not man's *anything.* The penalty for sin is death. When we speak of eternity, death would be an eternal separation from God, a payment that the infinite Son of God made in a moment of time; a payment that all men together could not make in a million years.

Secondly, there cannot be a second payment for sin. Christ's one payment was sufficient for all time and for all men. When someone dies in unbelief and goes to hell it is not to pay for their sins. That payment has already been made once and for all. Referring to Jesus doing the will of the Father,

Hebrews 10:10 says, *By that will we have been sanctified through the offering of the body of Jesus Christ once for all.* Verse fourteen adds: *For by one offering He has perfected forever those who are being sanctified.* And verse eighteen concludes the thought with: *Now where there is remission of these* (sins) *there is no longer an offering for sin.*

The person who dies in their unbelief will be separated from God, not as a payment for sin, but for failure to receive the One who made the payment for them. I recognize, of course, that when they die in their unbelief unsaved men will be separated from God forever (experiencing eternal death), but that separation is not another payment for sin in addition to the one Christ made on the cross. His one all-sufficient payment was for all sin of all men and for all time. God accepts no other payment in its place.

In **Romans 5:12-21** I'll simply highlight here the fact that through Adam's sinful disobedience to God sin's wages, which is death, was introduced into the human experience. *Therefore, just as through one man sin entered the world, and death through sin, and thus death spread to all men, because all sinned...death reigned from Adam to Moses, even over those who had not sinned according to the likeness of the transgression of Adam* (that is, in the same way Adam sinned)...*by one man's offense many died... For the judgment which came from the offense resulted in condemnation...by one man's offense death reigned through the one...through one man's offense judgment came to all men, resulting in condemnation...by one man's disobedience many were made sinners... so sin reigned in death.*

This dark, dreary picture of man's condition as revealed in God's Word is only surpassed by the greatness and completeness of God's provision in Christ. Notice these contrasts between what Adam brought to humankind to what Christ has brought and offers to all: *But the free gift is not like the offense. For if by the one man's offense many died, much more the grace of God and the gift by the grace of the one Man, Jesus Christ, abounded to many...the free gift...resulted in justification...through one Man's righteous act the free gift came to all men, resulting in justification of life...by one Man's obedience many will be made righteous...But where sin abounded, grace abounded much more, so that as sin reigned in death, even so grace might reign through righteousness to eternal life through Jesus Christ our Lord (vss. 15, 16, 18-21).*

So, in summary—

• Man is not, nor can he be perfect, which he would need to be if he is to enter God's new Heaven.

• Man being imperfect or sinful wouldn't be so bad if there was a way to atone for it or to undo it, but there is nothing man can do to earn, merit, or obtain this necessary perfection.

• Without a Savior all men are faced with the consequences of sin which is eternal death (separation from God).

• The only acceptable solution to man's problem must be something that God Himself provides—a way of escape, of deliverance, and that is exactly what He has done in giving His own Son to be our Substitute, our Savior.

For Personal Reflection and Application

❖ In this world in which we live we all have the same problem—we sin. Some sin one way; others sin another way, but we sin nevertheless. When witnessing to unbelievers, what would you say is the difference between "them" and you? Do you at times have feelings of superiority and tend to shun or condemn the very ones Christ came to save? It's true that without Christ we are hopelessly lost in our sin, but the only real difference between sinners who are lost and sinners who are saved is the grace of God. God's grace has made us what we are—children in His family and heirs to His eternal presence. It will prove a great benefit in your witnessing to constantly remind yourself that *grace alone makes the difference.*

How can anyone claim
to love the Lord Jesus well
who does not set out to
love what Jesus loves....
and have concern and
compassion over the very
thing dearest to the heart
of the Savior?

John R. Rice

7

Understanding the Message:
God's Provision

Nick was a Russian Jew who hosted a local call-in talk show in Charlotte, North Carolina. A friend, Julie, had sent him a copy of my book, Religion: Who Needs It? *and suggested the topic would be a good one for his show and that I, the author, just happened to live right there in Charlotte.*

About a week later I was invited to be on the two-hour show and we had a great time receiving calls and answering questions listeners had about God, the Bible, salvation and life. Of course, I gave the Gospel over and over again during the program, and during one of the commercial breaks Nick said something to me like, "Dick, am I understanding you correctly that you are saying that it's just Jesus God wants us to believe in—not religion, or church, or the synagogue?" I assured him that was exactly what I was saying based on Scripture, and I added, "Nor are we to trust in man-made dogma or tradition."

A few evenings later Nick and his wife were invited by Julie and her husband to have dinner at their home along with me and my wife, Kathy. We had a really enjoyable evening with just the six of us sitting around after dinner discussing "spiritual things." I'm not sure if Nick or his wife actually trusted in Christ to save them, but I'll never forget how clearly he saw that God's provision for our salvation was "just Jesus!"

$$\Longrightarrow\cdot\Longleftarrow$$

God's provision for our salvation is two-fold: 1) He has provided His Son as our Savior and, because of what Christ accomplished through His death and resurrection, 2) He offers salvation freely as His love gift to the believing sinner. We will see that the provision and the offer are completely sufficient to meet all the spiritual needs of man and the holy demands of God.

Jesus Christ, Our Savior

For the Son of God to be the Savior for all the world the debt of sin would have to be totally paid. The payment must be adequate to the debt. Man's need could not be met if even one sin was not included in the Savior's payment. But, assuming Christ's substitutionary sacrifice of Himself was adequate, that would take care of man's need insofar as the way of salvation being provided. Man's response to that provision is the other side of this story, which we will cover shortly.

God, on the other hand, also has a demand that must be met for any sacrifice to be acceptable to Him as sufficiently adequate. His demand springs from His character, particularly, His holiness. As we have already observed, God does not, nor can He, condone sin, tolerate it, or allow it to dwell eternally in His presence. Any payment for sin, to be acceptable, must allow God to remain God; must allow Him to maintain His absolute holiness while at the same time allowing Him to forgive sinful men so that they may live with Him in the beauty of His holiness.

God cannot just glibly say, "I forgive" without there being sufficient and righteous grounds from which such forgiveness flows. Forgiveness is made possible only because sin has been adequately dealt with. Sin cannot be glossed over, swept under the heavenly rug, or treated as if it isn't there. God is not a heavenly benefactor who simply says, "Ho, ho, ho. Don't worry about a thing; all is forgiven."

Fortunately for all of us, such a complete paid-in-full salvation has been provided and is offered freely to any and all who will have it. Especially note these important verses:

Isaiah 53:6: *All we like sheep have gone astray; we have turned, every one, to his own way; and the LORD has laid on Him the iniquity of us all.*

We have *all* gone astray (there are no exceptions) and the Father has laid on the Son "the iniquity of us *all*" (no exceptions). God the Father took the initiative in sending His Son and has adequately met our need in providing a Savior who is acceptable to Him.

Jesus paid for the sins of all men, but what if some say He

98

paid the sin debt for only those who would believe in Him, called the elect, the saints, believers? I discuss this in more detail in chapter ten, so I will just insert a word of warning here: If, as you read a passage of Scripture, it makes sense, don't seek any other sense or you'll only end up with nonsense!

It has been my experience that if I approach the Bible with no preconceived notions about what it ought to say, with no particular theological school of thought to defend, I will discover Scripture to be a well of refreshing spiritual water, a fountain from which I may satisfy my thirsty soul. But if in my study of Scripture I find myself trying to make certain passages say or mean things which they do not seem to mean in context, or I attempt to make them "fit" some theological system, I would do well to examine my approach to God's truth and not to worry one iota whether or not my understanding of Scripture fits into a humanly conceived notion or tradition.

You should always allow Scripture to interpret itself, "comparing spiritual things with spiritual" (First Corinthians 2:13). Observe God's admonition in First Corinthians 4:6 when He led Paul to write that we should *"learn...not to* (even) *think beyond what is written."* Scripture, and Scripture alone, is adequate in determining the doctrine we are to believe and preach, and the lifestyle we are to live (see Second Timothy 3:16, 17).

Now back to the point of showing that Christ's sacrifice was sufficient to meet the need of man's sinful condition.

First Peter 2:24 is another revealing verse: *Who Himself bore our sins in His own body on the tree, that we, having died to sins, might live for righteousness—by whose stripes you were healed.*

The "our" and "we" of this verse is a reference to believers, but the point is still clear that it is through the offering of His body that we have had our sins borne or carried away. It was upon the cross where the sin debt was paid. It is good to remind ourselves that the wages of sin is not a good life, it is not faithfulness, it is not enduring to the end, nor water baptism. Sin's wages is death and Christ—and only Christ—has paid that debt in full.

Just one chapter further we have **First Peter 3:18** which adds this thought: *For Christ also suffered once for sins, the just for the unjust, that He might bring us to God, being put to death in* *the flesh but made alive by the Spirit.*

Christ is the Just One. All the rest of us are unjust. He suffered once for the sins of the unjust. Having accomplished that feat in the flesh, He also rose from the dead—proof positive that the sacrifice of Himself was satisfactory to God. Though Christ's resurrection was not part of the actual payment, it was vital in verifying that sin's debt had been paid, and in validating the person of Christ, that He is all He claimed to be. Without the resurrection we, of course, would lack the greatest evidence of Christ being God, the Savior, and of the offer of salvation having any legitimacy. The entire Trinity, in fact, was directly involved in the resurrection of Jesus from the dead: the Father, Ephesians 1:17-20; the Son, John 10:17–18; and the Holy Spirit, Romans 1:3–4.

Acts 2:22–24 further emphasizes that it is Christ whom God has provided to be our Savior. The apostle Peter proclaimed: *Men of Israel, hear these words: Jesus of Nazareth, a Man attested by God to you by miracles, wonders, and signs which God did through Him in your midst, as you yourselves know—Him, being delivered by the determined counsel and foreknowledge of God, you have taken by lawless hands, have crucified, and put to death; whom God raised up, having loosed the pains of death, because it was not possible that He should be held by it.*

God was and is satisfied with His dear Son, especially in what He accomplished on the Cross. In fact, this verse states that it was by God's *"determined counsel and foreknowledge"* that Jesus was crucified and put to death. Men performed the actual deed and are, therefore, truly accountable for their participation in that sinful act although it was God who determined that the crucifixion of His dear Son would occur. As in so many areas of life, there is the Divine side and the human element blended perfectly into a complete whole, a complete picture. In this case, God the Father placed His stamp of approval upon His Son's death payment for sin by raising Him triumphantly over death.

Later, in the early days of the Church, it was the apostle Peter again who made the way of salvation clear to the Gentile, Cornelius, and his household. In **Acts 10:39-43** he preached: *And we are witnesses of all things which He did both in the land of the Jews and in Jerusalem, whom they killed by hanging on a tree. Him God raised up on the third day, and showed Him* *openly, not to all the people, but to witnesses chosen before by God, even to us who ate and drank with Him after He arose from the dead. And He commanded us to preach to the people, and to testify that it is He who was ordained by God to be Judge of the living and the dead. To Him all the prophets witness that, through His name, whoever believes in Him will receive remission of sins.*

What a great message! Jesus Christ is adequate to our need! The Father displayed His approval of His Son's sacrifice by raising Him from the dead. The early apostles proclaimed the great salvation message to all; then when Cornelius heard the Gospel message, he believed and he received forgiveness of sins as well as his entire household!

Notice the important emphasis in **First John 2:2:** *And He Himself is the propitiation for our sins, and not for ours only but also for the whole world.*

This concise verse contains one of the great words of the Gospel, *propitiation.* Basically it means *satisfaction.* When applied to Christ's payment for our sins it means that His sacrifice was a satisfactory one to the holy God of Scripture. His substitutionary sacrifice for our sins is adequate, not just for our sins, but also for the sins of the whole world. This means we may walk up to people anywhere on this planet and tell them that Jesus has paid the penalty for all of their sins and God has accepted that payment. Wonderful and liberating news for a desperately needy world!

This Completely-Paid-for-Salvation is Free.

With sin's debt paid by Christ, as evidenced by His bodily resurrection from the grave, with God's holiness being satisfied with that payment, salvation is now offered freely as God's love gift to the believing sinner. Salvation of sinful man is now possible, the way has been opened, the invitation is extended: Come! Believe in the Savior!

Some maintain that for salvation to be offered freely makes it cheap. They even refer to a freely offered salvation as being based upon "cheap grace." The real truth is that God's gift of salvation is free, not because it is cheap, but rather because it is absolutely *priceless*; there is no way any of us could ever gather up enough money, or accumulate enough good deeds, to pay for that which is beyond price. It is, as we often sing, "Amazing Grace, how sweet the sound, that saved a wretch like me." And verses like the following ones confirm this great truth.

Ephesians 2:8-9: *For by grace you have been saved through faith, and that not of yourselves; it is the gift of God, not of works, lest anyone should boast.*

Note the phrase, *it is the gift of God.* You don't pay for a gift, do you? Someone has to either pay for it, or make it, or both, but not the recipient of the gift. The recipient simply receives it. In addition, this salvation which is God's gift to the believing sinner, is not of yourselves and not of works to keep anyone from boasting, as if salvation could be attained by something they have done, or by something they are. Never forget, dear friend, that since salvation is by God's grace there is no room for boasting, and no human works, efforts, or sincere intentions could ever be adequate to obtain such a matchless gift as this. I am as convinced as I can be that the primary reason more people do not understand the Gospel message is because they do not comprehend G-R-A-C-E, which we will discuss in greater detail in the next chapter.

Then in **John 1:11-12** we read, *He came to His own, and His own did not receive Him. But as many as received Him, to them He gave the right to become children of God, even to those who believe in His name.*

Verse twelve makes it clear that *receiving* Christ is accomplished by *believing* in His name. Receiving Him and believing in Him are not two separate steps in the process of becoming saved. Sometimes you'll hear someone say, "It is not enough to believe in Christ; you must also receive Him, which you do by saying a prayer to receive Him, asking Him to save you." I have nothing against saying a prayer when one comes to Christ as long as it is understood that it is trusting in Christ (believing in Him) that saves—with or without a prayer. I prayed the night I trusted in Christ, but it wasn't my prayer that saved me. I was saved the only way anyone is ever saved, by believing on the Lord Jesus Christ. Receiving Him and believing in Him are synonymous. You will get a truer picture of what verse twelve is saying if you leave out the word *even* (which you should do because it was added by the translators as indicated by the fact that it is italicized in some

English translations). The verse would then read: *as many as received Him, to them He gave the right to become children of God, to those who believe in His name.* Must unbelievers receive Christ to be saved? Absolutely. And how do they do that? John 1:12 states it clearly: *By believing on His name.* Is it all right to lead the unbeliever in a prayer to lead them to Christ? Certainly—as long as faith in Christ is the issue, not the prayer.

Another verse that shows salvation is free is the often quoted **Romans 6:23:** *For the wages of sin is death, but the gift of God is eternal life in Christ Jesus our Lord.*

What is eternal life? Is it a reward for diligence, for faithful service, for hard work? No. It is the gift of God. And where is it found? In church? In the baptismal waters? In one's heart-felt, sincere beliefs? No! No! It is found in the Lord Jesus Christ alone. The focus is again upon Christ, not upon anything of merit that springs from us. To place the focus upon our performance is to miss God's point entirely. It is Christ who is the Great Focus of Heaven! For all eternity it will be so. God's greatest gift to mankind is all wrapped up in the Person of His dear Son, and in no one else.

Consider further **First John 5:11-12:** *And this is the testimony: that God has given us eternal life, and this life is in His Son. He who has the Son has life; he who does not have the Son of God does not have life.*

There are only two kinds of people in the world: those who have the Son and, therefore, have eternal life; and those who do not have the Son and, consequently, do not have eternal life. This life is given to those who have the Son, and only to those. One may have many religious "badges of honor" so-to-speak, but without Christ he is still lost. Being called Reverend, Holy Doctor, Pastor, guru, Esteemed Master, His Holiness, Sunday school teacher, deacon, elder, or choir member doesn't bring anyone any closer to "this life"— eternal life, which is found in Christ alone.

Here again, in **Second Timothy 1:9**, see the stress upon salvation being a gift: (God) *has saved us and called us with a holy calling, not according to our works, but according to His own purpose and grace which was given to us in Christ Jesus before time began.*

God has determined that salvation:
- would not be according to our works
- would be according to His own plan
- would be by His grace
- would be found in Christ Jesus, and
- would be a gift to be received,
 not a reward for work accomplished.

All of this was determined by Him "before time began." You might think of our redemption as one of God's primary long-range goals—*really* long-range, from eternity past. It was "according to His own purpose," what He wanted to do. There was no need to consult with anyone about this.

As a reminder, salvation was also "according to His...grace." That word *grace* keeps popping up all over the New Testament, doesn't it? It is so fascinating to me that God's testimony concerning the vital truths which are interwoven into the one grand doctrine of salvation is always consistent. He doesn't give one way of salvation in one place and an entirely different way to Heaven somewhere else. It is always by grace, through faith, and is a gift.

Are you picking up on the repeated themes concerning salvation contained in the great Gospel passages of the Bible?
- It is by grace.
- It is through faith.
- It is a gift to be received.
- It is not according to our works.
- It is found only in Christ.
- It is for all—whoever desires it (Revelation 22:17).
- Its origination is God Himself. He planned it.
 He offers it. He accomplishes it. He completes it.
 He keeps it.

Stay with me. It only gets better.

For Personal Reflection and Application

❖ Colossians 2:9, 10 reminds us that *in Him dwells all the fullness of the Godhead bodily; and you are complete in Him, who is the head of all principality and power.* Do you think it's accurate to say that not only is the Lord Jesus Christ God's provision for the world to be its Savior, but He is also our provision to live the Christian life? Is Christ all you need for salvation? Is He is all you need for victorious living? Is our salvation complete in Him—all the way from our initial trust in Him to save us, on through all of life here on earth, and on into eternity—Christ is everything?

❖ The resurrected Christ gives us an assurance that no religion or cult in the world could possibly offer. There is no certain forgiveness in Islam, in Hinduism, in Buddhism, or in any so–called "Christian" cult. Do you understand that in Jesus Christ alone we possess certainty of being forgiven and of spending eternity in the presence of our wonderful God? How does this reality affect you?

Man's part in salvation is merely to depend upon or trust God to perform, and to accept that which God freely gives. That is exactly what the words "through faith" mean.

J. F. Strombeck
in *So Great Salvation*

8

Understanding the Message:
Man's Response

At Gail's request, I was speaking to her priest and we were discussing whether or not keeping the sacraments was necessary for one's salvation. I asked, "What would you tell one of your parishioners to do if he was on his death bed and asked you what he had to do to be ready to meet God?" Father Murphy replied, "I would tell such a person to cast himself upon the mercy of Christ." I then asked, "If that is what your parishioners must do to be ready to meet God, why wouldn't you tell them that while they are healthy?" I was astounded by his reply: "I couldn't do that because then they would never show up for church."

———————◆———————

Throughout church history there have been debates of a theological nature in which those of varying degrees of agreement or disagreement would meet to discuss, argue, reason, and wrestle with the thorny issues facing the church at the time. Many more topics were discussed in lengthy church councils and in secluded conclaves, such as the Trinitarian nature of God, the human/divine natures of Christ, the personality of the Holy Spirit, the nature of the church, the canon of Scripture, eternal decrees, the nature of man, and the priesthood of believers.

Though official dogmas have been developed and authoritatively pronounced as God's mind on many of these issues, and volumes upon volumes have been written defending one position or another, total agreement on any of the issues has never been realized. It is still the same today.

Of all the Biblical and theological doctrines and issues debated over the centuries, one stands out as the doctrine which has been consistently argued throughout the church's history from the days of the first century church to the present. While other theological areas have been officially debated in large church councils once, twice, up to four or five times in the last twenty centuries, men have persistently wrangled over this doctrine during the entire 2,000 year history of the church. The debated question of which I speak was first asked of Paul and Silas while in a Philippian jail. The distraught jailer cried out, *"What must I do to be saved?"* (Acts 16:30).

The First Church Council Debate:
What Does God Require of Man for Salvation?

Sometime before Paul and Silas were asked the above question by the Philippian jailer, that issue arose and was debated at a church wide gathering in Jerusalem; thus it has been called The Jerusalem Council. The account of that gathering and the conclusions the church leaders reached is found in the fifteenth chapter of Acts.

And certain men came down from Judea and taught the brethren, "Unless you are circumcised according to the custom of Moses, you cannot be saved." Therefore, when Paul and Barnabas had no small dissension and dispute with them, they determined that Paul and Barnabas and certain others of them should go up to Jerusalem, to the apostles and elders, about this question (vss.1-2).

Physical circumcision of a male child was the sign God gave Abraham confirming His covenant with him (Genesis 17:1-14). In the process of time circumcision became a national and religious badge of honor, so to speak. By the time we open the pages of the New Testament *The Circumcision* was descriptive of the Jew, while *The Uncircumcision* was a way to describe the unclean Gentiles (Ephesians 2:11; Colossians 3:11).

The ones who insisted on circumcision as a condition for Gentiles to be saved were legalistic, religious Jews who did not understand the Gospel of God's free grace. Therefore, the church in Antioch (Acts 14:26-28) sent Paul, Barnabas, and others, to the recognized church leaders in Jerusalem to decide the true answer to the question.

Verse six states that "the apostles and elders came together to consider this matter." Certain ones then gave their reports and views. We're told "there had been much dispute" over this question (vs. 7). This was no casual issue. It was crucial. It still is. In fact, it may be the most crucial question of our day.

Here are summaries of the reports given:

Peter: God chose him to go the Gentiles (Cornelius' household, Acts 10:1-11:18). They heard the "word of the gospel" through Peter and believed (vs.7). These believing Gentiles received the Holy Spirit, thus demonstrating that God "made no distinction between us and them, purifying their hearts by faith" (vss.8-9). Peter's conclusion is powerful: *Now therefore, why do you test God by putting a yoke on the neck of the disciples which neither our fathers nor we were able to bear? But we believe that through the grace of the Lord Jesus Christ we shall be saved in the same manner as they* (vs.10-11).

Paul and Barnabas: God worked many miracles and wonders through them among the Gentiles. We know from the record that these miraculous feats were used by God to bring unbelieving Gentiles to faith in Christ (Acts 13:6-12; 14:1-4, 8-18).

James: He reminded the leaders that what Peter had shared concerning the Gospel being by grace through faith in Christ alone was in agreement with "the words of the prophets" (vss. 14,15). James' conclusion, therefore, was to write a letter to the Gentiles throughout the Roman Empire who were "turning to God" and admonish them to abstain from things polluted by idols, from sexual immorality, from things strangled, and from blood (vss. 19-20).

The letter itself stated: *We have heard that some who went out from us have troubled you with words, unsettling your souls, saying, "You must be circumcised and keep the law"* — *to whom we gave no such commandment* (vs. 24).

Let's summarize the conclusions of these first century Church leaders—the apostles and elders—whom God had placed in positions of authority to settle this vital issue:

- The Gentiles heard the word of the Gospel
- They believed in Christ.
- These Gentile believers received the Holy Spirit.
- Their hearts were thus purified or cleansed.
- This cleansing from God was by faith.
- The Mosaic Law is a yoke that no one can bear.
- The Gentiles were saved by grace just as the Jews.

- The Gospel message as preached by Peter, Paul, Barnabas, and James is in complete agreement with the Jewish prophets.
- Those who add anything to the Gospel are troubling and unsettling to the souls of men, and are not in agreement with the apostles, elders, and prophets.

It should come as no surprise, then, that some of us today also feel that contending for the faith of the Gospel as defined by Scripture alone—not by theological tomes—is of utmost importance. It is not a theological hobby horse; it is not majoring in the minor; it is not being divisive. When done in bold love it is following the path of Peter, Paul, Barnabas, James, all the apostles, the prophets, the original elders of the church, and the great witnesses and soul winners throughout the history of the church.

The Testimony of the Entire New Testament

It seems sensible to deduce that if this was the unified conclusion of the recognized leaders of the day—especially the divinely appointed apostles—whatever else God would later reveal to them to preach or to write would have to be in total agreement with this divinely preserved record. That is, in fact, exactly what has occurred. The inspired writings of the apostles, the New Testament, agree completely with the conclusions reached at that first Jerusalem Council.

That is not to say that there are no passages in the New Testament which may appear to contradict the freeness of God's gift of salvation, received by grace through faith in Christ. But keep in mind that if there truly are contradictory passages in Scripture, then we would not have the Word of God, for God does not lie nor contradict Himself. What we do have, instead, are statements which appear contradictory on the surface, but when carefully analyzed, are not in contradiction at all to God's salvation message as recorded throughout His Word.

Perhaps this will help to set your mind at ease: God's way of salvation is consistently presented in His Word. At least 160 times in the New Testament the Scripture is clear that the one condition for being saved is to believe in the Lord Jesus Christ, to trust Him, to depend on Him, to have faith in Him (virtually all synonymous terms). If you discover a few verses that seem to teach otherwise, before jumping to the conclusion that you have discovered some contradictions, or some added conditions for salvation, stop to consider: what are you going to do with these 160 verses that clearly teach salvation is by faith alone? You may need to humbly admit the passages that puzzle you may be teaching something entirely different than you thought at first. I will be covering some of those verses later in the book. For now, here are those passages revealing that salvation is by faith alone in Christ alone:

Luke 7:48–50; 8:12; 18:42; John 1:7, 12; 2:23; 3:15, 16, 18, 36; 4:39, 41, 42; 5:24, 45–47; 6:29, 35, 40, 47; 7:38, 39; 8:24, 29, 30; 9:35-38; 10:24–26; 11:15, 25, 26, 41, 42; 12:36, 46; 13:19; 14:1–6; 17:20, 21: 19:35; 20:29, 31; Acts 3:16; 4:4, 32; 8:12, 37; 9:42; 10:43, 45; 11:17, 21; 13:12, 39; 14:1, 23, 27; 15:7, 9; 16:31; 17:4, 5, 11, 12; 18:8, 27; 19:4; 20:21; 21:25; 26:18; Romans 1:16, 17; 3:22, 25, 26, 27, 28, 30; 4:3, 5, 9, 11, 13, 16, 23, 24; 5:1,2; 9:30, 32, 33; 10:4, 6, 8, 9, 10; 11:20, 30–32; 15:13; First Corinthians 1:21; Second Corinthians 4:4; Galatians 2:16, 20; 3:2, 5, 6, 7, 8, 9, 11, 14, 22, 24, 26; 5:5 Ephesians 1:13, 19; 2:8; 3:17; Philippians 1:29; 3:9; First Thessalonians 1:7; 2:10; 4:14; Second Thessalonians 1:10; 2:12, 13; 3:2; First Timothy 1:16; 3:16; 4:3, 10; Second Timothy 1:12; 3:15; Hebrews 4:2, 3; 6:12; 10:39; 11:6, 7, 31; James 2:23; First Peter 1:5, 9, 21; 2:6, 7; First John 5:1, 5, 10, 13; Jude 5.

The above verses are, of course, only from the New Testament. The means of salvation revealed in the Old Testament, though not stated as clearly or as often as in the New Testament was nevertheless also by faith. Whereas we look *backward* in faith to a finished work on the Cross, the believers who lived before Jesus came looked *forward* in faith to a coming Messiah/Redeemer who would deliver them from the consequences of their sins. *Salvation throughout Scripture is by grace alone, through faith alone, in Christ alone. Nothing more. Nothing less. Nothing else.*

Man's response to God's provision of His offer of salvation in His Son is to believe in the Lord Jesus Christ. What does it mean to believe in Christ? You sometimes hear people say, "I've always believed in Christ." Has anyone always believed in Christ? What is often meant by such a statement is: 1) they trusted in Christ at such an early age that they cannot recall the exact time when they believed; or, 2) they have been raised to believe in Christianity and they have never believed in anything else, so to their way of thinking, they have always believed.

To believe *in* Christ is not the same thing as believing certain things *about* Him, even correct things such as that He was born of the virgin Mary, or that He died for the sins of the world, or that He is the Son of God, or that He will come again. Believing truths *about* Him and believing *in* or *on* Him are two entirely different matters.

To hold correct views about Christ would be like me saying, "I believe in George Washington." That is, I believe what I've studied about him in history books: there was such a person; he was a general in the Continental Army, he served as our first President, and his wife's name was Martha, he chopped down the cherry tree, and told his father, "I cannot tell a lie. I did it with my little hatchet" (or did he?)

On the other hand, to believe in Christ is similar to me saying, "I believe in my wife, Kathy." Obviously I am not simply saying that I believe she exists. What I'm saying is that I *trust* her. That is the Bible meaning of believing in or on Christ; and that is the response—and the only response—God demands from unbelievers if they are to be saved. To "believe on the Lord Jesus Christ" for salvation is to be convinced of the truth concerning Him and thus to trust in Him, to depend upon Him to do the saving. You become persuaded that He died for you personally and so you count on Him to do for you what you could never do for yourself—impart eternal life and forgive all of your sin.

As simple as God has made it, it is not easy for a proud person, a person who is full of their own goodness, to admit to their own spiritual bankruptcy. Many good folks readily confess that they believe in Christ, but upon questioning their belief it often becomes apparent that they believe the proper truths about Him, rather than believing in Him as their Savior, as is evident by the fact that they are *depending upon* their own efforts or good works. Note the emphasis in these verses on believing *in* or *on* Christ.

John 3:16: *For God so loved the world that He gave His only begotten Son, that whoever believes in Him should not perish but have everlasting life.*

John 3:18: *He who believes in Him is not condemned; but he who does not believe is condemned already, because he has not believed in the name of the only begotten Son of God.*

Believing in Christ brings salvation and freedom from condemnation. The only thing that condemns a man is failure to believe in Christ. One may fail to do a hundred and one honorable things, but failure to do the one required thing is to be condemned forever.

John 3:36: *He who believes in the Son has everlasting life; and he who does not believe the Son shall not see life, but the wrath of God abides on him.*

The one who believes in Christ has everlasting life and the one who does not believe in Him is under God's wrath. That's the issue: to believe in Christ or to fail to do so. No other decision in life carries with it such a far reaching and eternal consequence.

John 6:28-29: *Then they said to Him, "What shall we do, that we may work the works of God?" Jesus answered and said to them, "This is the work of God* (what God requires of you)*, that you believe in Him whom He sent."*

It is interesting that these inquirers asked what "works" (plural) they could do which would be pleasing to God, and Jesus replied in the singular— *"this is the work of God that that you believe in Him whom He sent."* If there was more for man to do to be saved than to believe in Christ, what a perfect opportunity for the Lord to elaborate and to finally include—in one passage —all the conditions that would be necessary. But the Lord never says too little or too much. There are those who say that believing in Christ is only the first step to salvation, but Jesus Christ made it as clear as could be that believing in Him was the *one* thing God requires of man for salvation.

John 6:47: *Most assuredly, I say to you, he who believes in Me has everlasting life.*

Talk about utter simplicity! You believe in Christ and you have eternal life. It is yours the moment you believe! Please forgive me for being so repetitious. I am no more so than the Scriptures themselves. God is trying to drill it into our heads and hearts that this is His way of salvation, and there is no other. If we who believe in Christ do not grasp it, how can we ever expect the unbeliever to get it? If our understanding of the greatest message on planet earth is inadequate or warped, that is what we will communicate to others whom we are trying to win. We have got to strip our vocabulary of all Christianese and religious jargon and ask God the Holy Spirit to so burn these awesome truths into our very souls that these same grand truths will flow out from us in a spontaneous way.

Acts 16:30-31: *And he brought them out and said, "Sirs, what must I do to be saved?" So they said, "Believe on the Lord Jesus Christ, and you will be saved, you and your household."*

As with Jesus in John 6:28-29, Paul and Silas missed a grand opportunity here to give what some call "the whole Gospel" by failing to include other requirements in addition to faith, such as water baptism, lifelong obedience, living by the Golden Rule, keeping the Ten Commandments, joining church. They answered this suicidal man's desperate question as fully as God intended them to answer. Others may think Paul and Silas' answer was inadequate but that's only because they do not comprehend the depth of God's grace, the completeness of Christ's payment for sin, the freeness of salvation, the meaning of faith, or all of the above.

Romans 4:4-6: *Now to him who works, the wages are not counted as grace but as debt. But to him who does not work but believes on Him who justifies the ungodly, his faith is accounted for righteousness, just as David also describes the blessedness of the man to whom God imputes righteousness apart from works.*

This passage is so good in pointing out that:

- If we could work for our justification, it would be owed us in much the same way as when we work for a salary.
- On the other hand, to the ungodly one who does no work, but who believes on Christ, God accounts his faith as righteousness.
- Even in the Old Testament David understood the imputed righteousness of God, apart from any of his good works, and it made him happy.

Note: *Ungodly* normally refers to one who is *without God.* It is not so much describing the person's lifestyle, his morality, or lack of it. If I say someone is *un*popular I mean they are lacking in friends, they are without friends. If I describe someone else as being *un*wise I mean they are lacking in wisdom, they are without it. So, the ungodly person is without God. He may be a more upright, consistent person than you, but that is not the issue.The issue is, does he have God in his life or not. If not, he is ungodly.

Ephesians 2:8-9 (here are those key verses again): *For by grace you have been saved through faith, and that not of yourselves; it is the gift of God, not of works, lest anyone should boast.* Though these verses do not use the terminology of believing in or on Christ, they do make it extremely clear that the salvation God offers is by grace, through faith, and does not depend at all upon any works that we may perform.

These two verses are so descriptive of God's way of salvation that *I suggest you use Ephesians 2:8 and 9 as a focus, a standard by which to measure all other salvation verses.* When you do this you will be absolutely thrilled at how it enables you to understand the Gospel more clearly than ever. At the same time, however, you may become saddened at how often you hear messages called "gospel" which directly contradict the clear, literal statements of these grand verses. Stay positive. Remain focused! It pays rich dividends. You can never go wrong following the Lord on any subject as He leads you through His Word.

THE Issue When Sharing the Gospel

Protestant fundamentalists, evangelicals, moderates, and liberals, Roman Catholics and charismatics, all will agree that salvation is by God's grace. Even cultists verbally agree that salvation is by grace. For instance, *The Book of Mormon* states that man is saved by grace *after* he has done all he can do—which is not grace at all!

If you, as a witness for Christ, are not careful you will be deceived into thinking folks know the Lord because they will agree with you that we are saved by grace. However, if you tactfully question them you may discover that though they are *saying* that we are only saved by God's grace, they will *actually believe* we are saved by grace and works, not by grace alone.

Such a clever hard–to–detect counterfeit comes disguised in various ways. The sincere Protestant may admit that we are saved by grace but then add, "But God expects us to do our part, too." Our part may be anything from walking forward during the invitation, to saying a prayer, to making promises to God to do better, to joining church, to being baptized, to giving up certain sins, to living an obedient life. If you are speaking with a devout Roman Catholic you may be told emphatically that salvation is by grace because, after all, "We receive grace whenever we partake of the sacraments." Someone else may admit to the fact that salvation is by grace but also entertain the possibility of "sinning away our day of grace."

Write this indelibly in your brain; don't ever forget it: AS SALVATION IS THROUGH FAITH ALONE, SO IT IS BY GRACE ALONE! IT CANNOT BE BY GRACE and WORKS! This truth will at times prove to be the most difficult Bible truth for the unbeliever to grasp—especially unsaved church people who think they are already Christians—but it is absolutely essential that you personally understand it thoroughly and communicate it as clearly and as faithfully as you possibly can.

There are going to be "many" who will remind Jesus of how many "wonderful works" they did in their life times *in His name*, but He will say to them, *"I never knew you. Depart from Me you who practice lawlessness"* (Matthew 7:22, 23). Any dependence upon our own works or goodness will only land us in hell, not in Heaven.

Regarding this issue of grace, take special note of the following verses.

Romans 11:6: *And if by grace, then it is no longer of works; otherwise grace is no longer grace. But if it is of works, it is no longer grace; otherwise work is no longer work.*

In this all important matter of salvation, grace nullifies works, and works nullify grace. Salvation is not a blend of the two. It is—it *must* be—an either-or proposition. You cannot have it both ways. If a person to whom you are witnessing does not grasp this, you will only make it more difficult to really win him to Christ if you coerce him into making some kind of "decision" before he truly understands the Gospel.

Time and time again, just when you think someone is really understanding the Gospel, you will discover that they still have not understood the nature of grace. Apart from free grace there is no salvation. This doesn't mean that one cannot believe in Christ and be saved unless he fully understands grace. However, since the very heart of the Gospel is that salvation is only by God's grace through faith, you may not be clearly presenting the Bible way of salvation if you have failed to satisfactorily explain the true nature of grace to the unsaved. *Recognizing salvation by grace alone as the key issue of the Gospel will make you a much more effective witness for Christ.* Also, comprehending this grand truth will be the key that will open up so many other truths that have been puzzling to you for such a long time.

Take, for instance, the view held by some that there is merit in human faith. If that were true, it could not be *our* faith that saves us. God would have to give us the faith; it would have to be—as some contend—of divine origin, not our own faith. Otherwise we could boast and Ephesians 2:8–9 says we have been saved by grace through faith *in order to keep us from boasting.*

Well, what settles a question like this, our logic or Scripture? I trust you believe Scripture does. That being so, Romans also makes it clear that *faith is not meritorious and, therefore, is not a work*; there is nothing in or about faith that could cause us to boast.

We just read in Romans 11:6 that if salvation is by grace, it cannot be by works as well—(works: that which we do or perform, and to which we could point as having some merit). In light of this definition and in light of what Romans 11:6 reveals, consider this additional verse.

Romans 4:16: *Therefore it is of faith that it might be according to grace, so that the promise might be sure to all the seed, not only to those who are of the law, but also to those who are of the faith of Abraham, who is the father of us all.*

"It is of faith (in order) *that it might be according to grace!"* Can faith, then, possibly be a work? Can it have human merit that would allow the believer in Christ to boast? Not in light of Romans 11:6, and not if this verse is taken at face value. Does a drowning man boast because he trusts the lifeguard to save him? Does the trapped occupant of a burning building brag because he allows the fire fighter to carry him to safety? Does the dying patient, whose life is saved by the skill of a surgeon, take credit for the saving of his life? Of course not. Neither can any believing sinner boast of relying upon Jesus Christ to do all of the saving, to take him all the way to Heaven. Yes, salvation is through faith so that it might be completely compatible with God's grace. Faith is not the Savior; Christ is. It is the object of my faith that has merit, not my faith. The very nature of faith is to say, "I can't

do it. I'm trusting another to do it for me."

Having faith in Christ is looking away from self to the Savior, not looking within to find some saving merit there. Faith, you see, is not a work; it has no merit. Rather, it focuses on the One who has all the saving merit we need—the Lord Jesus Christ!

Salvation, then, is by grace and not of works. Neither is it by grace *and* works; nor can it be. The means by which God's great salvation comes to man is through faith as the helpless, hopeless sinner relies upon the saving merit of Another, counting upon Him to do what would be impossible for the unbeliever to do for himself—save his soul and give him eternal life in Heaven.

For Personal Reflection and Application

❖ Are you aware that you are not only saved by grace, but it is through God's grace that you are also trained by Him? Titus 2:11 and 12 reveals this grand truth. *For the grace of God that brings salvation has appeared to all men, teaching us that, denying ungodliness and worldly lusts, we should live soberly, righteously, and godly in the present age.* Romans 4:16 tells us that right standing with God is by grace so that the promise of salvation may be sure or certain. It is also a certainty that as we are taught by His grace we will honor Him with our lives. Grace never leads anyone astray.

❖ We are also reminded in Colossians 2:6 that *as you have therefore received Christ Jesus the Lord, so walk in Him.* We received Him through faith. We are to walk in the same way. Romans 10:17 says, *So then, faith comes by hearing and hearing by the Word of God.* Are you walking by faith? Can you trust the Lord to work in and through you to reach others?

❖ We need to pause periodically to thank our great God for such a full, complete, and satisfying relationship we are able to have with Him by His grace and through faith. How simple, yet majestic! Is it your habit to thank the Lord for such a complete salvation? Never lose sight of the Cross!

From the moment you
trust in Christ as your
Savior, God will always
treat you as His child;
never again will
He view you as one
outside of His family.
You will be His forever.

RAS

9

Understanding the Message: God's Guarantee

Nate was a sweet-spirited, mentally challenged young man and when he grasped the beauty of the Gospel tears welled up in his eyes. I asked, "Why the tears, Nate?" After a slight hesitation he replied, "Just to think, I'll be with the Lord forever and ever in a new body and with a new mind. I'll never again have to ask, 'Why'?" What an impact there is upon a believer when he is absolutely certain of having eternal salvation!

⇒•◇•⇐

The Security of the True Believer

As much as possible, try to remove from your thinking everything you have ever heard or read on this subject—all the logical arguments for or against the security of the believer. Especially forget all the labels and accusative phrases such as:

> Eternal Security
> Once-Saved-Always-Saved
> Once-in-Grace-Always-in-Grace
> Doctrine of the Devil
> Easy Believism
> Cheap Grace

When one can't support or defend a position with abundant Scriptural evidence, the next best thing is to conjure up mental pictures in the minds of the untaught causing them to cringe at the very thought of believing "something like that!" Politicians and the media resort to this sort of thing on a regular basis. In politics, one holding an opposite view of mine might be viewed as either an extreme ultra-conservative fascist, or a tax-and-spend, bleeding-heart liberal. Within the ranks of Christianity there is also the unfortunate name-calling, the mud slinging, the playing upon emotions, that ought to be below all of us who name the Name of Christ.

Our only authority should be the Word of God and we especially need to be reminded of some healthy principles that should govern our interpretation of God's Word. I mention them only briefly. There are several excellent books on the whole subject of *hermeneutics* (the art and science of interpreting Scripture) which you can study on your own (see Recommendations). For now, these reminders should prove helpful:

- Consider to whom any passage is addressed. Believers? Unbelievers? Israel? The Church?
- Consider the content of a verse—what is actually in the verse itself; or, sometimes what is not said—do not read into the verse or passage what is not there.
- Consider the context of a verse or passage, that which surrounds the statement you are studying. This will often prove to be the key to understanding difficult portions of the Bible.
- Where the Bible speaks literally, always interpret it literally.
- Always interpret the vague, unclear, or symbolic portions of Scripture (such as parables) by the plain, clear, and literal passages, never do the reverse of this.
- Study all the passages on the same subject so you will have a thoroughly balanced view of the topic under consideration.
- Avoid all personal prejudice. Do not force God's Word to fit your preconceived notions, or your experiences, or some theological school of thought that you embrace. Be honest with your treatment of Scripture, especially with those portions that don't seem to quite "fit" the way you feel they should fit. I remind you once again that God admonishes us in First Corinthians 4:6 to not even *"think beyond what is written."* In Second Corinthians 4:2 Paul gave this personal testimony of his own approach to Scripture: *But we have renounced the hidden things of shame, not*

walking in craftiness nor handling the word of God deceitfully, but by manifestation of the truth commending ourselves to every man's conscience in the sight of God.

- Do not hurry your interpretation, particularly when studying something new, or when delving into an area of study which may initially create negative feelings within you, or when tackling a difficult passage.

As we now turn to Scripture, allow God's Word to be your only authority concerning this subject, as well as with all topics you may study over your lifetime.

First John 5:9-13 is one of the most powerful and exciting passages in all the Word of God concerning our eternal position in Christ. Let it sink in as you read, and keep in mind that the truths revealed here are absolutely foreign to most people. So, as you share such a passage with one who is lost, go over it slowly so as to allow its grand truths to sink into their blinded souls. Here it is:

If we receive the witness of men, the witness of God is greater; for this is the witness of God which He has testified of His Son. He who believes in the Son of God has the witness in himself; he who does not believe God has made Him a liar, because he has not believed the testimony that God has given of His Son. And this is the testimony: that God has given us eternal life, and this life is in His Son. He who has the Son has life; he who does not have the Son of God does not have life. These things I have written to you who believe in the name of the Son of God, that you may know that you have eternal life.

In chapter twelve I give suggestions on how I present the Gospel, including the security of the believer. For now I just want to point out the following observations from this very important passage, plus a few more to follow.

From **First John 5:9-13** we observe:

- Whatever God says, His witness is greater, more reliable than any witness of man about anything at all. Applied to this subject of the believer's security, whatever God says about it is greater than anything and everything man may say to the contrary. If God says it, that settles it (v. 9).
- He who believes in Christ would normally have the

inner witness that he has believed God's testimony or witness (v. 10).

- Refusal to believe God is equivalent to calling Him a liar (v. 10). The reason: because he has not believed God's testimony concerning His Son.

- God has given eternal life to believers. Notice the tense: **has given** *us eternal life*, not will give, or is giving. It is done the moment one believes in His Son (v. 11).

- This eternal life, which is God's gift, is in His Son, Jesus Christ (v. 11). Here is an excellent reason for explaining why there must be only one way to Heaven. Only the life resident within Jesus Christ is eternal. It is a part of His very nature. No one else, nor any religion or church, or ritual, has it to give.

In speaking of Christ, the Bible states that He is *the only Potentate, the King of kings and Lord of lords, who alone has immortality* (First Timothy 6:15-16). The word *immortal* means not subject to death, so Jesus Christ is the only one who ever dwelt on earth who is immortal. Having paid sin's debt, He conquered death once and for all through His resurrection, and is not subject to it ever again. Man, on the other hand, is mortal. We do not have immortality within us. However, in Paul's last letter God spelled out how one may receive immortality, thus living forever. He said that salvation has now been revealed by the appearing of our Savior Jesus Christ, who has abolished death and brought life and immortality to light, through the gospel (Second Timothy 1:9-10). How do we receive eternal life or immortality? Through the Gospel.

- Those who have Christ have eternal life. Those who do not have Christ, do not have eternal life (v. 12).

- This particular passage was written expressly for the purpose of making the readers aware that if they indeed do believe in Christ, they may KNOW that they HAVE ETERNAL life! Imagine: a personal letter from God Himself letting believers in Christ know that He is giving us the privilege of being certain that we now have eternal life through His Son (v. 13).

So, dear reader, regardless what you may have thought previously, does it sound as if it's possible to be certain of having eternal life now, or does it sound as if we will have to wait until we die to find out? Don't hesitate to follow the Word of God wherever it leads.

Here is another great passage on the believer's security in Christ—**John 5:24:** *Most assuredly, I say to you, he who hears My word and believes in Him who sent Me has everlasting life, and shall not come into judgment, but has passed from death into life.*

Here are three stupendous guarantees to the believer:

- He *has* everlasting life. If the true believer has it and it is eternal, then there will never be a time when he doesn't have it!
- He absolutely will *not* be brought into judgment. Once one believes in Christ he will never ever be brought into judgment or condemnation. The believer's works will be judged or weighed—good and bad—to determine the degree of his rewards, but he will never be condemned (Romans 14:10-12; First Corinthians 3:11-15; Second Corinthians 5:10).
- He has *already passed* from spiritual death into life. Once one is born into God's family by faith in Christ (John 1:12; 3:3,7) there is no getting unborn. Believers have already entered into God's family and so already have spiritual life, which is eternal.

It keeps getting better and better, doesn't it? Consider further—**John 6:37:** *All that the Father gives Me will come to Me, and the one who comes to Me I will by no means cast out.*

This is such a beautifully simple promise that it grieves me deeply when unbelieving, religious men, who do not comprehend grace, twist it and pervert it so. Those who do not believe in the Bible doctrine of the security of the believer, sometimes say they believe in *conditional security* or *limited security* (meaning you are secure as long as you faithfully obey God). When they, therefore, come to this verse they must do something with it because it seems to be offering assurance that those who come to Christ by faith are secure in Him.

I maintain that unless one is predisposed toward their own interpretive slant, there could only be one meaning to the Lord's comment in this verse. But there are those who say, "Well, it certainly is true that He won't cast us out, but we may walk out on our own, exercising our own freedom of choice." Such an interpretation terribly dilutes the impact of the promise, doesn't it? But perhaps such interpreters are correct. Maybe that is what He meant. How would we go about finding out? Why, by reading further into the context of the verse, of course. By doing so we may find Jesus clarifying things for us. Did He mean we could walk away and be lost? Will any of His children be lost or will they all be raised?

Let's read on in the immediate context and find out, carefully observing what is said in **John 6:39-40:** *This is the will of the Father who sent Me, that of all He has given Me I should lose nothing, but should raise it up at the last day. And this is the will of Him who sent Me, that everyone who sees the Son and believes in Him may have everlasting life; and I will raise him up at the last day.*

Some of these same "conditional security" people will reply to verse thirty-nine by saying, "Oh, yes, He *should* raise us up at the last day, but it doesn't necessarily follow that He *will.* That depends on us." However, please note:

• It is the Father's will that Jesus should lose *nothing* (no one) whom the Father has given Him. And whom has the Father given Him? Verse thirty-seven tells us—"the one who comes to Me" or, in other words, the believer. Now, I may not be much but I'm at least something; and Jesus promised He would lose nothing!

• It is also the Father's will (vs. 39) that the one who believes in His Son, 1) may have everlasting life, and 2) the Son *will* raise him up at the last day. Notice that verse 39 does not say that Jesus *should* raise up every believer, but that He *will* raise everyone of them, thus losing none.

But there is still more good news! **John 6:47** states: *Most assuredly, I say to you, he who believes in Me has everlasting life.*

This is one of my favorite verses on the security of the believer because of its utter simplicity. Jesus is so straightforward in this statement. Can you imagine the shock (or awe) those folks felt as they actually heard Him, whom many believed to be only a carpenter's son, make such an astounding declaration. But there it is: everlasting life is for those who believe in Him, and when they believe they have it.

Oh, if only people could hear this message! If only upon hearing it they would believe! And if upon believing in Christ for themselves, they would only share it with others! It is the grandest, simplest, deepest, most wonderful message in all the world. Here's another outstanding passage on the believer's security.

John 10:27-30: *My sheep hear My voice, and I know them, and they follow Me. And I give them eternal life, and they shall never perish; neither shall anyone snatch them out of My hand. My Father, who has given them to Me, is greater than all; and no one is able to snatch them out of My Father's hand. I and My Father are one.*

This is one of the great salvation/security passages. Unfortunately, some dear folks get hung up on the Lord's statement in verse twenty-seven that His sheep *follow* Him. Several false conclusions have been built on that word *follow.*

Some say if you are a true believer or sheep you will follow Him, and if you don't that simply proves you are not really one of His. We are told that to follow Him means that true Christians follow Him *by living obediently throughout their lives.*

Another common view is that the promises of verses twenty-eight and twenty-nine *("I give them eternal life, and they shall never perish")* are *only* for those who follow Him. Verse twenty-eight begins with, *"And I give them eternal life..."* That is, He gives eternal life to the sheep of verse twenty-seven who follow Him.

The problem is not with whether or not the sheep follow the Shepherd. It plainly says that they do. The question that must be answered is, "What does it mean to follow Him?" Once again, the context tells us.

Throughout the chapter He contrasts Himself as the True Shepherd to all others who have pretended to be shepherds. He says of Himself: *"I am the door of the sheep ...I am the good shepherd."* All others are *"thieves, robbers, hirelings, and strangers"* to the sheep. A major point that He makes is that the sheep follow *Him*; they do not follow the other false shepherds. Note the contrast: the sheep hear His voice (the voice of the shepherd); and He calls his own sheep by name and leads them out... the sheep follow Him, for they know His voice. *Yet they will by no means follow a stranger, but will flee from him, for they do not know the voice of stranger...I am the door of the sheep. All who ever came before Me are thieves and robbers, but the sheep did not hear them... the hireling...(who) does not own the sheep, sees the wolf coming and leaves the sheep and flees* (verses 3-5, 7, 8, 12).

He continues the same analogy in verse 27, and the meaning should be clear: as members of His flock we follow Him, not false shepherds. We don't follow Buddha. Mohammed is not our shepherd. We do not fall down before one or more of the millions of Hindu gods. Our allegiance is not to any cult figure. We follow Christ, and we will follow Him all the way to Heaven because that is where He is leading us!

His promise of giving us eternal life and guaranteeing that we shall never perish is given to us because we are His sheep, not because we obediently follow in His every step—meaning we are consistently obedient, and only as we obey and because of that obedience, we have eternal life. Such an interpretation, dear reader, clearly advocates salvation by works, which we have already seen in many verses is not God's way of salvation at all.

Believe the precious promise. If you are one of His, He has given you eternal life and you shall never perish; neither shall anyone (including Satan or demons, or even you yourself) snatch you out of His or His Father's hand. Thank God, our eternal destiny and safety depends upon Him holding onto us, not us trying to hold onto Him in our feeble way! But there's more—

John 20:31: *But these are written that you may believe that Jesus is the Christ* (Messiah), *the Son of God, and that believing you may have life in His name.*

This is the key verse of the Gospel of John because it reveals the reason God inspired him to write it. It is evident throughout the book of John that the true identity of Jesus is a major emphasis. Beginning with the very first verse of the book where He is described as the Word, that is, God who took on flesh, it is also clear throughout all twenty one chapters that eternal life comes only through this One. The verse quoted above also clearly states that having "life in His name" is through believing. If eternal life could come any other way, if God had other steps in mind for us to take so as to guarantee our eternal salvation, surely here would have been an ideal place to state it. The one New Testament book above all others which was designed to lead us to faith in Jesus as our Savior would be the book to contain all the necessary steps for getting to Heaven. And it does that, only the steps turn out to be a single step—*"and that believing you may have life in His name."*

Believing in Christ is mentioned some ninety times in the Gospel of John as the one and only condition for receiving eternal life.

Then in **Romans 8:38-39** we read: *For I am persuaded that neither death nor life, nor angels nor principalities, nor powers, nor things present nor things to come, nor height nor depth, nor any other created thing, shall be able to separate us from the love of God which is in Christ Jesus our Lord.*

The "us" of verse thirty nine are the ones who are "in Christ Jesus" (verse 1), of whom He said "there is now no condemnation." As you walk back through these two verses you see that nothing, absolutely nothing, can or will ever separate us from God's love in Christ.

Nothing in life, nothing in death, no spiritual creature— whether good or evil (including Satan and demons), no earthly powers which can only destroy the body but not the spirit, nothing anywhere throughout any and all universes, nothing in the present, nothing in the past, nothing in our unknown futures, nothing in the depths of the earth, no created thing of any kind, *"shall be able to separate us from the love of God which is in Christ Jesus our Lord."* Whew!

I marvel that there are those who think the Bible does not promise security to the true believer in Christ. It is so crystal clear!

The Difference Between Security and Assurance

The one who believes in Christ in the Biblical sense of the word is saved forever. That is God's promise to him. *There is no salvation offered by God that is not eternal.* That's *security.* Those who trust in Christ need not know they are secure in order to be secure. As a true believer you are secure even if you are ignorant of this fact. Knowledge of your security equals *assurance.* Though all true believers in Christ are secure, not all believers know the Bible guarantees they are secure. But if someone is thoughtful enough to show them Scriptures which reveal their security in Christ, that new found knowledge would lead them to full assurance.

Security without assurance makes for a miserable child of God, full of anxiety, worry, unnecessary fretfulness, doubts, emotional agony, and even mental or emotional breakdowns at times. Sometimes, too, those believers who are ignorant of their security in Christ begin to stretch the truth concerning their personal lives. Thinking that being secure depends upon performance rather than depending solely upon grace, such believers tend to minimize their sins. Instead of admitting their sin they may call a lie "a slip of the tongue," or a lustful thought may be labeled "a demon of lust," thus relieving themselves of direct responsibility.

However, once you comprehend the awesome grace of God in securing your eternal destiny, the fear of losing that relationship vanishes and you can be totally honest with your Heavenly Father. Being secure in a family strengthens the family ties; it never weakens them. Insecurity in any relationship weakens and may destroy such a relationship, particularly in the spiritual realm. I love God more because I know I am secure in His faithful, infinite love.

To illustrate: suppose you were caught in the middle of the worst earthquake the world has ever experienced. Everything is shaking. You run outside for safety only to have trees and buildings fall all around you. The ground is heaving and cracking under your feet. You don't know where to run, or if you should move at all. There doesn't seem to be any place of refuge. Would you be scared? Would you feel safe? Might you perhaps even lose control of your senses and go berserk? All of those reactions would be pretty normal in such a devastating situation.

Now suppose before this traumatic event occurred, God appeared to you and described the earthquake in minute detail, explaining everything that was going to happen and giving you a personal guarantee that you would not be harmed, even going so far as to show you exactly where to stand so as to be safe from all harm. How do you think that would affect your emotional and mental state during the earthquake? If you saw before your very eyes the exact things happening which God had previously detailed for you, can't you imagine the deep calm you would have in the midst of the chaotic upheaval going on all around you?

Here's the lesson: if God determined that you would be safe in that earthquake but didn't inform you of it, you would still be completely secure in it, even though you might become completely unraveled emotionally by the quake. Your security would be no less certain because you did not know what God had in store. But as soon as God let you in on His plan, the knowledge that He had personally guaranteed your safety would produce deep assurance within you. Then you would be certain that no matter how bad the earthquake became you would be safe. A great calm would flood your soul.

The true believer in Christ may be certain of his or her salvation now. As good ambassadors for Christ it is our responsibility to share the Gospel with whomever we can, leading them into the full assurance of their salvation. The only salvation God offers is eternal, so we have not fully shared His message until we have presented *that* salvation to the unbeliever.

Summary: Presenting the Way of Salvation

God's Demand
Man must be perfect—*as perfect as God*—to qualify for Heaven.
Psalm 5:4; Habakkuk 1:13; Revelation 21:27.

Man's Condition
Man is not, *nor can he be*, perfect—he has already sinned.
Isaiah 64:6; Jeremiah 17:9; Romans 3:10, 23; 8:7,8; Ecclesiastes 7:20.

God's judgment or penalty on sin is death—*separation*.
Romans 6:23; Ezekiel 18:20.

Man can do *nothing* of himself to obtain this perfection.
Romans 4:5; 9:30-32; Ephesians 2:8,9; Galatians 2:16;
Philippians 3:9; Titus 3:5.

God's Provision
He sent His Son, the Lord Jesus Christ, to be our Savior, our Sin-Bearer.
Christ paid the penalty of our sin for us and rose from the dead,
thus proving the debt had been *paid* and *accepted* by the Father.
Isaiah 53:6; Second Corinthians 5:21; Philippians 3:9;
First Peter 2:24; 3:18; Romans 1:3,4, 16, 17; First John 2:2.

With sin's debt paid, salvation is offered *freely* to man as the *gift* of God.
Romans 5:15-18; 6:23; Ephesians 2:8,9; Second Timothy 1:9.

Man's Response
Man must personally *believe in* the Lord Jesus Christ
to obtain this gift of salvation.
(To "believe" means to rely upon, to trust in Him).
The Biblical response from the unbeliever can be summed up in the phrase:
By Grace Alone, through Faith Alone in Christ Alone—Nothing More
Nothing Less, and Nothing Else!
John 3:18, 36; 6:28,29, 47; 20:31; Romans 4:5.; 9:30-10:4.

God's Guarantee
The true believer in Christ may be *certain* of his or her salvation
***now* and salvation, once received, can *never* be lost.**
First John 5:9-13; John 5:24; 6:37, 39; 10:28-30; Romans 8:38, 39.

For Personal Reflection and Application

❖ Isn't it so kind and thoughtful of God to let us KNOW that we have eternal life through faith in Christ? No religion or cult anywhere in the world offers anything even remotely similar to what the true and living God gives to His children.

❖ Imagine for a moment the millions upon millions of devoutly religious people who strive, pray, labor and sacrifice with no hope, no certainty of where they will go when they die. Let your mind drift further to envision those same millions who have not even heard of the Bible or of Jesus. Could you perhaps be the means of carrying the Water of Life to some of them? Are you willing to be used in that way?

❖ How perpetually grateful we should be for the great salvation we have from so great a God. May we never cease praising and thanking Him, even throughout eternity.

THE

GOSPEL

PRESENTATION

We have not fully
preached a free gospel.
We have been afraid of
making it too free,
lest men should be led
into licentiousness;
as if it were possible to
preach too free a gospel,
or as if its freeness
could lead men into sin.
It is only a free gospel that
can make men holy.

Horatius Bonar

10

Sharing the Gospel:
The Need for Simplicity and Clarity

It was at a youth rally during which a number had indicated they were trusting in Christ to save them, that I afterwards engaged three of the teenagers in conversation. During our brief chat I asked why they had trusted in Christ. Each gave a good response, but the one I still recall is the girl who said, "It was clear and to the point. He (the speaker) was so simple that even I could understand it."

———≡•◇•≡———

I have been observing the drift away from a clear "Thus says the Lord" within Christian circles for more than fifty years. In America especially there seems to be a tidal wave of trendiness in ministry, and of meeting the felt needs of people (often at the expense of meeting their real needs), and of being accepted by the world. The words of Andrew Bonar (1810-1892) ring in my ears as I survey the current Christian scene: *"I looked for the Church and found it in the world; I looked for the world and found it in the Church."* I sense a kind of fanatical fervency on the part of many to be "state of the art" in everything that's done in the name of the Lord. This trendiness covers every aspect of the Christian's existence, from the way we dress, to our choices of entertainment, to the music we approve, to the things we read and watch, from the nature of our church services, to the principles employed in counseling, and to the methods used in designing and leading youth ministries.

Some changes, of course, are good and long overdue. For the most part, church services for many years have been far too stiff and intimidating to the average unbeliever or visitor. The move toward more casual gatherings could be healthy for the body of Christ, for when people are relaxed they tend to be more open and so fellowship with other believers develops in a more natural way. The influx of newer songs for the church has been generally good, as long as the great hymns of the church are not discarded in the process. The "great gulf" that has existed between clergy and laity (too often encouraged by the clergy throughout the church's history) is being gradually replaced by a more balanced and Biblical model where clergy and laity work together on a more level playing field as "God's fellow workers" in the harvest field (First Corinthians 3:5-9ff).

However, in the area of how we communicate God's message, I'm afraid we have created a strange marriage of traditional theological and evangelistic cliches with trendy catch-phrases that have pushed clear Scriptural statements and truths far into the background of our preaching, teaching, and witnessing. It is in this matter of being clear in our presentation of Bible truths that I am most concerned. If we do not convey God's truth to others in a clearly understood fashion we fail miserably in our roll as ambassadors and witnesses for Christ. We need to do our homework, saturating ourselves with a proper and thorough understanding of the Word of God; and we need to get the message straight, so that we are able to accurately pass that message on to others.

Man has concocted many techniques in the attempt to make eternal truths more palatable to an untaught, and often disinterested world, and it has created a problem of major proportions, though the church as a whole is oblivious to its presence, to say nothing of its magnitude.

When it comes to Bible truth, and especially presenting the Gospel, I take my stand with those who believe that communicating God's Word in a clear, understandable way is important—*very* important. It is vital to effective Biblical evangelism. In fact, it is the lack of clarity in communicating truth that has produced so much confusion and uncertainty in Christian circles. Failure to explain God's Word clearly has been the direct or indirect cause or catalyst leading to many false doctrines and cults.

When I emphasize the need for clarity in presenting the Gospel some wonder, "What's the big fuss? Why be so fervent in making sure everything is expressed in just a certain way?" I've been told, for instance, that the apostles and prophets didn't harp on the exact wording of phrases, or the precise definition of words, so why should we? Some feel that the matter of clarity is a mere side issue or even a nonissue in Scripture. Others claim, "The Bible doesn't emphasize the clarity by which one presents the truth; its emphasis is upon the truth itself, not upon the language in which that truth is couched."

I do not agree with that assessment. I believe clarity in presenting eternal truths is vitally important. Here's why I feel so strongly about it.

First, Words Have Meanings

It is an indisputable fact that words mean something. Not only so, but even the same word may convey different meanings when used in varying contexts. To say, as an example, that it doesn't matter whether we refer to the coming of the Holy Spirit to live within a believer as His indwelling, His anointing, His baptizing work, His abiding, His filling, or His sealing is to not only ignore the different meanings of the various terms used, but it is to bring unnecessary confusion in the minds of many concerning some vitally important Biblical truths.

How sad, for instance, for a true believer in Christ to be earnestly praying for the Holy Spirit to come as an indwelling presence when Romans 8:9 makes it crystal clear that if one has Christ he already has the Holy Spirit indwelling him. It's an automatic blessing from God for those who are in Christ. How comforting to know He is living within me because I trust in Christ as my Savior.

Or take the matter of salvation. What is required for one to receive eternal life? Ask the average person and you'll probably get answers like these: Do the best you can. Keep the Ten Commandments. Go to church. Pray. Be good. Be sincere.

By contrast, ask the same question of leading Christian communicators—pastors, Bible teachers, evangelists and others who should know the best ways to express God's truth—and you may be told to: Give your heart to Jesus. Commit your life to Christ. Turn from sin. Pray the sinner's prayer. Receive Christ as your Savior. Surrender to Christ as Lord of your life.

Confess Christ publicly.

All the things listed above in response to a simple question about what is required to receive eternal life cannot, nor do they, have the same meaning. Different words have different meanings! In response to the question, "What must I do to be saved?" we cannot answer "Believe on the Lord Jesus Christ" or "Commit your life to Christ" or "Keep the Ten Commandments" and logically contend all three answers are really saying the same thing. They are not. *It matters how we express truth!* We had better be certain we are correct when we proclaim, "Thus says the Lord." We dare not put our own words into His mouth.

Jeremiah 23:25, 26, 28, 30–32 provides some very sobering warnings to heed. *"I have heard what the prophets have said who prophesy lies in My name, saying, 'I have dreamed, I have dreamed!' "How long will this be in the heart of the prophets who prophesy lies? Indeed they are prophets of their own heart"..."The prophet who has a dream, let him tell a dream; and he who has My word, let him speak My word faithfully"..."Therefore behold, I am against the prophets," says the LORD, "who use their tongues and say, 'He says.' "Behold, I am against those who prophesy false dreams," says the LORD, "and tell them, and cause My people to err by their lies and by their recklessness. Yet I did not send them or command them; therefore they shall not profit this people at all," says the LORD.*

As long as those who see themselves as communicators of God's truth do not use precise Biblical words and phrases with accurate Biblical definitions, we will continue to flounder and to confuse other believers and, more tragically, we will keep perpetuating a condition of cloudiness in the already darkened minds of nonbelievers, keeping them from understanding the beauty and simplicity of the Gospel of God's amazing Grace.

The Impression Our Words Make Upon Others

What people perceive as we attempt to accurately convey God's truth may be nearly as important as what we actually say. For this reason I emphasize over and over again the importance of *using Bible words and phrases with Bible definitions expressed in such a way that anyone may understand*. This is the very heart of clear, accurate communication of the Gospel.

Probably the only thing worse than using Bible terms without also defining them biblically is using Bible terminology with incorrect man-made definitions. Yet, in our witnessing we often use correct words and phrases but leave it up to the unbeliever to supply their own definitions. And how does the unsaved know what we mean by what we say? Often their understanding comes from past perceptions of what they have heard or read.

Take, for instance, the phrase *born again*. The secular media use born again to describe everything from a true Christian, to a failing business that's been revived, to a losing team coming back late in the game to pull victory out of the jaws of defeat. The religious writers and pundits can speak of being born again and be referring to reincarnation (New Age), or regeneration through water baptism (Church of Christ), or of finding the key that restores true religion to earth (many cults). How, then, would the unbeliever understand you when you tell him he must be born again? He would probably attach a definition to the phrase by what his *perception* of it is or has been

Then there's a good, solid word like *repent*—another Bible word, and a word frequently used when the Gospel is preached. It is something every unbeliever automatically does when he shifts from his unbelief to faith in Christ. It is something every Christian must do to grow in their walk with the Lord. But if you tell a man he has to repent without defining it biblically, what will he likely think repentance means? Based on past exposures to the use of the word, his perception will probably be something like: "I've got to give up all my sinful habits. I've got to quit sinning. I've got to quit having any fun." So, you see, how one *perceives* what you are attempting to communicate is very important. Therefore, clarity of expression and accurate biblical definitions do matter.

The Testimony of History

One cannot peruse the events of the past without being repeatedly impressed with the tremendous influence and power of words. To give a few positive examples: Lincoln's *Gettysburg Address* after that pivotal battle of the Civil War; and Winston Churchill's 1940 speeches to the House of Commons during some of the darkest days of World War II when Great Britain was virtually in it alone and taking a pounding day and night from the German Luftwaffe. Then there have been the documents and books that have shaped and changed the course of history: *Mein Kampf* (Adolf Hitler's blueprint for world conquest), *The Communist Manifesto* (Marx and Engels), the *Declaration of Independence*, Luther's *Ninety-five Theses* and, of course, *The Bible*, to name a few.

Words, spoken and written, have created, built, changed, and destroyed whole civilizations, created new movements and religions, have turned individual lives around for good or evil. The record of history, including Church history, gives strong testimony to the influence clearly stated precepts have had on mankind whether those precepts have been for man's good or have led to his ruin. The clarity with which thoughts are expressed does matter!

The Testimony of Personal Experience

Any Christian who takes witnessing for Christ seriously is well aware of the literal multitudes who are completely confused concerning the way of salvation. I never get over the feeling I have when I hear an unbeliever, or a brand new Christian, exclaim, "Oh, I've never heard that before. I was always under the impression that _____ " (whatever false ideas they have had about salvation or assurance). Where did they get those ideas and impressions? More than likely from some who felt they were giving out God's truth, or from others who were deliberately and knowingly leading folks astray by twisting Scripture (Second Peter 3:16; Ephesians 4:14).

I spoke to a Muslim young man once who was brought to my apartment to refute Christianity and the Bible, but after I shared the Gospel of God's grace with him (we talked most of the evening) he said in utter simplicity, "I've never heard this before. It's the most beautiful story I've ever heard." He had, however, heard "gospel" presentations of one kind or another, but the real meaning of the one and only Gospel of grace had never been explained to him.

On two different occasions I've had Jewish men with whom I shared the Gospel state that they always knew that if there was a God "this is how He would have to be"—referring to Jesus their

Messiah who gave His life a ransom for all. In both instances they had been "witnessed to" by one or more Christians but had not heard the Gospel presented in a clear, biblical way. I realize, of course, that some unbelievers do not "hear" the Gospel when it is presented because they are not ready to hear it. By that I mean their lives are not at the point where they are willing to listen; but such did not appear to be the case with these two men. They simply had not heard the Gospel clearly enough where they could understand it.

My experience—that which I have lived—has revealed to me that clarity of expression is of utmost importance when I am attempting to accurately share the Word of God.

The Cults Prove the Point

Over the years I have repeatedly warned my students to beware of the cultists for they often use Bible phrases that are devoid of Biblical definitions. Or, as someone else has said, "The cults have our vocabulary but not our dictionary."

If ever there was an area where the need for clarity is urgent it is in cult evangelism. If clarity of expression is unimportant, if we are not to be concerned with the meaning of words, then it doesn't really matter what the cultists mean when they tell us:

Jesus died as a ransom sacrifice for our sins. What the Jehovah's Witnesses really mean is that one man, Jesus, paid the sin debt for one man, Adam, thus enabling the rest of us to work our way into Jehovah's Kingdom on Paradise Earth.

Jesus is God. When a cultist makes such a bold statement they normally mean Jesus was God in the same way we are, or in the same way we can be, or that He is god with a small g.

Salvation is by God's grace. Virtually all cults and traditional churches say this. The usual meaning is that God's grace enables us to do the necessary things—the good works—that are required to gain salvation. In fact, the Book of Mormon even says, *"...we know that it is by grace that we are saved, after all we can do"* (Second Nephi 25:23). However, if we only receive God's grace after doing all we can do, none of us would ever end up in Heaven or Paradise. Such a definition of grace is a travesty, and is not grace at all!

One more illustration from the world of the cults should

establish the importance of stating God's truth clearly and accurately.

Does it matter, for instance, which Greek word was used by Christ when He said, *"This is eternal life, that they may* **know** *You, the only true God, and Jesus Christ whom You have sent"* (John 17:3)? The *New World Bible* (the official "translation" of the Jehovah's Witnesses) translates the verse this way: *"This means everlasting life, their* **taking in knowledge of** *you, the only true God, and of the one whom you sent forth, Jesus Christ."* Accordingly, the Jehovah's Witness cult insists that one must study the Scriptures through God's Organization, the Watchtower Society, in order to take in the proper knowledge of Jehovah and of Jesus Christ. Only in this way can anyone hope to gain entrance into His eternal, earthly kingdom.

Well, what does the Greek New Testament reveal about the meaning: that we need to *know* the only true God, or that it is sufficient to simply *take in knowledge* of Him? Is it really that important as to what it means? I'm sure you will agree that there is quite a difference between these two concepts: knowing God personally and knowing certain facts about God.

Words do mean something, and different words mean different things. *Ginosko*, the word used in John 17:3, conveys the idea of *a personal, experiential knowledge* of the Lord— knowing Him; whereas, *epiginosko* is the word that could be used in *knowing a subject after having researched it.* In other words, "taking in knowledge" of a subject. This is not the word used in John. Does it really matter what word or phrase is used in the translation? I think it is clear that it does. It's the difference between one's personal salvation and one's eternal condemnation!

If words, phrases, and sentences do not have specific meanings, if how we express the most awesome, beautiful message in all the universe does not really matter, then let's not question the next cultist we meet. If, on the other hand, we dare not allow the cults to get by with their manipulative twisting of Scripture; if we insist on taking a stand against all such false prophets, then we are admitting by our actions that how concepts are expressed does matter. We do need to hold them, and ourselves, accountable for what is said and how terms are defined?

We dare not waffle back and forth on such pivotal truths as the way of salvation, the substitutionary character of the death of

Christ upon Calvary, the literalness of His resurrection, the authority and inerrancy of Scripture, and the certainty of His coming again—just a few areas where clarity of expression is absolutely vital if we are to correctly understand these truths for ourselves, and properly convey them to others.

Either there is only one way to Heaven (faith alone in Christ alone), or there is more than one way. Remember, it is either by grace or it is by works. It cannot be a combination of both grace and works. Scripture states unequivocally that it is *"by grace you have been saved through faith, and that not of yourselves; it is the gift of God, not of works, lest anyone should boast"* (Ephesians 2:8, 9). Romans 11:6 adds, *"And if* (it) *is by grace, then it is no longer of works; otherwise grace is no longer grace. But if it is of works, it is no longer grace; otherwise work is no longer work."*

Either Christ died for me on the Cross as my Substitute or He did not. Either Jesus came back from the dead bodily and literally or He did not. Either the Bible is completely accurate and authoritative in all areas of life and is infallibly correct in all that it states, or it is not. Either Jesus Christ is coming again, or we have no hope. *Cultic heresies remind us that we had better be very careful and precise in our attempts to convey divine truth accurately.*

The Most Important Testimony of All

Even if none of the preceding reasons for emphasizing clarity in presenting God's truth were valid, there is one overriding reason for believing that presenting the Word of God in a clear, understandable fashion is important: *the Scriptures themselves!*

Imagine for a moment that you are enrolled in a Christian Evidences class at the ABC Bible School. Your professor might present the following formula for you to consider as evidence that the Bible may be from God:

If God is our Intelligent, All-Powerful Creator, He would want to communicate with His created beings who are also somewhat intelligent. That being so, God would:

- Communicate His message simply, in terms easily understood, using earthly examples and illustrations to make the truth of His statements clear to the common man.

- Communicate His message accurately, saying only and precisely what He wanted conveyed. He would use the exact words or phrases that would get His intended meaning across. He would avoid using words that would confuse.
- Preserve His message so that generation after generation would have it available to them.

This is exactly what the Bible is—God's divinely revealed, accurately given and transmitted message to mankind, preserved throughout the generations so that we might know Him and His purpose for us. The doctrine of *Revelation* contends that *God has revealed to man those things that man would not otherwise know.* The word *revelation* (such as in the Book of Revelation) means an unveiling, an uncovering of previously hidden truths. If, by its very nature, the Bible is God's way of revealing what He wants us to know, then obviously He would do it in such a way that we would understand and comprehend the meaning God intended; otherwise it could not be said of the Bible that it was an unveiling of truth at all.

God initiated His revelation by guiding specially chosen men in such a way that His complete Word to man was recorded. *For prophecy never came by the will of man, but holy men of God spoke as they were moved by the Holy Spirit* (Second Peter 1:21). This verse tells us how God did it—how He got His message from His heart to ours, how He conveyed His exact thoughts through men to men.

Consider also the character of inspiration, that is, the degree to which the Bible can be rightly viewed as God's revelation to man. I believe in what is called *verbal plenary* inspiration of the Bible. By *verbal* I mean that every word of the original revelation from God was inspired by Him. By the word *plenary* I refer to the fact that the whole of Scripture in its entirety is thus inspired. I have been persuaded to embrace this view of inspiration from Scripture itself. Consider these Bible statements:

Second Timothy 3:16: *All Scripture is given by inspiration of God* (is God-breathed), *and is profitable for doctrine, for reproof, for correction, for instruction in righteousness.*

All Scripture would include both Testaments in their entirety. It would include the words of Jesus as well as those of Paul. It would span all topics discussed with no contradictions anywhere.

Matthew 5:18: *For assuredly, I say to you, till heaven and earth pass away, one jot or one tittle will by no means pass from the law till all is fulfilled.*

The *jot* (literally, iote or jod) refers to the smallest letter in the Hebrew alphabet and is nearly identical to our apostrophe sign. The *tittle* is a small horn shaped mark used to indicate accent in Hebrew. In current vernacular Jesus' statement can be understood to mean that not one crossing of the "t" or dotting of the "i" will by no means pass from the law till all is fulfilled.

Psalm 119:160: *The **entirety** of Your word is truth* (plenary inspiration), *and **every one** of Your righteous judgments endures forever* (this supports verbal inspiration) .

Psalm 119:126-128: *It is time for You to act, O LORD, for they have regarded Your law as void. Therefore I love Your commandments more than gold, yes, than fine gold! Therefore all Your precepts concerning all things I consider to be right; I hate every false way* .

Everything upon which the Bible speaks is God's Word—all of it, each word and phrase of it, no matter what the subject.

Finally, consider the Bible's own emphasis upon clarity. Some examples should make the point.

When God originally gave His Law to Israel through Moses He had it inscribed on stones, and He commanded, *"You shall write **very plainly** on the stones all the words of this law"* (Deuteronomy 27:8). God wanted to make sure there was no misunderstanding of what He was commanding His people; He did not want them to miss it, so He had it written "very plainly."

Much later when the rebuilding of Jerusalem's wall was completed under Nehemiah's leadership, he gathered together *"the nobles, the rulers, and the people, that they might be registered by genealogy"*—nearly 50,000 people (Nehemiah 7:5, 66, 67). A short time later *"all the people gathered together as one man in the open square that was in front of the Water Gate; and they told Ezra the scribe to bring the Book of the Law of Moses, which the LORD had commanded Israel"* (8:1). The people stood from "morning (first light) until midday" (8:3) as Ezra and others read aloud. And how did they read? *"So they read **distinctly** from the book, in the Law of God; and they **gave the sense**, and **helped them to understand** the reading"* (8:8).

153

No ambiguous religious jargon or opinion here. They read God's Word plainly, provided clear interpretation, and showed them how to apply it to their own lives. That's clarity.

And what are we to think of the apostle Peter on the Day of Pentecost? He who cowered before a young Jewish maiden a few days previously now stood before thousands and boldly declared God's message of salvation through Jesus, the Messiah. Listen to his clear, ringing words: *"Therefore let all the house of Israel know assuredly that God has made this Jesus, whom you crucified, both Lord and Christ* (Messiah)*"* (Acts 2:36). Could there be any misunderstanding here? Hardly. The people's response was exactly what you might expect from such a straightforward declaration: *"Now when they heard this, they were cut to the heart, and said to Peter and the rest of the apostles, 'Men and brethren, what shall we do?'"* They clearly understood Peter's message, did they not?

Certainly one of the clearest communicators of God's message was the apostle Paul. In expounding upon the New Covenant which we are to preach today (as opposed to the Old Covenant), Paul declared that it is God who has *"made us sufficient as ministers of the new covenant, not of the letter but of the Spirit; for the letter kills, but the Spirit gives life"* (Second Corinthians 3:6). He then wrote, *"Therefore, since we have such hope, we use great boldness of speech"* (v. 12). The word *boldness* is translated in the King James Bible as "plainness" of speech, which may be a more preferable rendering in this case. You see, the boldness referred to here has nothing to do with loudness or rude bluntness. Vine says that it means "to speak without ambiguity; plainly; or without figures of speech." The same Greek word is translated "openly" in John 7:13 where it states that *"no one spoke openly of Him for fear of the Jews."* Because of the fear of what others might think or what they might do to them, the people in this instance did not make it clear what their feelings were concerning this Jesus of Nazareth.

In his first letter to the Corinthians Paul reasoned that every language has its own significance or meaning. He illustrated his point in this way: *"Even things without life, whether flute or harp, when they make a sound, unless they make a distinction in the sounds, how will it be known what is piped or played? For if the trumpet makes an uncertain sound, who will prepare himself for battle? So likewise you, unless you utter by the tongue* **words easy to understand**, *how will it be known what is spoken? For you will be speaking into the air"* (First Corinthians 14:7-9).

Traditional cliches or slogans (I call it *Christianese*) have no place in the communication of God's eternal message. The growing practice of using current trendy means of presenting Bible truths should also be shunned. They do not really help in conveying truth. They are, in fact, great hindrances to a clear presentation of any and all Bible doctrines. Think twice before you get caught up in the latest Christian fads. Make sure they are Biblically sound. Our purpose should be to *accurately* communicate Bible truth, not to just make it sound hip or cool.

The Need for Simplicity *and* Clarity

There is an important difference between being simple and in being clear in your presentation of the Gospel. To be simple is to state something in easy-to-understand terms. But I remind you that to be *clear,* in the context of communicating the Gospel, is to *state Bible truths with Bible definitions in every day language people readily understand.*

In the summer of 1969 I was on my way to a large pastor's conference in Saint Louis, Missouri. I had been on one of my speaking tours, driving from place to place, and was headed back to Florida from Minnesota, making stops along the way. I had been invited to speak at a church in a small Missouri town. I had never met the pastor but he had known of my ministry and asked me to speak on the Sunday morning before the pastor's conference was to begin. He also requested that I speak on evangelism, which I was happy to do.

Apparently during my message I made a comment to the effect that I never tell a lost person, "Give your heart to Christ," or "Open your heart to Christ," or "Invite Christ into your heart or life." After the service was over and he and I were on the parking lot getting ready to go to lunch, he said, "Dick, I have a question for you. You said in your message that you never ask an unbeliever to give his heart to Christ, or to invite Him in. I'd like to know why you don't because I always do."

I gulped and shot a prayer up to the Father (this pastor was over six feet tall!), and I asked him, "When you tell a nonbeliever to 'invite Christ into your heart' or 'to give Him your heart,' what is it you want him to do?" He thought for a moment and replied, "I want him to trust in Christ to save him." I replied, "So, why not say it that way?" He looked at me as if that simple thought had never dawned upon him in his entire life. A silly looking grin came over his face as he exclaimed, "Oh, you mean just *say* it that way?!?"

To tell someone to "invite Jesus into your heart" or to "just repeat this prayer after me" are simple concepts to understand and to follow, but they are not clear in the sense of being Biblical. As a faithful witness for the Lord, I must be careful to give the unbeliever clear Bible statements, not man made cliches which often cloud the issue of salvation rather than making it understandable.

The Ignorant Masses

Who will stand in the gap to defend the unbeliever's right to know the truth of God accurately? Not the unbeliever. He may not even be aware of being ignorant or confused about spiritual matters. The cultist or unsaved religionist won't bother because they already think they've got the "key" to truth. The average Christian could take up the burden of the unsaved person's lack of knowledge of the truth, but he usually doesn't. Christians are often unaware that there is a serious communication problem between believers and nonbelievers or even between believers and believers; or, if they are aware, it is usually not that important to them. Some may think there are other weightier matters to concern oneself with like the construction of a new church building, or increasing the giving of members, or the various church programs, or buying new choir robes, and the list goes on.

God warned Israel, *"Cursed is the one who makes the blind to wander out of the way... "* (Deuteronomy 27:13, KJV). A major influence upon the spiritually blinded is what they hear from the mouths of Christians, especially from the Christian professionals. Could it be we are causing those who are spiritually blind "to wander out of the way" through our failure to accurately and clearly communicate as we should? If this is possible, could clarity then ever be a trifling matter? I hardly think so. Therefore, we dare not approach any part of God's Word in a casual or cavalier fashion.

Somewhere, somehow we have lost our deep reverence, even fear, of the holy Word of God. Isaiah states, *But on this one will I look* (approvingly).*: on him who is poor and of a contrite spirit, and who trembles at My word* (Isaiah 66:2b). A few verses later he adds, *"Hear the word of the LORD, you who tremble at His word... "* (v. 5). I am personally convinced that if we had the deep reverence for the Word of God that we should have, we wouldn't question for a moment the importance and the absolute necessity of stating His Word in an exact and plain manner.

The early Jewish scribes who made copies of the Hebrew manuscripts certainly evidenced this reverence for God's Word. Consider these comments by Sidney Collet in his book, *All About the Bible:*

"In making copies of the Hebrew manuscripts...the Jewish scribes exercised the greatest possible care, even to the point of superstition—counting, not only the words, but every letter, noting how many times each particular letter occurred, and destroying at once the sheet on which a mistake was detected, in their anxiety to avoid the introduction of the least error into the sacred Scriptures, which they prized so highly and held in such reverent awe. Moreover, each new copy had to be made from an approved manuscript, written with a special kind of ink, upon sheets made from the skin of a 'clean' animal. The writers also had to pronounce aloud each word before writing it, and on no account was a single word to be written from memory. They were to reverently wipe their pen before writing the name of God in any form, and to wash their whole body before writing 'Jehovah,' lest that holy name should be tainted even in the writing. The new copy was then carefully examined with the original almost immediately: and it is said that if only one incorrect letter was discovered the whole copy was rejected."

People who are regular church attenders ("pew warmers") are often more gullible than they should be. We want to believe the best of our spiritual leaders (and that's only proper), but we tend to believe whatever comes from behind the pulpit. It never dawns upon many that since Satan is the Great Deceiver and Counterfeiter, the most logical places for him to gain influential power is in the pulpits of our churches, in the Chair of Theology in our seminaries, through the mass produced books of some of our most widely read and respected writers, or through the lyrics of the songs sung by some of the most popular "Christian" recording artists of the day.

We are in a bitter, do-or-die spiritual battle, a struggle between God and all of the demonic forces of the wicked one. This is not Sunday School 101. It's war! The battle field is the mind of man. The weapons and ammunition are thoughts that bombard the human mind constantly. These thoughts are expressed in words. Words convey thoughts and concrete thoughts have far reaching consequences! The more precise and accurate our words are, the more freedom the Holy Spirit has to wield His sword, which is the Word of God (Ephesians 6:17). The more engrossed we are in vague religious cliches while the enemy is precise and clear in what he wants others to believe, the less effective we will be while he gains ground by leaps and bounds.

By current standards the war to capture the minds of men seems as if it is being won by Satan, forfeited by the Church without so much as a wimper. This is not God's design or purpose. However, God has ordained that the means through which others learn of His truth (especially salvation truth) is through the life and lips of His own children. Scripture teaches that the Gospel is to be conveyed to the world through those who are already redeemed:

For whoever calls upon the name of the LORD shall be saved. How then shall they call on Him in whom they have not believed? And how shall they believe in Him of whom they have not heard? And how shall they hear without a preacher (one to proclaim)*?....So then faith comes by hearing, and hearing by the Word of God* (Romans 10:13-14, 17).

But as we have been approved by God to be entrusted with the Gospel, even so we speak, not as pleasing men, but God who tests our hearts (First Thessalonians 2:4).

Let the redeemed of the LORD say so, whom He has redeemed from the hand of the enemy (Psalm 107:2).

And He said to them, "Go into all the world and preach the Gospel to every creature (Mark 16:15).

I am not saying that the key to winning multitudes to Christ lies in plainness and accuracy of speech, but I am certainly saying that without such Biblical clarity believers become major stumbling blocks in conveying God's saving message to unbelievers. It would be a terrible thing to stand before the Lord and realize that I had often confused the unsaved by my fuzzy presentation of the Gospel.

The following simple but important principles should provide you a standard by which to judge if you are communicating the Gospel correctly and with clarity.

Develop the habit of using Bible words and phrases utilizing Scriptural definitions only. If Scripture does not define something don't give in to the temptation of manufacturing your own definition. It seems that more and more people are quick to dogmatically provide their own definitions for some of the gifts of the Spirit as if those definitions were straight out of the Bible; the word of knowledge, for instance, (First Corinthians 12:8) has been twisted in such a way as to serve the kingdom building purposes of more than a few televangelists.

Do not add to Scripture. Don't read into it what is plainly not there. You are entitled to your opinion as to what a passage may mean, but if your interpretation or application is not clearly revealed in the pages of Scripture, it may be wise to keep such opinions to yourself.

Thoroughly study the message of salvation. Memorize it. Reherse it. Make sure the message you pass on to others as "the Gospel" really is.

Faithfully share the wonderful Gospel of Christ. The more you share the Gospel the more confident you will become, and the more it will sharpen your ability to do so effectively.

It's Time for Clarity! It's *Past* Time!

For Personal Reflection and Application

❖ Have you had occasions when you heard a false gospel preached, and you *knew* it was false? What were your feelings? What was your reaction? How do you think God must have felt?

❖ Is your presentation of the Gospel always true? Is it thoroughly Biblical? If it is, you will focus on Christ—His Person and His Work on Calvary. You will never place an emphasis on any merit or work of man, either before receiving salvation or after one is saved.

**For let us keep in mind
that we are in the
business of *winning* men
to Christ. We cannot win
by antagonizing...It certainly
has no place in the work of
individual soul–*winning*.**

Charles Galludet Trumbull
Taking Men Alive

11

The Winning Attitude

They had just played for the state high school football championship—and lost. After the game, as the loss began to really sink in, Nat, their all-star tackle, stood in the middle of the locker room and wept. Everyone thought he was weeping over not winning the championship. Instead, as he shared with them through his tears, "This is my last year and tonight was my last game with you guys, and I know that some of you still do not know Christ as your Savior. I'm weeping because if you die in your unsaved condition you'll spend an eternity separated from God in hell and I don't want you to go there."

They didn't all trust in Christ that night, but they took their football buddy's pleading to heart because they knew that he cared!

As important as it is to speak in clear, simple terms so that you are understood, there is one other quality that is nearly as important, and sometimes more so. I call it *The Winning Attitude*. The apostle Paul refers to it in three of his letters.

First, he describes it in Ephesians 4:14, 15:

That we should no longer be children, tossed to and fro and carried about with every wind of doctrine, by the trickery of men, in the cunning craftiness by which they lie in wait to deceive, but speaking the truth in love, may grow up in all things into Him who is the head—Christ.

There are many religious leaders who deliberately and cunningly "lie in wait to deceive" and they often deceive through what they say or teach—their doctrine and their promises. In contrast, we are warned against being as children, "tossed to and fro." Rather, we are to "speak the truth in love." From these verses we see that our assignment is threefold:

SPEAK the Truth in Love

*Yes, we are to **speak***. Remember Paul's question in **Romans 10:14:** *"...how shall they believe in Him of whom they have not heard? And how shall they hear without a preacher* (or one to tell the message)." People must hear the Gospel for *"faith comes by hearing and hearing by the Word of God"* (Romans 10:17). Of course, the "hearing" may be through the printed page, or a tape or video recording, but however it comes, the unbeliever must be exposed to the saving message of the Gospel.

No one will ever be led to Christ by your good life. (You might want to read that last sentence again to let it sink in). They may be influenced for good, they may be softened up to listen because of the good testimony you live before them, but in order to know how to be saved—that is, *what* to do—they must somehow be told. Speaking, preaching, telling, is God's method of reaching those outside of Christ. He has no other plan.

Then we are to speak the *TRUTH* in love

Sometimes we attempt to tell another person how to come to God but we ourselves are not quite sure exactly what to say. So, there is the second element in the above verse: we are to speak *the truth*.

Opinions won't do, regardless how sincere the person is who holds them. When I hear or read a Gospel message and come to the invitation portion of the message where the speaker or writer is telling the unbeliever what to do, I often find myself shaking my head and asking myself, "Where is *that* found in the Bible?" We tell the lost they've got to pray a prescribed prayer, or come to the altar, or surrender all to Christ, or commit their lives to Him, or promise to do better, join the church, get baptized, and on-and-on; none of which is found in Scripture as a means to or a condition for getting saved.

Jeremiah had the proper understanding when he wrote, *The prophet who has a dream, let him tell a dream; and he who has My word, let him speak My word faithfully. What is the chaff to the wheat? says the LORD. Is not My word like a fire? says the LORD, and like a hammer that breaks the rock in pieces?* (Jeremiah 23:28, 29). And Isaiah adds, *To the law* (the Word) *and to the testimony! If they do not speak according to this word, it is because there is no light in them* (Isaiah 8:20).

In answer to life's most important question—What must I do to be saved?—Paul and Silas repied to the jailer, *Believe on the Lord Jesus Christ and you will be saved* (Acts 16:30, 31). That's it. There are no four steps to climb to salvation, no nineteen things to do to have eternal life, as one so–called study Bible asserts. Believing in Christ is the one and only condition for receiving salvation. We need to clearly and fearlessly proclaim this truth, and to do so faithfully.

Finally, we are to speak the truth *IN LOVE*

In my early attempts at witnessing I'm afraid I drove quite a few people away from the Lord. I was very argumentative. Every discussion about the Gospel turned into a debate. I wasn't very effective, but I soon recognized the problem and I began asking God for a tender heart, a love for people, especially toward those who are lost.

What a difference it made as God began to answer my prayer! I've discovered that I can even let an unbeliever know he or she is hell-bound without Christ and they will take it from me as long as they know I genuinely care for them. I don't mean they will necessarily believe it, but they won't feel I'm attacking them either. People can tell if you really care or if you are just performing a religious duty as you witness to them. So be sure to speak the truth *in love.*

Secondly, Paul describes *The Winning Attitude* in Colossians 4:5, 6.

Here Paul discusses more of the how-to of speaking the truth in love. He says, *Walk in wisdom toward those who are outside, redeeming the time. Let your speech always be with grace, seasoned with salt, that you may know how you ought to answer each one.*

Note how clearly the necessary ingredients are spelled out here so that no one need miss the point, plus God's precious promise.

The Necessary Ingredients

Ingredient number one: *Walk in wisdom toward those who are outside.* Obviously the "outside" in this verse does not refer to being outside of the local church or outside any particular group or denomination. The reference is to being outside of Christ. It's referring to unbelievers and the need for wisdom on our part in dealing with them.

How foolish we are sometimes when speaking to the unsaved. We embarrass them, offend them, ridicule them, belittle them, and then we come to the oddest conclusions such as: *the Spirit didn't have them prepared*, or, *they were so hardened*, or, *it was the wrong time or place to witness.*

Ask yourself: How would I react if I was witnessing to someone who was drinking a beer while I spoke? How *should* I react? One pastor-evangelist taught that when he would visit in a home and the television was on, he would turn it off. Would you? Might it not be more thoughtful to at least ask permission to either turn it off or to turn down the volume?

One of the major things that used to aggravate my dad and me before I was a Christian was the pushiness of visiting evangelists who would come calling during "revival" at the local church. The pastor of the small church where some of the family members attended displayed a great deal of tenderness and tact but I cannot recall any visiting speaker who did—and, of course, the "revival speakers" are usually considered the experts in reaching the lost community.

It is essential to meet people where they are (as Jesus did repeatedly) and to *lead* them into truth rather than attempting to push them into it. You may see yourself as being too blunt or— the opposite—not forward enough to be an effective witness, but **James 1:5** is applicable to any believer: *If any of you lacks wisdom, let him ask of God, who gives to all liberally and without reproach, and it will be given to him.* And the wisdom God will provide is His own, which is described so beautifully in **James 3:17:** *But the wisdom that is from above is first pure, then peaceable, gentle, willing to yield, full of mercy and good fruits, without partiality and without hypocrisy.*

Oh, how the unbelieving world needs to see this kind of wisdom shown to them by those of us who belong to Christ. God never calls upon you to do something—like to "walk in wisdom" —without providing the ability to do it. In this case, you can have His wisdom by *asking* for it in faith. Do it!

Ingredient number two: *Redeem the time.* To "redeem the time" in this case means to look for and to take advantage of opportunities. William McCarrell who founded "The Fisherman's Clubs" years ago used to promote C.I.O.—Contact Is Opportunity! The "opportunity" may be nothing more than offering a tract to a check-out clerk in a store, or sharing the Gospel with someone asking for directions, or (for you men) engaging someone in a conversation while sitting on a bench in the mall as you wait for the ladies to finish their shopping!

I believe one of our greatest lacks is the failure to take advantage of daily opportunities to share Christ. We tend to be desensitized to those around us because we become so hurried to get the shopping done, to get the kids to their ball games, to stay on schedule, that the people God brings into our lives become nothing but blurs during our daily rush; or worse, we see them as a nuisance and an aggravation, when in reality they are our mission field. How consistent is it to pray for and to support foreign missions when we ourselves don't recognize the mission field all around us? Opportunities are everywhere! Ask God to show them to you, and then gobble them up for Jesus' sake.

The third ingredient: *Let your speech always be with grace, seasoned with salt* If your speech is "with grace" it will be gracious, tactful, kind, loving, thoughtful. If it is "seasoned with salt" it will be in good taste; it will not be crude, crass or rude; it will cause a thirst in others (as salt tends to do) to want to know more about your Savior.

Some belittle the importance of *how* we speak to others, saying it is not important, and that the only essential thing is the truth itself. If that were true, I wonder why God would lead Paul to pen such admonitions as these. And why would He have recorded this incident concerning Paul's preaching: *Now it happened in Iconium that they went together to the synagogue of the Jews, and so spoke that a great multitude both of the Jews and of the Greeks believed* (Acts 14:1). Obviously our words, the tone in our voices, even the expressions upon our faces, may either attract others to Christ or repulse them. This is not a difficult concept to grasp. We see it in operation in all areas of life. In business, the way one communicates to others can be the difference between making a sale or losing the customer. The same kind of principle often applies to the spiritual plane as well.

If we have the above ingredients in our talk and walk He promises—*That you may know how to answer each one.* Please note that the promise is *conditional.* It follows 1) walk in wisdom, 2) redeem the time, and 3) be gracious and tasteful in your speech. There is no guarantee that you will know how to answer unbelievers if these conditions are not met. So, rather than concentrating on God's promise—what *He* will do—you should focus on the necessary elements in your life that will bring about the promised blessing of knowing how to answer others.

Without stretching this point too far, it is interesting that the promise is not *that you may know **what** to answer each one.* The promise is *that you may know **how** to answer each one.* There is a difference. Knowing *what* to answer focuses on having the proper *information*, the *facts.* Knowing *how* to answer revolves around *the proper way* of answering someone so that they are more responsive to the facts you give them.

Many times the *way* you respond to another's questions or objections is more important to winning them than having the correct facts at your finger tips. Not only that, but questions that nonbelievers ask in the midst of your Gospel presentation are often not the real questions that interest them. They may be nothing more than smoke screens. To you they may even be irritants. If you do not handle these questions or objections properly (knowing *how* to answer), they may never open up their hearts to you, revealing those things that are of a genuine concern to them.

The third passage in which *The Winning Attitude* is expressed is Second Timothy 2:24-26.

In this last letter of Paul, knowing he was soon to die (4:6–8), God led him to write the following as a final admonition on this topic of reaching the lost. *And a servant of the Lord must not quarrel but be gentle to all, able to teach, patient, in humility correcting those who are in opposition, if God perhaps will grant them repentance, so that they may know the truth, and that they may come to their senses and escape the snare of the devil, having been taken captive by him to do his will.*

As a further description of The Winning Attitude, this passage is so clear in providing certain ingredients of its own.

First, *a servant of the Lord must not quarrel.* It is never right to argue the Gospel. Obviously when you are witnessing to a nonbeliever, there will be differences of opinion; there may be conflicts; there may even be some heated words thrown at you. However, you must not allow the conversation to sink to the level of argumentation. If the unbeliever raises his voice, lower yours; if he begins to attack what you are telling him, the verse above continues with what you should do—*be **gentle** to all.* This is the same principle as recorded in Proverbs 15:1. *A soft answer turns away wrath, but a harsh word stirs up anger.*

Secondly, a servant of the Lord must be *able to teach.* Now before you convince yourself that this statement disqualifies you as a soul winner because you are not a teacher, consider this: Do you know you are saved? Are you going to Heaven? Has God forgiven you of your sins? Do you know you have eternal life? Do you know any Bible verses—*any*—that you could show to a nonbeliever that may open his eyes to one of these aspects of the Gospel truth? If *yes*, then you are able to teach an unbeliever, using God's Word. You see, the above statement is not necessarily speaking of a public performance, but a one–on–one situation where one person is the student (the nonchristian) and another person is the teacher (you)!

Thirdly, a servant of the Lord must be *patient.* Like gentleness, this is another quality listed as part of the Fruit of the Spirit in Galatians 5:22, 23. There it is called *longsuffering.* It is so essential that we allow God to nurture this grace in us. There certainly will be times when you may lead someone to Christ in ten or fifteen minutes, but there will be other situations where you may have to spend hours on end, and perhaps many hours on numerous occasions, before you see any positive evidence of good coming out of your talks. It probably will not be a common occurence for you to win someone to Christ in a few minutes time who has been steeped in a false religion, a cult or in philosophy for many years. Patience is needed, and it is a powerful virtue which God uses in your life to bring others to Christ.

Finally, the servant of the Lord must be humble—*in humility correcting those who are in opposition.* In sharing the Gospel there usually comes a time when the views and opinions of the one to whom you are speaking must be challenged and corrected. However, please note, the correction should always be in *humility*, not out of arrogance or pride, and never to belittle the one to whom you are witnessing. Charles G. Trumbull pointed out that, *"Fishermen do not thrash the water or throw stones at the fish."* Neither should we approach the "fish" we are trying to catch in any way other than in humility of spirit.

Apparently the means (or, at least, a *major* means) of God *"granting them repentance, so that they may know the truth, and that they may come to their senses and escape the snare of the devil..."* (vss. 25, 26) is directly associated with the *way* in which we approach them: being gentle, able to teach, patient, and especially, correcting them in humility. How very important, then, that we plead with God for this *Winning Attitude* to be the chief characteristic we display as we reach out to those who are lost, helpless, and spiritually blinded—people to whom we are commanded to carry the Gospel!

For Personal Reflection and Application

❖ Proverbs 15:1 says, *A soft answer turns away wrath, but a harsh word stirs up anger.* Can you recall times in your own life when either of these maxims (or both) have been observed—when someone's anger was abated by a soft, kind response, or when one's anger was aroused by an unwise, critical word? I'm sure you can see—from the stand point of winning others to Christ—how the *way* we speak to others is extremely important, and may either turn others toward the Lord or drive them away from Him.

❖ What should your response be when someone you are trying to win to Christ invites you to participate in something you don't approve of? Can you think of a way to decline without offending the person or without leaving the wrong impression—like you think you are better than they?

**We must remember
the saddest failure is
to fail to obey the
commission of Jesus
Christ and the prompting
of the Holy Spirit. To be
unsuccessful may be a
disappointment; to be
unfaithful is a sin.**

**Edward Last
in *Hand Gathered Fruit***

**You claim you are following
Jesus. Are you fishing
for men? If you are not
fishing, you are not following.**

Charles M. Alexander

12

Leading Others to Christ

I had asked Bill at the beginning of our talk if he knew whether or not he would go to Heaven when he died. He assured me that he did not know where he would go when it came time for him to die. I then proceeded to share the Gospel with him. The time finally came when I was convinced he understood the Gospel and might be ready to trust in Christ. I said, "Bill, does what the Bible says about having eternal life make sense to you?" He replied that it did. I then said, "Well, since you admit that it does make sense, would you trust in Christ right now?" His response took me completely by surprise, for he said, "I already have." In my mind I was thinking, "You're lying to me because at the start of our talk you said you didn't know whether or not you had eternal life; now you say you do." With somewhat of a skeptical tone I asked, "When did you trust in Christ?" His reply to this question was an even greater surprise. Without any hesitation he said, "Just a few moments ago when you showed me John 6:47!"

Even though I felt Bill wasn't ready to trust Christ until I was ready—until I had covered all of my points—God made it crystal clear to him through His Word that by believing in Christ he would receive eternal life right then and there. Bill didn't have to wait on my little presentation to be completed before he placed his faith in Christ. It's a lesson I will never forget.

⟫•◆•⟪

Getting Started

What would you say is the most difficult part of *actually* witnessing to someone? If you answered, "Getting started" you gave the most common reply I've encountered over the years. Over and over again the number one reason Christians give for not witnessing can be summed up in the statement: "I don't know how to start."

I'll briefly give you a few suggestions, but I believe there is far too much emphasis on this aspect of witnessing. Instead of memorizing "conversation openers" our time and efforts would be far better spent in saturating ourselves with Scripture, relying upon the power of God's indwelling Spirit, and pleading with Him to give us the kind of burden for the unsaved that would compel us to *"seek and to save those who are lost."* I know that when my own heart is broken and tender before the Lord, getting a conversation started is not nearly the obstacle it normally is during those times when I am not spiritually sensitive to Him.

Nevertheless, here are some general suggestions as to what you might be looking for to turn a conversation toward the Gospel.

First, *keep in touch with what is happening in the world,* especially tragedies and earth shaking events like wars, earthquakes, large scale financial depressions, the deaths of well known personalities (particularly when suicide is involved). Use these current events to get a conversation on a more serious level than the weather or the latest football scores. One series of events that I've used on a number of occasions were the terrorist bombings that took place in America on September 11, 2001. What I say usually goes somethng like this: "Other than the suicidal terrorists, I don't believe a single person who died that day in the various crashes left their homes thinking, 'This is going to be the last day of my life'—and, yet, it was. None of us ever knows when our 'day' has arrived."

Secondly, *use personal trials*—yours or theirs—to introduce the Gospel. If *you* are going through a difficult time, give a testimony to God's faithfulness and then move right into the Gospel. If *they* are going through a hard time, give a personal testimony to God's faithfulness and then move right into the Gospel. Either way, you see, you can use personal trials and set-backs as opportunities to focus on God and the great love He displayed in sending His Son to be our Savior.

Thirdly, *carry carefully selected Gospel tracts with you at all times—and use them.* A word of warning here: a great number of Gospel tracts that I've read over the years have presented a pretty good message until the writer comes to the invitation. It is at this point that many tracts fail miserably to present a clear Biblical answer to the age-old question, "What must I do to be saved?" Most contain several things the reader must do in order to be saved. Steer clear of those tracts that usually have two or more things you must "do" in order to be saved. There have been some good tracts that contained "Four Things You Must KNOW to be saved." That's different than "four things you must DO to be saved."

The best kind of tracts are those with a lot of Scripture relating to salvation, when used properly—not yanked out of context. The least effective are probably those that are mostly stories or illustrations with only a smattering of Scripture. God honors and uses His Word, not necessarily our stories and illustrations.

Few emphasize God's grace or the completeness of Christ's payment on the cross. When you find a really effective tract, read it over and over again until you virtually know it by heart. Then when you present it to someone, as they are looking it over, you can walk them through it without even lookng at it yourself because you will know it so well.

When I present a tract to someone, I usually say something like this: "Here's something I read one day that really meant a lot to me. I think you'll enjoy it, too." Using words similar to these, you are not just shoving a piece of literature at someone as if you are trying to unload it. It's meant something to you and you want to pass on the blessing. You'll get better responses when your attempts with tract distribution are coupled with a personal word.

Here's one final word regarding the use of tracts. There are an amazing number of Christians who look down on passing out tracts. For whatever reasons, they are totally negative about the use of tracts. Some have been victims of a well meaning Christian pushing a tract under their noses and saying something like, "Here, read this." Others will make some nonsensical comment like, "The apostle Paul never used tracts!" Of course, Paul never used the radio, or television, or airplanes, or a thousand and one other modern means of spreading the Gospel either, but that doesn't mean we shouldn't. Then there are those who simply do not believe that tracts are effective. I've been told on several occasions that "no one ever gets saved by reading a tract." Obviously these dear people have not read the kinds of books I have on my shelf that contain a number of testimonies of folks who came to Christ through the means of simple Gospel tracts. On the foreign mission fields literature distribution has proven to be a mighty force in bringing multitudes to a saving knowledge of the Lord Jesus Christ.

Fourthly, *sometimes just be straightforward in stating what you want.* Some people really appreciate the upfront honesty of this approach. You might ask, "Would you mind if I ask you a personal question?" When they reply, "No, I don't mind" then you could follow with any number of questions, such as:

"Has anyone ever shown you right from the Bible how you can be sure of going to Heaven?"

"Do you know if you will go to Heaven when you die?" Do not use this one when visiting someone in the hospital. They will think you know something they don't and you may cause them to have a heart attack on the spot!

"What do you think you would have to do to go to Heaven?" One boy replied, "You gotta die!"

"If you were to stand before God and He would ask you, 'Why should I let you into My Heaven?'—what would be your reply?"

Just remember that God is far more interested in that lost sheep being found than you or I could ever be. If you are genuinely serious about reaching the unsaved, God will always come through to aid you in "how to answer each one" (Colossians 4:5, 6).

The Most *Natural* Way to Share the Gospel

I stress the word "natural" because that's what it is—the sharing of *your own personal* salvation testimony. Usually when you share your salvation testimony you should include 1) what you thought about God, Heaven or salvation before you trusted in Christ, and 2) how you discovered the truth of the Gospel.

In my case, I often share the fact that when I was very young I thought "good boys go to Heaven and bad boys go to hell." As I got older—and meaner—I went from *thinking* I was one of the good little boys to *knowing* I was one of the bad boys. By the time I was in high school I had stopped going to church altogether and thought I had turned my back on God, if there was One. Then, at nineteen, I understood the Gospel for the first time and three weeks after first being exposed to it, I trusted in

Christ as my Savior.

Your testimony may be entirely different, but as you share it don't preach or sermonize, just tell in simple terms how you came to know the Lord. Be sure to include some Scripture. If you don't have any memorized, or there's no Bible handy, share what you know.

There are some who are reading this who were saved at a very young age—so young, in fact, you cannot recall the details. The last thing you want to think is, "I don't have a testimony." Oh, yes, you do! You have the best kind of tesimony of all. How I would love to be able to say that I was saved at a very young age. If I had, then all through my twenty-one surgeries I would have known I would have gone to Heaven if I died on the operating table. Nor would I have had the haunting memories of foolish and hurtful things I did (mostly as a teenager) that had I only known Christ, I may not have done.

If you are a person who was saved early in life you can say, "I thank the Lord that I trusted in Him at an early age and He has been faithful all through my life." And, then, go on from that point to share the Gospel.

The important point in sharing a testimony is to make sure it is *your* testimony, not someone else's, and make sure it is true. Don't yield to the temptation of embellishing your testimony in order to make it more interesting or exciting to the listener. Most people you'll witness to will prove to be just normal folks and they'll relate to what is real and genuine. You don't have to stretch the truth about yourself to make the truth about Christ more appealing.

The Most *Effective* Way to Share the Gospel

There is no more effective means of sharing the Gospel than by using the Word of God. There's power in it, God promises to bless it, and faith comes by people being exposed to it. Keep in mind, also, that the Gospel is a part of Scripture. The power is not in our well thought out arguments or dazzling personalities; it's in God's Word.

Take these verses to heart.

Romans 1:16, 17: *For I am not ashamed of the Gospel of Christ, for it is the power of God to salvation for everyone who* believes, *for the Jew first and also for the Greek. For in it* (the Gospel) *the righteousness of God is revealed from faith to faith; as it is written, "The just shall live by faith."* Note that the Gospel is God's *"power to salvation."*

The power is in the Message not necessarily in the messenger, but when both the message and the messenger are correct and in agreement, there is double-barreled power the Holy Spirit can use!

Romans 10:17: *So then faith comes by hearing, and hearing by the Word of God.* There is no salvation apart from the Word of God.

Isaiah 55:10, 11: *For as the rain comes down and the snow from heaven, and do not return there, but water the earth, and make it bring forth and bud, that it may give seed to the sower and bread to the eater, so shall My word be that goes forth from My mouth,; It shall not return to Me void, but it shall accomplish what I please, and it shall prosper in the thing for which I sent it.*

Make sure your use of God's Word is in harmony with its purpose. Don't use "Christian life verses" for salvation.

Jeremiah 23:28, 29: *The prophet who has a dream, let him tell a dream; and he who has My word, let him speak My word faithfully. "What is the chaff to the wheat," says the Lord, "Is not My word like a fire?" says the Lord, "and like a hammer that breaks the rocks in pieces?"*

Only God's Word can burn into the heart and conscience of man. Turn it loose in your life.

Mark 13:31: *Heaven and earth will pass away, but My words will by no means pass away.*

There is no substitute for God's Word. Use it faithfully. As you learn it, people will gradually be drawn to you because they will sense you know the Scriptures well enough to know what you are talking about.

I worked temporaily in a bank in Hialeah, Florida after finishing Bible school. From day one I let others know that I knew Christ as my Savior. The kidding began almost immediately. I was called "Rev" or "Holy Joe" on more than one occasion, but it was somewhat amusing that when individuals were going through some really hard times, they would get me off in a corner and ask me, "What does the Bible say about _____?" (whatever their concern was). I was able to lead several to the Lord. So use God's Word faithfully.

How to Witness to Those Who Have More
Questions than You have Answers

In my younger years I was witnessing to students in the University of Miami's student center. As I shared the Gospel with one young man he asked, "Do you believe God is all-powerful?" I confidently replied that I did. He then said, "Well, if God is all powerful, He can do anything. Right?" I said, "He sure can." To this he responded, "Well, if God can do anything, can He make a rock so big He can't pick it up?" I was floored. I'm not sure how I replied, but I know it wasn't very convincing. I left the campus after that conversation like a dog with its tail between its legs. When I got home I went into my bedroom, sat at my desk, and told God, "That will never happen to me again. Whatever it takes, I'm going to find an answer to that question."

I began asking all of the Christian leaders I knew how they would answer such a question. The answers I received from them did not even satisfy me, so I knew those answers wouldn't work with an unbeliever. I read a number of books trying to find an adequate reply to the question—all to no avail. Finally, one day when I wasn't even thinking about it, an answer popped in my head that I felt would do the trick. I couldn't wait for someone to ask me that question again. But I did wait—for a few years, in fact.

It happened back at the U of M campus when they were dedicating their brand new multimillion dollar student union building. I had taken some Bible school students with me to witness. As I was sharing the Gospel with one university student he asked, "Do you believe God is all-powerful?" I could hardly believe what I was hearing. I thought, "Aha! I've been waiting a long time for you." To his question I replied that I did indeed believe God was all-powerful. He then proceeded with the next question (I think that both of these students must have taken the same faith-destroying course at the university). He said, "Well, if God is all powerful, He can do anything. Right?" To his surprise, I answered, "No, He can't."

"Wait a minute," he said, "if God is all-powerful, then He can do anything."

Again I replied, "No, He can't."

To this he responded as I hoped he would by saying, "Name

something God can't do."

So I calmly said, "Well, He can't lie. He can't go back on His Word. And He can't do anything stupid, like make a rock so big that He can't pick it up!"

When I ask Christians the question, "Why do you think we don't witness more than we do?" most Christians answer, "Because we're afraid people will ask us something we don't have the answer to." Or, "We don't want to be intimidated by not knowing how to answer people's questions."

Well, I have some wonderful news for you: lack of knowledge can be one of the least of your worries when it comes to sharing the Gospel. In fact, *not* knowing the answers to the questions of nonbelievers can be a great advantage to you. I'll now explain how this can be.

Imagine for a moment that you are sharing the Gospel with Sam Skeptic and in the middle of your presentation he says, "I have a question. Where did Cain get his wife?" You didn't even know Cain had a wife, much less where he got her. And, besides, who's Cain anyway?

Now, either you are going to know the answer to a question like this, or you're not. Before I share what to do in either situation, I want to share another little secret with you.

When I'm giving the Gospel to someone and they insert a question into the conversation that has nothing to do with salvation, I know that that question has been introduced to get me off of the Gospel and onto something else that really doesn't matter that much. One thing I do not want to happen is to get side tracked from the Gospel. This is one of the devil's favorite tricks: get the Christian to dump the Gospel in order to chase some unimportant issue, and he has won the victory. I don't mean that the person asking the question has the motive of getting you bogged down in mundane matters; what I mean is that the devil uses such questions to accomplish his purposes whether or not that is the thought in the mind of the person to whom you are witnessing.

So, here is the very simple procedure I recommend.

First, thank them for the question. I've heard the "where did Cain get his wife" question over and over again, but I remind myself when I hear it for the umpteenth time that I've never heard it from *this* person before, and so I thank them for asking it.

Secondly, you may want to compliment them by saying something like, "I'm glad to see you are thinking."

Thirdly, ask permission to set the question aside for a few moments and then you'll come back to it. I normally say it something like this: *"You know, Sam, I'm right in the middle of a train of thought, and I'm such a lame brain that if I stop now I'm liable to forget where I am. So, if you don't mind* (notice: I'm asking persmission), *could we put your question off to one side— just for a few minutes—and let me finish my train of thought, and then I'll come right back to your question. Would that be all right with you?"* I cannot recall how many times I've done this and the response has always been the same: "Sure, that'll be fine." In this way—by having his permission to proceed—you can finish your presentation of the Gospel, usually without further interruptions of this sort.

Incidently, it is amusing how often the question does not come up again. But suppose it does. You've finished giving the Gospel and now he wants the answer to his question. Remember, what I said earlier: either you will know the answer or you won't. Knowing the answer is not necessarily to your advantage. Here's why.

If you know the answer to the question, and if you are not careful, you may tend to overwhelm this person with your great knowledge, giving him Scripture after Scripture to demonstrate your answer. In doing this, you may—without realizing it—be detracting from the Gospel you just shared. So, *when I know the answer to one's question, I normally give him as brief of an answer as will satisfy him* and then I reiterate the Gospel again.

But most of you who are reading this are not concerned with what to do when you have the answer; what bothers you is what to do when you do *not* have the answer. Here's where I want you to pay close attention and to see that not knowing can be a great advantage to you.

Back to Sam Skeptic. He allows you to put off answering his question about Cain's wife until you are through with your little "religious talk" and now he puts the question to you again: "Where did Cain get his wife?" And you don't have a clue. Here's what I recommend.

First, you compliment him for his question. You might say, "Sam, that's such a good question that I'm afraid I don't have the answer."

And then, right on the heels of admitting your ignorance, you *obtain a way of contacting him after you find the answer!* I usually say something like, "But I'll tell you what, give me your address, or phone number, or email address, and I'll find the answer to your question and get back in touch with you."

Putting him in this position will reveal something very valuable to you—Sam's sincerity. If he says, "Hey, don't worry about it. It's not really that important to me" then you know he was probably trifling with you and was insincere in asking the question.

BUT—and this is where the advantage of not knowing comes in—if he gives you a way to contact him, do your homework; find the answer to the question, and get back in touch with him. *This will give you **a second opportunity** to share the Gospel with him!* What an advantage, and all because of something you were initially hesitant about—the fear of not knowing the answer to people's questions. You should never hide behind this excuse again. It's one of the devil's tactics to keep your mouth shut concerning Christ.

The Effective Use of Questions

The master at using questions effectively was *THE* Master, the Lord Jesus Christ, and using questions effectively can often give you an edge in controlling the conversation and keeping it focused on the Gospel. Look at how Christ used questions to make *His* points rather than allowing the questions of others to fulfill their purposes.

In **Luke 20:1–8** Jesus' authority was questioned. *Now it happened on one of those days, as He taught the people in the temple and preached the gospel, that the chief priests and the scribes, together with the elders, confronted Him and spoke to Him, saying, "Tell us, by what authority are You doing these things? Or who is he who gave You this authority?" But He answered and said to them, "I will also ask you one question, and answer Me: the baptism of John—was it from heaven or from men?" And they reasoned among themselves, saying, "If we say, 'From heaven,' He will say, 'Why then did you not believe him?' But if we say, 'From men,' all the people will stone us, for they* *are persuaded that John was a prophet." So they answered that they did not know where it was from. And Jesus said to them, "Neither will I tell you by what authority I do these things."*

It's not always essential to answer one's questions, especially if you have reasons to believe that they are only attempting to lead the conversation to an unprofitable end.

In **Luke 20:20–26** insincere men attempted to trap Him in His conversation. *So they watched Him, and sent spies who pretended to be righteous, that they might seize on His words, in order to deliver Him to the power and authority of the governor* (vs. 20).

The question was: *"Is it lawful to pay taxes to Caesar or not?"* (vs. 22). *But He perceived their craftiness, and said to them, "Why do you test Me? Show Me a denarius. Whose image and inscription does it have?" They answered and said, "Caesar's." And He said to them, "Render therefore to Caesar what is Caesar's, and to God the things that are God's." But they could not catch Him in His words in the presence of the people. And they marvelled at His answer and kept silent* (vss.23–26).

I often use questions to set up people, as Christ did. This is an important tool in evangelizing those who are involved in cults, but I often use this "Set Up Technique" with all kinds of people. Seldom are the questions I ask of a very deep nature intellectually. They are simple and to the point.

Here are the ones I call "The Big Four."

- *Why?* or *Why not?*
- *How do you know?*
- *What do you mean by _____?*
- *Let me see if I understand you correctly. Are you saying___?* I then reword the statement I'm questioning into my own words.

An example or two may help you see the value of using questions correctly. The one you are speaking with says, "I believe it is only by the grace of God we can be saved." So you ask, "What do mean by being saved by *grace*? What is grace in your understanding?" Then you let them explain—without interrupting them. By allowing the person to explain themselves you'll discover what they *really* believe rather than what it sounds like they believe. (This is the "what do you mean by" question).

Here's another example. As you are sharing with another

person they bluntly say, "I don't believe the Bible." You could gently say something like, "Well, you know, that's interesting because I've been studying the Bible a little and I've come to believe in it. If you don't mind telling me, I'd like to know why you don't believe in it. Maybe I'll learn something." (This is the "why" or "why not" question).

Then there's the atheistic thinker who says, "There is no God." A very simple, "How do you know?" question is in order. But you must then allow them to talk so you'll know where they are coming from in their reasoning.

Don't think you have to know all the answers. It's not true, as I demonstrated earlier. And don't think you have to do all the talking. I am as convinced as I can be that THE BEST SOUL WINNERS ARE THE BEST LISTENERS, not necessarily the best talkers. This truth ought to be a real encouragement to those of you who are shy and somewhat of an introvert.

Talking is not so much the name of the game; *intelligent, prayerful listening* often is. As you listen, ask a few well chosen questions and observe how much more you accomplish. The conversation will usually go a lot smoother as well, because you will be including the other person more into your sharing time. Natural born "talkers" sometimes face real difficulties in letting others talk, but it is so essential to allow others to express themselves. It's the only way to discover what's under the surface; what makes this person think the way they do. So be a good and careful listener.

Leading Someone to Trust in Christ

I'm afraid that leading others to Christ has become for some a simple matter of learning sales techniques to get a name "on the dotted line." However, that is not the way it should be.

As I'm sharing the Gospel—usually emphasizing one of the five points I covered earlier in chapters five through nine—I'm showing the person to whom I'm speaking one Bible verse after another. If I'm discussing man's condition, I might turn to Romans 3:23 (*For all have sinned and fall short of the glory of God*), and then I'll often ask, "According to this verse, how many have sinned?" They will reply, "All." Then I might say, "Would that include you?"

Do see what I'm doing? I'm getting them into the Word, plus I'm making them see what it actually says by the use of questions, and I'm applying it directly to them. In this way my presentation of the Gospel is very personal, direct and to the point, and based solidly on what the Bible says.

No matter which point of the Gospel I'm emphasizing my approach is the same: I point them directly to the Scriptures; as they are looking at the verse, I ask them questions about it so I know they understand what it says, and then I lead them to apply it to themselves.

Here are some examples of how I might ask questions concerning various verses I would use under the five points I covered in the earlier chapters.

Regarding God's Demand—Perfection, I could show them Psalm 5:4—*For You are not a God who takes pleasure in wickedness, nor shall evil dwell with You,* and ask one of these questions:

"Is God pleased with wickedness?"

"Will evil dwell with God?"

"If not, and we are evil in His sight, can we dwell with Him?"

Regarding Man's Condition—he is sinful, I might turn to Isaiah 64:6—*But we are all like an unclean thing, and all our righteousnesses are like filthy rags; we all fade as a leaf, and our iniquities, like the wind, have taken us away,* and ask:

"According to this verse, how many are clean?"

"What would 'all our righteousnesses' be—the worst that we do, our average performance, or our best?"

"How does God see 'all our righteousnesses'?"

Regarding God's Provision—His Son, I've often turned to Luke 2:11—*For there is born to you this day in the city of David a Savior, who is Christ the Lord,* and ask:

"Who is the Savior according to this verse?"

"Does it say that _____ is the Savior?"

"Why do you think God would send a Savior?"

"What do you think a Savior would do?"

Regarding Man's Response—to believe in Christ, I may share a verse like this one: *Believe on the Lord Jesus Christ and you will be saved* (Acts 16;31), and ask:
"What does this verse say you must do in order to be saved?"

"What do you think it means to 'believe on' the Lord Jesus Christ?"

"Does it say, 'Believe on the Lord Jesus Christ and join the church, and you'll be saved'?"

Regarding God's Guarantee—eternal life to those who believe in Christ, a good verse to share would be John 5:24—*Most assuredly, I say to you, he who hears My word and believes in Him who sent Me has everlasting life, and shall not come into judgment, but has passed from death to life*, and then to ask:
"What kind of life does it say a believer receives?"

"How long is everlasting?"

"When does a believer in Christ receive everlasting life?"

"Will the believer in Christ ever come into judgment?"

Over and over and over again, I place Scripture in front of folks—either from a Bible or a printed tract—and ask enough questions until I am convinced they truly understand the Gospel.
Once I am persuaded they really do understand, I am then ready and willing to lead them to trust in Him as their Savior. I need to emphasize here that *I never attempt to lead someone to Christ unless I am convinced they understand the Gospel and what they must do to be saved.* It's easier than you might imagine to get someone to shake your hand and say *yes* to your admonition to trust in Christ, or to get them to repeat a prayer

after you, than it is to make the Gospel so clear that they do *indeed* place their faith in Him. So, when I am convinced they understand the Gospel—and not before—I will usually ask one or more questions like the following:

- *"Can you think of any reason why you shouldn't trust in Christ as your Savior?"* If they say, "No," I then ask, "Then, *do* you trust in Him?"

- *"If you were to stand before God right now and He were to say to you, 'Why should I let you into My Heaven?' what do you think you would say?"*

- *"Does what the Bible says about obtaining eternal life make sense to you?"*

If their answer is *no*, I attempt to find out what does not make sense and go back over that point until it is clear to them. If their answer is *yes*, I proceed to the next question:

- *"Well, since you admit that it does make sense, do you trust in Christ as your Savior?"*

Obviously, I want a *yes* answer to this question. If I get a negative response, I normally inquire, "Can you put your finger on why you wouldn't trust in Christ to save you?" I then listen intently and clear up any lingering misconceptions they may have, or attempt to answer any question or objections they may still be entertaining. After that, I will come back once again to invite them to trust Christ.

You may have just read the above comments about leading others to Christ and be wondering, "Where's the prayer?" What prayer? "The prayer to recieve Christ," you might reply. What prayer to receive Christ? "The sinner's prayer," you add. What sinner's prayer?

What's my point? Simply this: one *must* believe in Christ to be saved; they *may* pray when they do it, but prayer is not a prerequiste to salvation. Neither is walking an aisle, raising the hand, standing, or any number of other things we ask unbelievers to do because "we've always done it that way."

When I extend a public invitation for folks to trust in Christ, I often have them raise their hands to indicate their decision. I normally do this with heads bowed. However, I always make it clear that raising the hand does not save anyone; neither does my prayer. What they *must* do is to believe in the Lord Jesus Christ—with or without a raised hand or a prayer.

The same is true when dealing with someone one-on-one. If you have been showing them for thirty minutes that all they can do to receive salvation is to believe in Christ, why at the moment of decision would you tell them to do something else like repeating a prayer after you? Do not include anything else to God's one condition of faith in Christ to your invitation. Keep it strictly Biblical.

So, what do I do to be assured that one has recieved Christ? I explain the Gospel thoroughly (as I've demonstrated), ask a lot of questions, and then invite them to trust in Him when I think they understand enough to do it. If they assure me that they are trusting in Him, here's what I do from that point on.

Leading New Believers to the Assurance of Salvation

First, I *never* tell anyone they are saved. I don't excitedly grab their hand and say, "Praise the Lord, brother, you're saved!" Why do you think I'm careful about this? It's simple: I do not know their hearts, only God does (Jeremiah 17:9, 10; First Kings 8:39). You might wonder why anyone would say they are trusting in Christ if they're not. That, too, is simple. They may just be a nice person and they don't want to disappoint you; or they may feel that if they don't say yes to you the conversation could go on and on, and they have other things they need or want to do; or they may respond favorably to your invitation, but still not really understand the Gospel or what they are doing.

So, when I receive a favorable response to my invitaiton for them to trust Christ to save them, I usually do what is natural (in America's culture, not necessarily elsewhere): I shake their hand and say something like this: "God bless you, _____, if you really are trusting in Christ as your Savior, let me show you what God has for you." I then go over some of the verses we covered earlier in chapter nine on God's Guarantee. In this way their assurance will come from Scripture, not from a prayer, or from an

190

emotionally high experience, or from me telling them that they are saved. Let me illustrate with a true story.

My student, Lee, asked if I would consider coming to her house for dinner and witnessing to her father. I told her I would be happy to, and we had a delightful dinner a few evenings later. As we talked around the table that night, Lee's father began to criticize his own church. After a while I began turning the conversation toward the Gospel. Lee and her mother got up quietly from the table and went into the family room. I discovered later that they sat in the dark and prayed for me the entire time.

Once I fully explained the Gospel to her dad and felt he understood, I asked him if it made sense, and he replied that it did. I then asked him, "Since it does make sense to you, do you trust in Christ as your Savior?" He said, "Yes, I do."

I shook his hand and said, "God bless you. Now if you are trusting in Christ to save you, let me share with you what God promises you." I then turned to John 6:47. I was using the King James Bible back then (and so was virtually every other Christian in the English speaking world).

I turned to the verse, placed the Bible before him and quoted it as he read it. *Jesus said, "Verily, verily, I say unto thee, 'He that believeth in me hath everlasting life."*

I said, "I'd like to ask you three questions, and the answers to all three questions are found in this one verse. Here's the first question. According to this verse, who has everlasting life?"

He thought a moment and then replied, "He who believes in Christ."

I said, "Does that include you?"

He quickly responded, "Yes, it does."

So then I asked, "What does it mean to 'believe in' Christ?"

He gave me a very clear answer: "To trust in Him."

"And do you do that?"

Again, his reply was a very firm, "Yes."

"O. K." I said, "Here's my next question. Remember, the answer is in this verse. According to John 6:47, what kind of life does a believer in Christ receive?"

He quickly read over the verse and replied, "Everlasting life."

"And how long is 'everlasting,'" I asked.

He correctly said, "Forever, never ending."

"Good," I said. "Now here is the third question. The answer

may be a little more difficult, but it's found in the verse. Here it is. When does the believer in Christ receive this everlasting life?"

After glancing at the verse again, he said, "When he believes."

"How do you know that?" I asked.

"Because," he said, "it says that he 'hath' it. That's present tense."

I said, "Great! Now tell me, do you 'hath' it?"

He looked at me with a kind of strange look on his face and said, "Do I *what?*"

"Do you 'hath' it. Jesus said that if you believe in Him you 'hath' it. Do you 'hath' it?"

He responded to that by saying, "Yes, I think I do."

I said, "Let's read the verse again. 'He that believeth on me *can think that he hath* everlasting life.'"

"No," he said, "it says he 'hath' everlasting life."

"Well," I replied, "do you 'hath' it?"

His reply this time was, "I feel as if I do."

So I said, "Let's read the verse again: 'He that believeth on me, *if he feels he hath everlasting life*, hath it.'"

He displayed a slight smile and said, "No, it doesn't say that. It says he 'hath' it."

"Do you 'hath' it?" I responded once again.

This time I could tell he really felt he had the right answer when he said, "If what Jesus is saying is true, then I do."

I said, "Let's read the verse again. 'He that believeth on me hath everlasting life, *if what I am saying to you is true.*'"

The next time around I said, "I'll tell you what we'll do. You read John 6:47 to yourself slowly. Take your time. And when you are done, tell me if you 'hath' everlasting life or not."

Ever so slowly and quietly he read the verse. As he was reading he got this most amazing look on his face. I could almost see *eureka!* written on his eyes, and he excitedly exclaimed, "Hey, I 'hath' it!" And truly he did. What a happy Christian family that threesome became.

There is hardly a greater joy in the whole world than to lead someone to the full assurance of salvation that comes solely through God's precious Word. What a privilege we have to share such a liberating message to those who are in spiritual darkness.

Decisional Regeneration

A strange dichotomy has developed within Christian circles concerning the necessity of unsaved people "making a decision" to trust Christ.

On the one hand we have those believers who say that no "decision" is necessary. All the unsaved person has to do is to believe in Christ. It doesn't require a decision; it requires a proper knowledge of who Jesus is and what He did for them when He died and rose again. Then—on their own, or as the Spirit leads them—they either believe or they don't. Christian workers in this group, such as pastors and missionaries, do not usually extend a personal invitation to audiences for those who are trusting in Christ to indicate it in some way, say, by raising the hand or coming to the altar.

In contrast to this are those who insist that there must be a defining moment when a person passes from spiritual death into spiritual life. This requires a conscious decision. Some, not the majority, even go so far as to preach that if you do not know the exact time when you trusted in Christ, you are not even saved for, they reason, how can you be born again and not be aware of when it happened? The Christian workers in this camp will nearly always give a public invitation for those who are trusting in Christ to indicate it in some way.

This either-or approach to what some have called "decisional regeneration" is unfortunate. It is obvious in Scripture that there were those who believed in Christ and their decision was definite and public. The book of Acts gives several examples of those who believed and were almost immediately baptized to declare their faith. There was Lydia, the first known convert in Europe, in Acts 16:14, 15. In the same chapter, the Philippian jailor was another who publicly bore witness to his faith (vss. 27–34). Earlier in Acts, Philip led the Ethiopian eunuch to the Lord and he wanted to be baptized right away (Acts 8:26–38).

But there are others in the Bible who "believed" because they were convinced Jesus was the Messiah/Savior, but there was no public display or initial evidence of their faith until sometime later, if at all. The Gospel of John records some of these. Joseph of Arimathea was one of these. John 19:38 says that he *"was a disciple of Jesus, but secretly, for fear of the Jews."* I've heard some wild explanations of Joseph's "secret" faith from those who are convinced that there is no such thing as a secret believer. Nevertheless the Word of God stands sure. You can believe what it says; you cannot always believe how men interpret His Word. Nicodemus, who is always referred to as he who "came to Jesus by night" was another secret believer (John 3:1-16 and 19:39). Then there were the unnamed "many" in John 12:42-43 who "believed in Him" but who did not confess Him for fear of being put out of the synagogue.

You have no doubt become aware from reading this far in this book that I normally attempt to lead an unsaved person to make a conscious decision to trust in Christ for salvation. I believe that it is fitting to do so, as long as there are no attempts at forcing one to make such a decision. One does not need to know *when* they trusted in Christ. I know when I trusted in Christ as my Savior almost to the very minute, but my wife Kathy does not know the time or place when she actually trusted in Christ to save her. The important thing is that she knows she does trust in Him alone as her Savior.

Defective Gospel Invitations

Gospel invitations are similar to Gospel messages in that some are simply unclear or confusing, while others are false. Many salvation invitations do not really convey what the Bible means by "believing in" Christ. Therefore when I refer to *defective* Gospel invitations, I mean everything from invitations that are Biblically deficient, ineffective, and inaccurate, to some that are just plain wrong. In my analysis of the following invitations you will find examples both of the unclear and of the downright unbiblical.

The first question you want to ask when you hear anything that purports to be Biblical is the question, "Where is that found in the Bible?" If it isn't in Scripture, it may still be all right. For instance, church membership, church buildings, and worship teams are not in Scripture, but neither are they unbiblical— meaning *contrary* to the Bible. But when something is not found in Scripture, we should at least examine it in the light of Scripture to ascertain if it is in keeping with the Bible's teachings and principles. That's what I am doing with these invitations—

comparing them to what the Bible clearly states one must do in order to be saved. So, let's get to it.

Ask Jesus to come into your heart, or
Ask the Lord to forgive you, or
Pray to receive Christ.

These are very popular invitations which may seem to have a Biblical basis springing primarily from three New Testament verses.

The first one is **John 1:12** which says that *"as many as received Him, to them He gave the right to become children of God."* The common deduction from this statement is that "you receive Christ when you invite Him into your heart."

Then there is **Romans 10:13**: *For whoever calls upon the name of the LORD shall be saved.* How do you call upon Him? We are told that you call upon Him by praying to invite Him into your heart.

Probably the most used verse to justify "asking" Jesus to come into your heart is **Revelation 3:20**. It states: *Behold, I stand at the door and knock. If anyone hears My voice and opens the door, I will come in to him and dine with him, and he with Me.*

It is interesting, and very revealing, that in none of these verses is asking or praying to be saved mentioned or even implied.

For instance, the last part of John 1:12 defines "receiving" Christ as "believing in His name." There are not two steps to salvation—receiving and believing—there is only one—*receiving* which is done when one believes in Christ.

Romans 10:13 must be understood by its context. The *calling* of verse thirteen is shown to be the result of saving faith in verse fourteen. It is not a means to salvation; it is a response from one who is already a believer. Here is what it says: *How then shall they call on Him in whom they have not believed? And how shall they believe in Him of whom they have not heard? And how shall they hear without a preacher* (one to proclaim, a witness). Note (working backwards), that there must be a proclamation of the message before one can hear it. Then in order to believe the message, there must be the hearing of it. Finally, before one calls on the Lord, he must believe in Him. Therefore the calling of

195

verse thirteen is a call springing *from* faith, not a call *for* faith.

In Revelation 3:20 we again go to the context. First, we notice that it is clear (as it is in all seven of these messages–2:1–3:22) that it is a message to a church; in this case, the "church of the Laodiceans" (vs. 14). It is not a message directly slanted to the unbelieving world. That being so, the *door* mentioned in verse twenty is not the door of an individual's heart, it is the door of the church. Secondly, the reference to "anyone" in verse twenty is specifically directed to anyone within the church, not to unbelievers. Thirdly, the invitation is an invitation to "dine" with the Lord, not to "know" Him. This speaks of fellowship, not salvation. Finally—and this is vital—the promise to the one who "opens the door" is not, "I will come *into* him." Instead, the promise is, "I will come in *to* him." This is not a mere play on words. The Laodicean church was a very lukewarm body of believers (vs.15). If you are lukewarm in your relationship with the Lord, you will not be having much sweet fellowship—you won't be "dining" with Him. But if you find yourself in a church situation much like that described in this passage, Christ promises to have that fellowship with you if you allow Him room to do so. So, Revelation 3:20 is an invitation to believers to have fellowship with Him. It was never intended to be an invitation to salvation.

Give your heart to Christ.

There is one verse in the entire Bible that states something close to this invitation. It is found in Proverbs 23:26: *My son, give me your heart, and let your eyes observe my ways.* It goes on from there to warn of the harlot who "lies in wait for a victim" (vss. 27, 28). It well could be that the "me" of the verse is Solomon, not necessarily the Lord. But even if it is the Lord speaking, He is speaking to His *son* about observing His ways. It is not referring to how to be saved. With one hundred and sixty New Testament verses which clearly point out that salvation comes to one who believes in Christ, it is not a good policy to go to one verse which says nothing about salvation, forgiveness, or eternal life, and apply it as a condition for salvation. Salvation, you see, is not a *give* proposition; it is the *receiving* of a gift. We don't give God anything in order to obtain eternal life. If we did, eternal life could not be rightly called "the gift of God" (Romans 6:23). It would be a reward for what we gave. That would then lead to our boasting, which will never be allowed by God (Ephesians 2:8, 9).

Confess your sins and come to Christ.

What is often meant by "confess your sins" is to confess your sinfulness. If that is the meaning, then it could be stated: *admit you are a sinner and come to Christ.* I have no problem with that slant to the above invitation as long as it is made clear. However, nothing is said about having faith in Christ in such an invitation—simply to "come" to Him. So it is still an ineffective form of a salvation invitation. You can do better than this, and you should.

Repent of your sins, or
Forsake your sins.

I deal with repentance and its relationship to salvation later in the book, but for now I'll simply point out that repentance—when applied to salvation—always means a change of mind; particularly, a change of mind toward God and Christ. Paul preached it that way, as he clearly stated in **Acts 20:21:** *Testifying to Jews, and also to Greeks, repentance toward God and faith toward our Lord Jesus Christ.*

The Greek word translated repentance does not carry with it the idea of either sorrow for sin or a turning away from sin, though both of these thoughts are commonly preached as repentance. But analyze this view of repentance with me for a moment. Let's say one did turn from or forsake his sins, is that really the problem? Outward sins (plural) are not the issue in salvation. The issue is the sin of unbelief (John 3:18). As I've already pointed out, it is the only sin that condemns the unbelieving sinner.

Christ has taken care of the sin problem when "He became sin for us" (Second Corinthians 5:21). The sins of the world were laid upon Him. **Second Corinthians 5:19** tells us: *God was in Christ reconciling the world to Himself, not imputing* (charging) *their trespasses* (sins) *to them.* The trespasses of the world were

197

charged to Christ; He bore them in His own body on the tree (First Peter 2:24 and 3:18). Why should we—some 2,000 years later—now tell sinners to do anything more concerning their sins than what Christ has already accomplished?

Not only that, but think on this: Biblically speaking, is sin primarily outside of me or inside of me? It's inside, isn't it? Some twenty-five years after his conversion, Paul stated: *I know that in me (that is, in my flesh) nothing good dwells* (Romans 7:18). No matter how many outward sins a nonbeliever may turn from or forsake, he is only dealing with symptoms, not the real root problem, which is his sinful nature—that from which all outward sins spring. So, the sinner should really be invited to come to Christ as he is. The Lord will receive him and He will then begin the cleaning up process from the inside with the presence of the Holy Spirit within this brand new babe in Christ.

Alas, we Christians—especially the professionals—seem terrified at the prospect of inviting a despicable sinner to come to Christ in his filthy rags of unrighteousness. Yet I seem to remember Jesus responding much differently to the outcasts of His day. We read about one incident in **Luke 5:30-32:** *But their scribes and the Pharisees murmured against His disciples, saying, "Why do you eat and drink with tax collectors and sinners?" And Jesus answered and said, "Those who are well do not need a physician, but those who are sick. I have not come to call the righteous, but sinners, to repentance."* He met with, He ate with, and He drank with *sinners*; and in *their* environment He invited them to repentance. And, oh, what a change of mind they must have had! This Representative of God was so different to what they were used to from those other supposed representatives—the sanctimonious scribes and Pharisees. That's one of the real beauties of sharing the Gospel of grace to lost sinners—it is such a stark contrast to most of what people have thought all their lives. So I invite them to think differently; to think along the lines of what God has revealed in His Word.

> *Surrender your life to Christ, or*
> *Commit your life to Him, or*
> *Make Jesus the Lord of your life.*

A complete surrender of all that I am and all that I have or ever hope to have, is absolutely essential if I ever hope to be the Christian God intends for me to be. However, such conditions are not found anywhere in Scripture as mandatory for the unbeliever to fulfill. I deal with the subject of Lordship Salvation in detail in chapter sixteen and so I won't go into it here other than to point out that: 1) in all of the New Testament church letters (that's Romans through Jude—twenty–one books in all) there are admonitions, urgings, warnings and commands for those who are *already* saved to yield to Christ's Lordship over them. Why would God urge His own children to yield themselves unreservedly to Him if they already had to do that in order to be saved in the first place? 2) Why would God ask the unbeliever who has no spiritual appetite, desire, or power, to do that which seems at times nearly impossible for His own children to do—and His children are indwelt by the Spirit of God to enable them?

I'm afraid that many well-meaning believers are putting the cart before the horse in trying to get unbelievers to do that which only believers are able to do. Peter had the right idea about this type of thing when he gave his report to the First Jerusalem Council. The debate revolved around whether or not Gentiles had to be circumcised and keep the Law in order to be saved. Acts 15:10, 11 records part of Peter's reply: *"Now therefore, why do you test God by putting a yoke on the neck of the disciples which neither our fathers nor we were able to bear? But we believe that through the grace of our Lord Jesus Christ we shall be saved as in the same manner as they."* Making Christ Lord of one's life is a *yoke* that no unempowered nonbeliever could ever fulfill.

For Personal Reflection and Application

❖ If you have attempted to lead others to Christ, what have been some of the most difficult hurdles for you to overcome in leading others to a decision to trust in Christ? How do you think you might overcome those hurdles?

❖ Think of the folks you would like to win to Christ. Analyze each one's personality—their strengths and weaknesses, their likes and dislikes, their outlook on life in general. Do you pray for these you want to win in an informed and intelligent way? The more specific your prayer requests are for these individuals, the more specific will be the answers to your prayers. You may well find that after you have prayed for them in this way, that getting through to them will become easier.

"God, if there is an answer to any man's excuse, I promise You I will never be caught on the same excuse twice."

Prayer of Dawson Trotman
Founder of *The Navigators*

13

Answering Questions and Objections

When I came to Christ in 1953, there were several very helpful books on the market dealing with witnessing. The best ones usually contained a chapter or two showing the reader how to deal with different types of objections unsaved people have.

Since those days fifty years ago there have been quite a number of books written on the subject of evangelism (I have more than one hundred books on this subject in my own library). However, there has been a noticeable lack in most of these volumes in providing simple, to-the-point answers to men's questions and objections. I vividly recall how helpful it was to me as a young growing Christian to have Dr. R. A. Torrey and others, spell out brief answers with Scripture. I can't help but think that a new generation of believers may be similarly strengthened and equipped by such direct responses to the questions and objections men often have.

In practically every witnessing opportunity I've ever had, questions and objections from nonbelievers have been raised during the course of the conversation. Such questions and objections should not be considered as walls blocking the Gospel's penetration; rather we should look upon them as bridges to carry the Gospel message with even greater clarity to the lost one. Keep the truths mentioned in chapter eleven—The Winning Attitude—in mind as we consider a number of questions, objections and obstacles that are frequently inserted into our conversations by the ones we are attempting to reach. To that end I include the next two chapters in this volume. First we consider questions and objections you will often encounter from those with whom you speak.

"I live as good a life as anyone else" (the self-righteous).

They may not come right out and say it but the bottom line of their thinking is: "I'll be saved by good works." *Agree with them that salvation is obtained by good works—not by our good works, however, but by Christ's good works!*

*Not By **Our** Good Works.*

Romans 4:5: *But to him who does not work but believes on Him who justifies the ungodly, his faith is accounted for righteousness.*

Ephesians 2:8-9: *For by grace you have been saved through faith, and that not of yourselves; it is the gift of God, not of works lest anyone should boast.*

Titus 3:5: *Not by works of righteousness which we have done, but according to His mercy He saved us....*

*But By **Christ's** Good Works.*

Romans 5:6-10: *Christ died for the ungodly...while we were still sinners, Christ died for us...having been justified by His blood, we shall be saved from wrath through Him...we were reconciled to God through the death of His Son...we shall be saved by His life.*

Ephesians 1:7: *In Him we have redemption through His blood, the forgiveness of sins, according to the riches of His grace.*

Hebrews 9:12: *Not with the blood of goats and calves, but with His own blood He entered the Most Holy Place once for all, having obtained eternal redemption.*

First Peter 1:18-19: *Knowing that you were not redeemed with corruptible things, like silver or gold, from your aimless conduct...but with the precious blood of Christ as of a lamb without blemish and without spot.*

First Peter 2:24: *Who Himself bore our sins in His own body on the tree....*

First Peter 3:18: *For Christ also suffered once for sins, the Just for the unjust, that He might bring us to God....*

"I can't believe it's that simple."

Receiving the gift of eternal life is simple for us on two accounts. First, without salvation being freely offered by a merciful and compassionate God, it would not be possible to obtain. Keep in mind that God's demand for anyone living in His presence is perfection. No one can deliver it. We are all condemned under the righteous hand of our holy God. So, salvation must be free or else there would be no salvation at all. This is why the cults and religions of the world have nothing certain to offer. Their followers can only cling to a weak "I hope so" uncertainty.

Secondly, God has done the hard part—that which would be impossible for us to accomplish. He sent His Son who for the joy that was set before Him voluntarily went to the cross in place of us, though He despised its shame (Hebrews 12:2).

For God to offer eternal salvation any other way than as a gift, would not make it difficult; it would be impossible. Thank God that it is as simple as it is.

⇒•◇•⇐

"You mean I can just believe in Christ, live as I please, and still go to Heaven when I die?"

This may sound strange, but I just love it when someone reacts this way as I'm presenting the Gospel. It's a loaded question, to be sure, but it often indicates that this person is probably on the verge of really understanding the true heart of the Gospel—not that we live as we please, but that the way one lives has nothing to do with receiving salvation. *Good* works, remember, have nothing to do with either receiving salvation or with keeping it, and *bad* works have nothing to do with either being eligible or ineligible for salvation.

So how do I respond to such a radical question? First, I always encourage the unbeliever to come to Christ *"just as you are."* I invite him to come without any pretenses, without making impossible promises to God which he won't be able to keep anyway. If he has sin in his life (and who doesn't?), he is to come *with* that sin, *with* those hangups, *with* those puzzling questions and doubts and *with* his skepticism. God will meet him where he is, receive him when he places his faith in Christ, and God will become his Heavenly Father with all the privileges of a Father. Once he places his faith in Christ certain things will then become realities.

First, **John 1:11, 12** states that he will become a child of God. *He* (Christ) *came to His own, and His own did not receive Him. But to as many as received Him, to them He gave the right to become children of God, to those who believe in His name.*

Secondly, **Hebrews 13:5, 6:** *Let your conduct be without coveteousness, and be content with such things as you have. For He Himself has said, "I will never leave you nor forsake you." So we may boldly say: "The LORD is my helper; I will not fear. What can man do to me?"* God will never leave him and will always be present to help him.

Thirdly, **Hebrews 12:6, 11:** *For whom the Lord loves He chastens* (trains, disciplines), *and scourges every son whom He receives... Now no chastening seems to be joyful for the present, but grievous; nevertheless, afterward it yields the peaceable fruit of righteousness to those who have been trained by it.* God disciplines and trains everyone of His own children. This is perhaps the most important passage to share because it shows that there is no such thing as an untaught, undisciplined child of God.

I usually tell this kind of person, "When you truly trust in Christ alone for your salvation you do become God's child; He then has all the privileges of a Father and you have all the pivileges of His child. And though you may try to 'live as you please' God will be forever present in your life to teach and train you to walk as He wants you to walk."

As a witness for Christ, you don't want to ever leave the impression that (1) as long as someone *says* they believe in Christ, nothing else matters, including their behavior; or (2) one cannot be saved if they are still holding onto some habit that you might deem as sinful. Let the Scripture guide you in leading such a person to the truth.

———◆———

"I've gone to church all my life.
Why haven't I heard this before?"

This was precisely the first question I had when I heard and understood the Gospel. The implication of such a statement is that "if what you are telling me is true (the Gospel), I would have heard it during all the years I've attended church. So maybe it's not true. Maybe you have a wrong or warped slant on things"

When speaking to someone with this objection I usually try to relate to them by admitting that I had the same question, but then I'll show them some clear salvation verses and say something like, "You know, these verses (and all the other verses in the Bible on salvation) have been in the Bible for thousands of years. I didn't put them there. But I, like you, was unaware of their presence for nineteen years of my life. The issue for me was: Am I going to believe what is clearly stated in Scripture or will I continue to hold to religious views that have no foundation in God's Word. If I believe in what the Bible says, I'll find forgiveness and freedom. If I continue as I have for years, I will remain in my darkness and uncertainties. I have a feeling that the same issue is facing you right now. Which will you believe, the traditions of men or the truth of God's Word?"

<hr/>

"It's just too hard to be a Christian."

Those who feel this way have probably been exposed to either a false gospel or, at best, a very unclear presentation of the real Gospel during which the distinction between *becoming* a Christian and *living* as a Christian are confused. Obviously they do not comprehend *grace*, it hasn't been made clear to them that eternal life is a *gift*, and that salvation is something one *receives*—not something that one does.

In such instances it is usually good to turn to a few clear verses on salvation and ask, "What's so difficult about _____?" For instance, in John 3:16, What's difficult about "believing in Him?" In Romans 6:23, What's difficult about receiving a "gift?" In Revelation 22:17, What's difficult about "taking" the water of life "freely?"

You might also want to point out to this person that *becoming* a Christian is easy (Acts 16:31), but *living* the Christian life is not hard—*it's impossible!* Then, to prove this second point, show them verses like Ephesians 4:29-32, Second Corinthians 10:3-5, and First Thessalonians 5:18. How are the commands in these verses humanly possible to obey? They are impossible. So, we need God's grace to save us, and we need His grace to enable us once we are in His family. Urge the one you are speaking with to not put the cart before the horse: tell him to trust in Christ first; *then* He will be in his life to empower him from within to live a life pleasing to God.

⇒·◆·⇐

"I have no problem believing Jesus will get people to Heaven, but I can't believe He is the only way to get there."

You might ask, "Do you think Jesus would lie to you?" Usually the person will say He wouldn't lie to them. If that's the response you get, point out what Jesus Himself said about this issue. For instance, consider **John 10:7-11:** *Then Jesus said to them again, "Most assuredly, I say to you I am the door of the sheep. All who ever came before Me are thieves and robbers, but the sheep did not hear them. I am the door. If anyone enters by Me, he will be saved, and will go in and out and find pasture. The thief does not come except to steal, and to kill, and to destroy. I have come that they may have life, and that they may have it more abundantly. I am the good shepherd. The good shepherd gives His life for the sheep."*

Notice that He did not claim to be "a" door, but "the" door. He is not "one of several" shepherds; He is "the" shepherd. *"All who ever came before Him"* (whom He called "thieves and robbers") would certainly include seers, prophets, and so-called holy men, as well as ancient religious belief systems.

Then there is Christ's statement in **John 14:6:** *Jesus said to him, "I am the way, the truth, and the life. No one comes to the Father except through Me."*

Pretty clear and to the point, isn't it? Agree with such a person that Jesus certainly would not lie, especially about something so very important. When discussing an issue like this, I will often say something like, "You know, if I want to know how to come back from the dead, it just makes sense to me to listen to the *only* Person who ever did come back by His own power." Then, depending on the personality of the person you are speaking to, and how much freedom you have in being straight forward, I sometimes will go as far as to point out that Buddha is dead, Mohammed is dead, the founders of the various cults and religions are all dead; Jesus Christ alone came back from the dead. No wonder He is the only way to Heaven.

After sharing what Jesus said about being the only way, you might want to share other Bible verses on the same subject. For instance, in speaking of Jesus, Peter said in **Acts 4:11,12**, *"This is the 'stone which was rejected by you builders, which has become the chief cornerstone.' Nor is there salvation is any other, for there is no other name under heaven given among men by which we must be saved."* There is "no other name" because there is no other Savior.

Isaiah 43:11 adds, *I, even I, am the LORD, and besides Me there is no Savior.*

Isaiah 45:21 continues by saying, *Tell and bring forth your case; yes, let them take counsel together. Who has declared this from ancient time? Who has told it from that time? Have not I, the LORD? And there is no other God besides Me, a just God and a Savior; there is none besides Me.*

First Timothy 2:5,6 is very clear: *For there is one God and one Mediator between God and men, the Man Christ Jesus, who gave Himself a ransom for all, to be testified in due time.* One may not believe there is only one way to God and Heaven, but it certainly is clear enough that the Bible teaches that the Lord Jesus Christ is the only way and the only Savior. Christ has never been wrong about anything else; it's not logical to think that He would be mistaken about this.

⇒•◇•⇐

"I can't believe an all loving God would send anyone to hell."

There are two things wrong with this sentiment. First, God is not *"all* loving." By saying God is "all loving" it is often implied that that's all that He is—a loving God. He *is* loving to an infinite degree, but whatever He is, He is to an infinite degree—including His justice, righteousness, and holiness.

The second flaw in the above statement is that God "sends" people to hell. In reality, everyone outside of Christ is already hell bound. There is nothing that they or God must do to "send" them there. Hell was originally intended for the devil and his angels, not for man. However, men end up there for refusing to believe in the Lord Jesus Christ.

Here are some good verses to share on this point.

Matthew 25:41: *Then He will also say to those on the left hand, "Depart from Me, you cursed, into the everlasting fire prepared for the devil and his angels.*

John 3:18: *He who believes in Him is not condemned; but he who does not believe is condemned already because he has not believed in the name of the only begotten Son of God.*

John 3:36: *He who believes in the Son has everlasting life; and he who does not believe the Son shall not see life, but the wrath of God abides on him.*

Humanly speaking, I do not like the doctrine of hell, and I readily admit that to unbelievers. For years I did not believe in hell, but my unbelief did not change the fact of it; nor does my belief in it now mean that it's real. Jesus Christ and His infallible Word determine that. As with so many other truths, the One who has never lied, nor been wrong about anything upon which He has ever spoken, taught more about hell than He did Heaven. Not only that, but the final hell (from the Greek word *gehenna*) is only mentioned twelve times in the Bible; eleven of those twelve times the truth about hell came from the lips of Christ.

As much as hell may bother me emotionally, I must submit my feelings and intellect to the all-knowing One. I may not like it or fully understand it, but it is real. Therefore, while one may not believe God would allow anyone to go to hell, it is essential that he believes in the Deliverer, Jesus Christ, to avoid being separated from God forever. Jesus was not merely making a suggestion when He told Nicodemus, "You MUST be born again" (John 3:3, 7). There is no other way to see or enter God's kingdom and thus to escape hell other than to believe on the Lord Jesus Christ.

<hr />

"That's your interpretation."

The vast majority of the time when someone says this, their objection is a smoke screen. The real issue is usually a matter of belief, not a matter of interpretation. To prove it, turn to a clear and simple salvation verse, read it to them, and ask them, "How would you interpret this?" For instance you might say, "In **John 3:16,** how would you interpret these phrases: *God so loved the world? He gave His only begotten Son? Whoever believes in Him? Have everlasting life?*

Get the picture? Put the ball in their court so they will perhaps begin to see that it really is an issue of "do I believe what it says" rather than "do I believe how someone is interpreting it?"

———⫸•◆•⫷———

"What about infants who die, or the millions of aborted babies? What happens to them?"

There is a great statement that Abraham made to the Lord as he was reasoning with God over the impending destruction of Sodom. He said, *"Shall not the Judge of all the earth do right?"* (Genesis 18:25). And I think this testimony by Abraham concerning God's character is certainly appropriate to the question of babies. He will do what is right.

Not only that, but the Scripture seems to indicate that anyone who dies who is incapable of understanding the Gospel, and therefore unable to believe, is covered by Christ's substitutionary death on their behalf. Here are some Scriptures that may bear that out.

Second Samuel 12:15-23. David's child by Bathsheba became ill. While the baby was was still living David fasted all night and mourned over his baby's illness, and he pleaded with the Lord to cure the child. Then the child died and David washed himself and ate, which surprised the servants and they asked him about this sudden change of behavior that came over him. His reply is found in verse twenty three where he said about his dead child, *"I shall go to him, but he shall not return to me."* We know David went to Heaven and so it seems he is saying his baby went there before him.

First John 2:12-14 contains an interesting arrangement that may throw further light on this subject of the destination of babies who die before they are able to believe in Christ. Notice to whom John says he is writing—

little children, vs. 12.

fathers, vs. 13.

young men, vs.13.

little children, vs. 13.

fathers, vs. 14.

young men, vs. 14.

In the English translations each of the categories is repeated—little children, fathers, and young men, but not in the Greek. The word translated "children" in verse 13 is the word for "young growing child." The "little children" of verse 12 is the Greek word meaning "infant." Notice that in each case except the "infant" of verse 12 the person has *done* something: the fathers have *"known* Him" (v. 13 and 14), the young men have *"overcome* the wicked one" (v.13) and *"are strong, and the word of God abides in you, and you have overcome the wicked one"* (v. 14). The little children (growing child) have *"known* the Father." But what about the infant? *"I have written to you, little children* (infants) *because your sins are forgiven you for His name's sake!"* They don't do anything—they can't; yet they are forgiven, they belong to Him. So, logically, if they were to die in that infant stage they would be where He is—in Heaven (Psalm 115:2, 3; 123:1).

In **Matthew 18:10** Jesus said this concerning young children, *"Take heed that you do not despise one of these little ones* (see vss. 2-4—a little child)*, for I say to you that in Heaven their angels always see the face of My Father who is in Heaven."*

Hebrews 1:14 is very clear that angels are *"ministering spirits sent forth to minister for those who will inherit salvation."* So, it appears that little children, who have angels in Heaven, inherit salvation.

At what age, therefore, is someone accountable before God? Consider this statement in **James 4:17**: *Therefore to him who knows to do good and does not do it, to him it is sin.* If a person does not "know to do good"—that is, they are *incapable* of knowing right from wrong (not that they are simply ignorant or untaught)—God apparently sees them as blameless. This would include infants and those born with a physical handicap that keeps them from comprehending right from wrong, even though they may live enough calendar years to be considered adult.

Obviously this "age of accountability" is not a set age for everyone. Some children understand enough to trust in Christ as their Savior when they are three or four years old, but not all three or four year olds would grasp concepts such as *sin, salvation,* or *judgment.* It is an individual matter and only God knows for sure when one is truly there.

The issue of who has eternal life, however, is clear enough in Scripture.

John 3:18 is a key verse concerning this. It says, *He who believes in Him* (Christ) *is not condemned; he who does not believe is condemned already* **because** *he has not believed in the name of the Son of God.*

There are people (like infants or severely mentally challenged individuals) who are *not capable* of believing; that is, they *cannot* understand that it is *right* to believe and that unbelief is *wrong* (James 4:17). Such individuals are apparently not accountable for their state. They would be like the "infant" in First John 2:12—*"forgiven for His name's sake."*

In light of all of this, and the fact that *the Judge of all the earth will do right,* would God *demand* that we believe in Christ for our salvation, condemning us if we don't, and then withhold salvation from those who *would* believe if they *could*—those who are incapable of believing? The key word here is "incapable." This word does not apply to those who have simply never heard the Gospel. They are capable of believing it if they only know what to believe. So let's move on to that question.

=≻·◇·≼=

"What about those who have never heard of Christ?
God wouldn't let them go to hell, would He?"

To begin with it's important that we are aware of what the Bible actually teaches concerning this entire subject. A lot of people feel that God has just left a bulk of humanity out in the cold with no chance of ever hearing His salvation message through Christ. Others, on the other hand, think that God will save anyone who is sincere in their beliefs, especially if they have never had the opportunity to hear about the Gospel. Well, let's look at the question from the Bible's viewpoint.

First, let's consider what God *has* done to make salvation available to all.

We begin with **Romans 1:18-20.** Read the passage and you will see that He has revealed Himself *in* those who *"suppress* (hold down) *the truth in unrighteousness."* This is an inborn

God-awareness. He has also revealed Himself *to* them through creation. This is a God-awareness through nature. Neither of these are sufficient to bring salvation to anyone, but they are sufficient to cause one to seek after the God of creation—to respond to the inborn awareness of God they already have.

John 3:16, 17 reveals that God gave His only begotten Son to be our Savior and when He came to earth He provided salvation for all through His death and resurrection. All men may not know He has done this but the fact is, He did it, and He did it for *all* the world.

Luke 2:10, 11 adds this important insight: *Then the angel said to them, "Do not be afraid, for behold, I bring you good tidings of great joy, **which will be to all people***. *For there is born to you this day in the city of David a Savior, who is Christ the Lord." All people* does not leave anyone out.

Jesus told us exactly why He came in **Luke 19:10.** *For the Son of Man has come to seek and to save that which was lost.* "That which was lost" would include everyone outside of Christ, even those who are not yet aware of His coming.

In addition, there's **Hebrews 2:9** where it clearly states that Jesus "tasted death for *every* man"—not just the civilized or the elect.

First John 2:2 is another unmistakable confirmation concerning Christ's death being for everyone. *And He Himself is the propitiation for our sins, and not for ours only but also for the whole world.* Since Christ was the satisfactory payment (*propitiation*) for the *whole* world, that would certainly include the so-called heathen person who has never heard the Gospel.

Finally, **Titus 2:11** says, *The grace of God that brings salvation has appeared to all men.* God's grace "that brings salvation has appeared to *all* men"—all men would include those who have never heard. You might be thinking, "But these Scriptures do not really shed any light on whether or not those who have never heard the Gospel are lost."

So, let's take a look at what God *is* doing now to make salvation available to all.

We begin with **John 1:9:** *That was the true Light which gives light to every man who comes into the world.* Since Jesus is that true Light which gives light to *"every man who comes into the world,"* everyone, then, is born with Divine light from God—an

214

inborn God-awareness. People are not born with a bent toward atheism, but toward God. No one comes into this world without this *initial* light from God. How an individual may respond to that light we'll see in a moment.

The present ministry of the Holy Spirit lends further light on what God is currently doing to reach all the world. **John 16:7-11** gives us a vivid picture of His present ministry with the world. *Nevertheless I tell you the truth. It is to your advantage that I go away; for if I do not go away, the Helper* (the Holy Spirit) *will not come to you; but if I depart, I will send Him to you. And when He has come, He will convict the world of sin, and of righteousness, and of judgment: of sin, because they do not believe in Me; of righteousness, because I go to My Father and you see Me no more; of judgment, because the prince of this world is judged.*

Jesus promised that once He left to return to the Father in Heaven He would send the Holy Spirit, and when the Spirit came the promise was that He would "convict" (persuade) the world of the sin of unbelief, of its need for righteousness, and of coming judgment. Jesus did go back to Heaven and He did send the Holy Spirit *who is doing His convicting work now.*

Jesus is also involved in drawing the lost to Himself, as He said in **John 12:32:** *And I, if I be lifted up from the earth, will draw all peoples to Myself.* Jesus was "lifted up from the earth" on the cross at Calvary, and He is drawing" all peoples" to Himself—"all" is all, and He is doing it *now.* He draws, but not all respond to His drawing.

Jeremiah 29:13 gives God's promise that those who seek Him—whether or not they know of Him—will find Him. He wrote, *And you will seek Me and find Me, when you search for Me with all your heart.*

God guarantees that those who seek Him will find Him—written to Israel in captivity in a heathen country, Babylon. The "seeking" is man's responsibility. Those who seek receive more and more spiritual light until they are exposed to the Gospel message. Those who do not respond to the light they already have, sink into greater spiritual darkness.

Here's another passage that urges unbelievers to seek the Lord. **Isaiah 55:1, 6:** *Ho! Everyone who thirsts, come to the waters: And you who have no money, come, buy and eat. Yes,. come buy wine and milk without money and without price...Seek* *the Lord while He may be found, call upon Him while He is near.*

Acts 17:16-34 is the New Testament equivalent to the Old Testament passages we just read. Paul was in Athens and he saw that *"the city was given over to idols"* (v. 16). He witnessed to the heathenistic philosphers on Mars Hill and told them that God *"has made from one blood every nation of men"* in order that they *"should seek the Lord...though He is not far from each one of us"* (vs. 24-27). He then proceeded to tell them of Christ and some of them believed (vs. 29-34).

There are four primary passages that record the Great Commission—Christ's last "marching orders" to His troops, the apostles. They are **Matthew 28:18-20; Mark 16:15; Luke 24:46-49; Acts 1:8** All of these verses record Christ commanding His disciples to go into all the world and preach the Gospel to every creature. They obeyed and all the world heard the Gospel in the first century according to Colossians 1:5, 6, and 23: *Because of the hope which is laid up for you in heaven, of which you heard before in the word of the truth of the gospel, which has come to you, as it has also **in all the world**, and is bringing forth fruit, as it is also among you....if indeed you...are not moved away from the hope of the gospel which you heard, **which was preached to every creature under heaven**, of which I, Paul, became a minister.*

Important Point: If those who have never heard the Gospel can be saved by sincerely believing in their own gods or religions, then the worse thing Christians could do would be to take the Gospel to them, for then they would be condemned if they failed to believe in Christ (John 3:18, 36). Would Jesus Christ command us to preach the Gospel to the world if these people were already saved through their own pagan beliefs? Not hardly.

Now we turn to the question of why some have not heard the Gospel.

Romans 1:18-28 contains the answer: They surpressed (held down) the Truth in their unrighteousness (v. 18). *"When they knew God* (literally: when they were aware of God), *they did not glorify Him as God, nor were they thankful, but became futile in their thoughts and their foolish hearts were darkened"* (v. 21). Cause and effect is in operation here: what you sow, you reap. *"They became fools and changed the glory of the incorruptible*

216

God into an image made like corruptible man and birds, and four-footed beasts and creeping things" (vss. 22, 23). This is what pagans continue to do. They *"exchanged the truth of God for the lie, and worshipped and served the creature rather than the Creator"* (v. 25). So, *"God gave them up to uncleanness...gave them up to vile passions...and gave them over to debased minds"* (vs. 24, 26, 28). Cause and effect again.

It is a strange phenomenon that the parts of the world where the Gospel was first introduced in the first century are now some of the darkest areas of the world spiritually—the Middle East, all of the Arab countries, North Africa, Egypt. What happened? The above passage tells us: When they were aware of the truth concerning God, they did not glorify Him as God, were unthankful, and became futile in their thoughts; they exchanged the truth of God for the lie; so, God gave them over to debased minds.

God's remedy, of course, is His way of salvation through faith in His dear Son, and this is where you and I come in. God's methods in reaching the unreached is clearly revealed in His Word. He often sends *witnessing* believers to *seeking* unbelievers, as Philip was sent to the Ethopian man on his way back to Africa (Acts 8:26-39). God also sends *seeking* unbelievers to *witnessing* Christians, as God told Cornelius to send for Peter in Acts 10:1-11:18.

At other times God will send a witnessing Christian to someone who does not show any signs of seeking the Lord, but through the witnessing an interest is ignited and they come to faith. Such was the case of Christ speaking to the Samaritan woman at the well (John 4:4-42), and of Paul in Athens (Acts 17:16-34).

I do not normally give as elaborate a response to this question as I have laid out for you here. I summarize this information for them. You, on the other hand, want to impress upon the person you are witnessing to that although it is good to be concerned about those who have not heard, it is mandatory that those who have heard respond to the Gospel—like this person in front of you. Failure to do so means eternal condemnation, but to trust in Christ to save them means eternal life in the presence of God.

I was witnessing to Mr. Aaronson on Miami Beach when he angrily asked, "Where was your God when Hitler massacred six million of my people?" I already knew he believed in God, so I replied, "I guess He was the same place your God was. You see, Mr. Aaronson, the question is not, 'where was God,' the question is where were the hearts of the people? Your prophets, including the greatest one, Moses, warned over and over again that if Israel deserted God, He would leave them to their own devices and cause other nations to rule over them." This became the turning point of our conversation and he later admitted that his people may have been reaping what they had sown. Mr. Aaronson did not trust in Jesus as his Messiah that day, but when we parted he was much more receptive to the Gospel than he had been at the beginning of our time together.

The above question is not an easy one to answer. The framing of the question does not always revolve around Hitler's treatment of the Jews. It might concern itself with the death of innocent children, or why God allowed the terrorist's bombing of the World Trade Center and the Pentegon, or the attack on Pearl Harbor. But regardless of the example given in the framing of the question, the *nature* of the question is basically the same: how can a loving God permit so much meaningless evil in the world; why does He allow so much injustice to go on and on; if He is all powerful why doesn't He put a stop to it?

I normally bring folks who ask this type of question back to the truths pointed out earlier in Romans 1:18-32, especially verses 20-26, and verse 28. If people consistently leave God out of their lives, they remove themselves from His protective hand. It shouldn't then be a surprise if, when they begin to experience the results of ignoring or denying Him, that they have been left by Him to fend for themselves, and to reap what they have sown. The world without God can be a horrible place, a place where the Hitlers of life can wreak havoc on others before coming to their own horrific ends.

Life is not fair, but God is just, and as such He allows man to make his own choices, but with every choice there are con-sequences—some good, some bad. You need to impress upon others that they have a clear-cut choice: they can trust in

Christ or reject Him. In either case, they will reap the results of the choice they make.

For Personal Reflection and Application

❖ Listening to the Lord as He speaks in and through His Word is absolutely the best way to find the answers to questions—yours and those of others—and to discover the most effective responses to the objections of nonbelievers. Do you "listen" to God—*daily*—by meditating on His Word? As you do, answers and helpful insights will pour into your life.

❖ On a more personal level, when you have painful questions of your own—they usually begin with *why*—be encouraged and comforted by David's comment in Psalm 119:49, 50: *Remember the word to Your servant upon which You have caused me to hope. This is my comfort in my affliction, for Your word has given me life.*

For every difficulty that keeps a person from Christ, there is a Biblical solution. Our task is to act as spiritual doctors— diagnosing the patient's spiritual, intellectual and emotional needs, and prescribing the proper Scriptural remedy.

RAS

14

Overcoming Obstacles

I distinguish between questions and objections, and obstacles for this reason: there may be an obstacle in one's path to salvation which is not really in the form of questioning God or the Bible, and they may not be objecting to anything within Scripture; they sometimes are simply bogged down with *feelings* or *impressions* about themselves, or others, or God, that hinder them from seeing the truth. We want to remove those obstacles or change them from being obstructions to being bridges to the Gospel. Here are a few that you may encounter.

"There are too many hypocrites in the church."

It is important that you *agree with the unbeliever* about this. There shouldn't be *any* hypocrites in the church! Also ask something like, "Can you think of anything about Jesus Himself that you don't like or that you think was hypocritical?" Their response will almost always be a *no* reply. Then you can remind them that you are speaking of them knowing *Him*, and that you are not speaking to them about getting involved in a church. Then proceed to give the Gospel.

This doesn't mean that church is unimportant, but it is simply an affirmation that what saves is faith in Christ, not church attendence or identification. We need to keep first things first, and what is always first when it comes to salvation is Christ.

———≫·◆·≪———

"I live as good a life as a lot of Christians I know."

I usually say, "I don't doubt that one bit, and if getting to Heaven was a matter of being good, then you would probably have a good chance of making it. However, it is not goodness God demands, it's perfection." Then I use this truth of what God demands as my stepping stone into giving the Gospel.

⊸⬥⬰

"I'm too sinful for God to save."

No one is *that* sinful. Show them that Christ came to die for sinners and that the worse sinner of all has already been saved, so anyone may now trust in Christ and be saved.

First Timothy 1:15-16 is an excellent place to start. *This is a faithful saying and worthy of all acceptance, that Christ Jesus came into the world to save* **sinners**, *of whom* **I am chief**. *However, for this reason I obtained mercy, that in me first Jesus Christ might show all longsuffering,* **as a pattern** *to those who are going to believe on Him for everlasting life.*

In these verses we see that not only has God already saved the "chief" of all sinners (Paul was a murderer of Christians before he himself became one), but also that the reason behind saving this chief of sinners was "as a pattern" so that anyone coming after Paul would know that since God saved the likes of Paul, they too can be saved. That's something to really shout about!

For someone who is truly plagued by their sins, you may have to go over verses like these over and over again, emphasizing God's grace, mercy and lovingkindness.

Romans 5:6, 8 are other great verses to show a person who feels they are too sinful for God to save. *For when we were still* **without strength**, *in due time Christ died for the* **ungodly** .... *God demonstrates His own love for us, in that while we were* **still sinners**, *Christ died for us.*

As you point to these verses, emphasize the highlighted words. If someone feels they are too great a sinner for God to save, they need to be reassured that there is no such creature. The very ones Christ died for were without any moral strength of their own, were ungodly, and were still sinners.

It's also very important to point out that they are invited to come to Christ as they are—with all of their sins, their doubts and questions, their hang-ups, and their hurts.

There are some good verses that make this truth clear, and here are some of my favorites.

John 4:3-30, 39-42, the example of Jesus with the Samaritan woman, is a classic illustration of a person living in sin and coming to Christ as they are. When Jesus was speaking to the Samaritan woman at the well, there came a point in their conversation where Jesus said to her, *"Go, call your husband, and come here." The woman answered and said, "I have no husband." Jesus said to her, "You have well said, 'I have no husband,' for you have had five husbands, and the one whom you now have is not your husband; in that you spoke truly"* (vss. 16-18). Notice that although Christ revealed to her that He knew the sinful life she was living, He did not come down on her in a harsh way. In fact, He commended her for speaking truthfully about not having a husband. Many a Christian worker would have taken a different slant, condemning her for attempting to mislead them.

The woman, in her excitement, *left her water pot, went her way into the city, and said to the men, "Come, see a man who told me all things that I ever did. Could this be the Christ?" Then they went out of the city and came to Him* (vss 28-30). Later, *many of the Samaritans of that city believed in Him because of the word of the woman who testified, "He told me all that I ever did"* (vs. 39). Later still, *many more believed because of His own word* (vs. 41).

All kinds of lessons can be gleaned from this wonderful story, but in light of the one who thinks he cannot come to Christ because of his sin, I'll focus on these few facts: Christ loved this very sinful woman and she knew it! He impressed upon her His identity as her Messiah, and the overriding issue is always who Jesus Christ is and what will lost sinners do with Him. The issue is never how sinful is the lost person you are attempting to reach. The old hymn says, "Christ receiveth sinful men," but we don't always convey that to sinful men, do we? We sing, "Just as I am, I come" but then we often turn to the lost one and tell him how much he has to stop or change before he may come. How hypocritical, and how unlike Christ is such an approach to the lost.

Luke 5:27-32

In this passage Jesus calls Levi (Matthew), a hated tax collector working for the Roman government, to follow Him. *Then Levi gave Him a great feast in his own house. And there* were a great number of tax collectors and others who sat down with them. But their scribes and the Pharisees murmured against His disciples, saying, "Why do You eat and drink with tax collectors and sinners?" And Jesus answered and said to them, "Those who are well do not need a physician, but those who are sick. I have not come to call the righteous, but sinners, to repentance" (vss. 30-32).

I'm afraid the truth of the matter is that most of us do not feel comfortable around outwardly sinful people. Not only that, but some of us detest being in their presence. We attempt to get them to clean up before we will even invite them to trust in our precious Savior. Such an attitude is obviously not the attitude of one who is led by the Spirit of Christ. Until we get rid of our own self-righteous spirit of superiority (snobbery), we will never be able to genuinely display Christ's love for the sinner while disapproving of their sinful ways.

Revelation 22:17: The last invitation in the Bible. *And the Spirit and the bride say, "Come!" And let him who hears say, "Come!" And let him who thirsts come. And whoever desires, let him take the water of life freely.* If one is thirsty and desires to have his or her thirst quenched by Jesus Christ, they are invited to come to Him. On what condition? Simply that they thrist and want to drink of the water of life freely. We need to keep it that simple.

"I'm afraid I've committed the unpardonable sin."

You might ask them what they understand the unpardonable sin to be. Their answer will almost always be wrong. I can only think of two instances where someone who thought they had committed this sin were even close to possessing the Bible's description of it. The best description of it is **Mark 3:28–30:** *Assuredly, I say to you, all sins will be forgiven the sons of men, and whatever blasphemies they may utter; but he who blasphemes against the Holy Spirit never has forgiveness, but is subject to eternal condemnation—because they said, "He has an unclean spirit."*

Only Mark's account of this sin tells why the one who commits it is condemned: *because they said, "He has an unclean* (evil, demonic) *spirit.*" In other words, all the miracles Jesus performed were performed by a spirit of the devil rather than by the Spirit of God. They did not believe He was who He claimed to be—God in human form, the Savior, their Messiah. This is nothing less than unbelief, and anyone who dies in unbelief will be separated from God forever in hell.

By the same token, anyone who is currently an unbeliever is already condemned *because* of their unbelief, so be sure to show them **John 3:16–18:** *For God so loved the world that He gave His only begotten Son, that whoever believes in Him should not perish but have everlasting life. For God did not send His Son into the world to condemn the world, but that the world through Him might be saved. He who believes in Him is not condemned; but he who does not believe is condemned already, because he has not believed in the name of the only begotten Son of God.*

If the unbelief of the one who is currently an unbeliever condemns him, what's the remedy? *Belief,* of course. A friend of mine used to say, "The answer to unbelief is belief!" So even if one has committed the "unpardonable sin," they may still believe in Christ while they are living and escape the eternal condemnation which follows all those who die in a state of unbelief. The fact that one is concerned that they may have committed this sin, is a strong indication that they have not; otherwise, they would have no concern about it whatsoever.

To make the point more obvious, you might misquote a verse to alleviate their fears; a verse such as **John 6:47:** *Most assuredly, I say to you, "He who believes in Me has everlasting life."* Try misquoting it like this: *"He who believes in Me has everlasting life unless he has committed the unpardonable sin."* This should get them to see that there is hope for them and that Christ's invitation to salvation is open to all regardless of what sins they've been guilty.

"There are so many denominations. How can we know which one is right?"

No denomination, cult or local church is the way to salvation. None of them are right all the time about all things (though there certainly are religious people who think their group is the only true one). Besides that, which church to align oneself with is not really the issue. Here's another good verse to *mis*quote—**Acts 4:12:** *Nor is there salvation in any other, for there is no other name under heaven given among men by which we must be saved other than the First Bapterian Episcolopian Church of the Firstborn Brethren!* The issue, as always, is the Gospel. *Share it!*

━━━━━◆━━━━━

"When God wants to save me He will. There's nothing I can do about it."

There is nothing in the Bible to support such a conclusion. In fact, just the opposite is the case. Take special note of **Second Corinthians 6:1-2:** *We then, as workers together with Him also plead with you not to receive the grace of God in vain. For He says, "In an acceptable time I have heard you, and in the day of salvation I have helped you." Behold,* **now** *is the accepted time; behold,* **now** *is the day of salvation.*

God's time to be saved is always *NOW.* He never promises to save anyone tomorrow; instead He warns about putting things off in **Proverbs 27:1:** *Do not boast about tomorrow, for you do not know what a day may bring forth.* **Hebrews 3:7-8** also warns, *Therefore, as the Holy Spirit says, "Today, if you will hear His voice, do not harden your hearts... "*

━━━━━◆━━━━━

"I probably will believe in the Lord one day, but not now."

Procrastination, when it comes to spiritual matters, can be a deadly weakness or even a sin, so along with Proverbs 27:1, and Second Corinthians 6:2 quoted above, you might also share this verse with a person who insists on putting off the matter of trusting in Christ—**Hebrews 2:3:** *How shall we escape if we neglect so great a salvation, which at the first began to be spoken by the Lord, and was confirmed to us by those who heard Him.* Though they may feel they have plenty of time to think it over, none of us can be sure how much longer we have to live. Kindly but firmly plant the thought in such a person's mind that they are neglecting God's offer of salvation and if they continue to do so there will be no escape. Urge them to place their faith in Christ right away.

⸺⸻◈⸻⸺

"I really couldn't care less about what you are telling me."

This kind of attitude can be a tough one to overcome. Many times a person feels this way because of having been turned off to everything religious in the past, and they think what you are attempting to share with them is "just more of the same." Be patient and try to understand that it may not be you or God they are angry with. The problem is often found in their misconceptions about Him. I was this way before I came to Christ, and my Dad was this way until the day he died.

You want to dwell upon God's love and His eagerness to receive them into His family. If some of their misconceptions surface during your talk, help clarify their thinking by the wise use of Scripture. Some teachers of personal evangelism believe in coming down hard on a person like this, but I believe such an attitude is often a cover–up for deep hurts and disappointments If all else fails, you then may feel a need to warn them while still being their friend.

The passage I prefer to use in situations like this is one that holds out the loving offer of the forgiveness of sins, coupled with an earnest warning to those who refuse God's offer. It's important to impress upon this type of person that God's first choice for them is salvation and that He will do all He can to draw them to Himself short of making them respond to Him. That they must do on their own.

The passage I mentioned is **Acts 13:38-41:** *Therefore let it be known to you, brethren, that through this Man is preached to you the forgivenss of sins; and by Him everyone who believes is justified from all things from which you could not be justified by the law of Moses. Beware therefore, lest what has been spoken by the prophets come upon you: "Behold, you despisers, marvel and perish! For I work a work in your days, a work which you will by no means believe, though one were to declare it to you.* Notice the offer: the forgiveness of all sins through faith in Christ. Then the warning: the very real prospect of perishing without Christ.

Here is another verse you may choose to use from time to

time. **Proverbs 29:1:** *He who is often reproved, and hardens his neck, will suddenly be destroyed, and that without remedy.*

"I do not want to talk about it, period!"

You may ask this person why they do not want to talk about the Lord and, if they give you reasons, you may build upon those to introduce the Gospel. Using the vehicle of your own testimony might be good here. However, often this type of person will not even give you any reason for refusing to discuss anything spiritual or religious.

You must respect their right to refuse you and/or your message. There is no law that says they must listen to you. If they absolutely will not talk about anything to do with God, I usually thank them for their honesty and let it go, meanwhile lifting them up in prayer. If you live, or work, or attend school with such a person, the life you live before them will be of tremendous importance in possibly breaking down barriers, but don't be surprised if they persecute you for they, too, may be reacting to some very unpleasant experiences in their past.

On rare occasions you may attempt something like this. I was wanting to witness to a gentleman one day and he made it very clear to me that he did not want me to say anything to him "about religion or God." I could not find an opening because of his stubborn refusal to allow any "God talk" to enter the conversation. Finally, I said, "O.K., if you don't want to hear that God loves you, and that Christ died to pay for your sins, and offers you the gift of eternal life when you trust in Him, I'm not going to tell you!" He gave me that "aren't you cute" look and smiled ever so slightly, and then I did have the opportunity to share the Gospel with him. Just don't try to use this approach unless you feel the person to whom you are speaking really does have a soft spot somewhere underneath his or her exterior.

"I'm not worthy of God's love.

Emphasize the truth that none of us are worthy and that's where the importance and meaning of God's *grace and mercy* comes in. *Mercy* is **not** receiving what we deserve—hell and judgement, while *grace* is **receiving** the exact opposite of what we really deserve—Heaven and forgiveness. Use **Matthew 9:12-13** to emphasize that Jesus said, *"Those who are well have no need of a physician, but those who are sick. But go and learn what this means: 'I desire mercy and not sacrifice.' For I did not come to call the righteous, but sinners, to repentance."*

Romans 5:6, 8, 10 is also a good reminder that Christ died for us while we were *"without strength,"* while we were *"still sinners,"* and while we were His *"enemies."* Worthiness is not the issue; God's character, His love, is what determines if we are saveable, and we are!

"I haven't been in church in years."

In the back of this person's mind is probably a feeling that "going to church" has something to do with eventually going to Heaven—in other words, good works are essential. Use any of the clear salvation verses to show them the error of this kind of thinking. Ephesians 2:8, 9, Romans 4:5, Titus 3:5 are all good to share. You might try misquoting again. Take, for instance, the first phrase of Ephesians 2:8. You might read it to them this way: *For by grace you have been saved through church attendence.* Make sure they understand that the verse does *not* say that; then make it clear what it *does* say and *present the Gospel.*

"I used to be a Christian but I failed—I couldn't hold on."

Either this kind of person has never really heard or understood the Gospel or, if they have, they are now very confused. The confusion will probably revolve around the works issue, the lack of understanding concerning grace, the false teaching that they can lose their salvation, or a combination of all three. It will be important for you to make the Gospel clear, emphasizing all of those issues.

Also, stress that being saved is not our holding on to the Lord, but Him holding on to us. That's what security is all about. **John 10:28–30** is the classic passage on this. *And I give them eternal* *life, and they shall never perish; neither shall anyone snatch them out of My hand. My Father, who has given them to Me, is greater than all; and no one is able to snatch them out of My Father's hand. I and My Father are one.* He holds on to us. We are in *His* hand, not He in *ours.* If being saved or staying saved depended on *us* holding on to Him, the likelihood is very real that we would all "let go" at one time or another. Salvation, then, would depend upon our faithfulness rather than His faithfulness. Thank God, it depends solely upon His ability to save and keep us, and not upon our fickle attempts at saving ourselves.

"I thought I was a Christian but I guess I'm not; I've still got too many bad habits."

When I encounter someone with this kind of fuzzy thinking it is almost always true that they got this idea from preaching they've heard. Unfortunately there is far too much preaching that declares that if you haven't gotten rid of all of your besetting sins, then you probably are not saved.

Make sure the Gospel is clearly understood by this person and then share some verses like the following. **Hebrews 12:1:** *Therefore, we also, since we are surrounded by so great a cloud of witnesses, let us* (believers) *lay aside every weight, and the sin which so easily ensnares us, and let us run with endurance the race that is set before us.* Why would God inspire the writer of Hebrews to urge his fellow believers to *"lay aside every...sin which so easily ensnares us"* if there was no possibility for any such sin to be in a true Christian's life?

A careful reading of the following verses should convince any open minded individual that Christians can be beset by sin: **First Corinthians 1:1, 2; 3:1-4; 5:1-5; 6:1-6; 11:17-22.** Trace these verses through and you will see the book of First Corinthians is written to *"The church of God at Corinth... with all who in every place call on the name of Jesus Christ our Lord..."*—in other words, it is written to true believers in Christ. And these true believers were divisive in following after men (3:1-4), one was guilty of gross immoral sin and the church was puffed up about it instead of mourning over it (5:1-5), they were taking one another to court before unbelievers (6:1-6), and they were even being gluttonous and drunk at the Lord's table (11:17-22). For this reason—partaking of the Lord's table *"in an unworthy manner"*—many were weak and sick, and many died prematurely. This church obviously had a sin problem and yet there is no suggestion that they were not saved; rather God handled the problems by reminding them of their true relationship with Him by saying, *"Do you not know that your body is the temple of the Holy Spirit who is in you, and you are not your own? For you were bought at a price; therefore glorify God in your body and in your spirit, which are God's"* (6:19, 20).

"All my friends will be in hell, so I may as well join them" (frivolous).

I label this statement as *frivolous* while the one to follow I consider to be *serious*. The reason for the distinction lies in the attitude of the one making the statement, and I approach the ones making these statements in a different way. To the frivolous person (often a teenager or young adult) I will often go straight to the Scriptures to point out certain frightening things that are revealed concerning hell. In **Luke 16:19-31**, for instance, is the story of the rich man and a beggar, Lazarus. They both died and Lazarus went to Paradise. The rich man *"died and was buried. And being in torments in Hades, he lifted up his eyes and saw Abraham afar off, and Lazarus in his bosom. Then he cried and said, 'Father Abraham, have mercy on me, and send Lazarus that he may dip the tip of his finger in water and cool my tongue; for I am tormented in this flame'"* (vss. 22-24).

A little later Abraham told the rich man, *"between us and you there is a great gulf fixed, so that those who want to pass from here to you cannot, nor can those from there pass to us."* Then he (the rich man) *said, "I beg you therefore, father, that you would send him to my father's house, for I have five brothers, that he may testify to them, lest they also come to this place of torment"* (vss. 26, 27).

It's important to observe several facts that are apparent from this story. First, Hades or Hell is "a place of torment." There is never a "party time" in hell. No one is ever going to air-condition it! Secondly, once a person is in hell, there is no escape. There are no "Exit Signs" in hell. Thirdly, once a person wakes up in hell the last thing he or she wants is for any of their friends or loved ones to join them there. Please note that the rich man did not turn to anyone in hell to talk to, to have fellowship with. His gaze went immediately to Paradise where he saw the peace and enjoyment that Lazarus and Abraham were having.

Some believe that this story is not true, that it is just a parable. Rather than arguing the point, it might be better to ask, "If this is only a parable and not reality, what *is* the reality? What is it supposed to be illustrating?" If this is only a shadow of the real, then the real must be far worse than what is pictured here. I'd rather take it at face value; after all, in each of Christ's many parables He never named anyone by name. At the beginning of this story we are told, "...there was a certain beggar named Lazarus." Now, either there was such a beggar or there was not. I firmly believe there was and, therefore, the story is a true account.

Jude 7 gives some more striking and somewhat frightening insights regarding hell. It says: *As Sodom and Gomorrah, and the cities around them in a similar manner to these, having given themselves over to sexual immorality and gone after strange flesh, are set forth as an example, suffering the vengeance of eternal fire.* The citizens of Sodom and Gomorrah had been dead, and their cities destroyed, hundreds of years before God led Jude to write these words; yet they were still "suffering (present tense) the vengeance of eternal fire."

Pretty solemn thought, isn't it?

As I'm sharing the Gospel, if I feel that the one making this statement about hell is treating it very lightly I sometimes like to remind him that "you may laugh your way into hell, but you will never laugh your way out." Or, "Your friends may laugh you into hell, but they'll never be able to laugh you out." When I have made statements like this to individuals (or sometimes to a group, like at a camp where some of the campers may be acting up), I'm always *very* serious, *but equally loving*. **Never** make such statements as if you have a chip on your shoulder, or as if you wish they *would* to go to hell.

=>•◇•<=

"If what you say is true, then all my loved ones are

either already in hell or are headed for it. If that's
the case, then I want to be in hell with them,
not in Heaven" (serious).

Those who express this sentiment in this way are usually quite serious and sincere. I've had statements made to me on numerous occasions by Jewish folks, by dedicated Roman Catholics, and others who have had a long line of family and ancestors who have "always believed this way."

This, then, is not the time to be harsh or to attempt to shock them out of their entrenched belief system. Love, tenderness and understanding are what is called for in situations like this. I attempt to reason with this kind of person along several lines.

First, I might say, *"You don't really know what anyone else truly believes, especially relatives and ancestors who lived before you were even born. Only God knows the thoughts of the hearts of men."*

This is supported in Scripture in **First Kings 8:39.** King Solomon, praying at the dedication of the Temple, asked God to *"forgive, and act and give to everyone according to all his ways, whose heart You know (for **You, only You**, know the hearts of all the sons of men)."* Probably all of us entertain thoughts and feelings that no one else on planet earth is aware of; that would certainly include thoughts about God, Heaven, hell, death, and life after death. God, however, knows our every thought.

Jeremiah 17:9, 10 elaborates further that *The heart is deceitful above all things, and desperately* (incurably) *wicked; who can know it? I, the Lord, search the heart, I test the mind...*

Secondly, I may reason this way with them: *"Assuming you are right about your ancestors, wherever they are—Heaven or hell—they long for you to be in Heaven, not in hell."*

At this point I would point out such things as hell being a constant state of death, which literally means "separation" (the Second Death—Revelation 20:14, 15). Those who are there are not only separated from God, but from each other as well. There will be no comfort for anyone because a loved one has also come there. That, in fact, may add to the sorrow.

Thirdly, I may remind them, "Jesus has never been wrong about anything, so He certainly is not wrong about this matter of hell. He spoke more about it than He did about Heaven. He wants you to be in Heaven, and that's why He came and died, and rose from the dead. He offers you the gift of eternal life and if you really care about those in your family or among your friends who are still living, you could well be the instrument, the catalyst, of seeing whole generations (from the present going well into the future) coming to Christ and spending eternity with Him in Heaven."

Then, come back to the Gospel and urge this dear person to reconsider, and to place their faith in Christ alone.

>—◇—<

Those who lack assurance

Due to Ignorance.

The key here is to educate them from Scripture. Share the Gospel and especially emphasize *God's Guarantee*—what He promises to the one who puts his or her faith in Christ. I remind you once again to use verses like those listed here: John 3:18, John 3:36, John 5:24, John 6:37-40, John 6:47, Romans 8:31-39 and First John 5:13.

Due to Sin.

Few things will rob a believer of assurance quicker than allowing sin to dominate the life. This is particularly true regarding the thought life. If someone is struggling with the assurance of salvation because of recurring sins in their life try misquoting Scripture. For instance, **John 6:47:** *He who believes in Me has life until he sins;* or, *He who believes in Me has temporary life.*

Due to False Teaching

Examples:
"I used to be saved but fell away."
"I've sinned away my day of grace."
"I've fallen from grace."

Due to Looking at Something Other than Christ,

for Instance, Emotional Experiences, Visions, etc.

In each case go directly to clear, literal Scriptures which cannot be misunderstood. Make sure they understand the Gospel before getting into the "eternal security" debate, but then share such verses as mentioned above under *Due to Ignorance.*

For Personal Reflection and Application

❖ Are you patient, loving and understanding with nonbelievers, knowing that they are often confused and bewildered by all the inconsistencies of life because they allow intellectual, moral or emotional obstacles to stand in the way of their coming to Christ?

❖ Do you only care about having the flawless answer, or do you make friends and give support that causes unbelievers to want to hear you?

Always be ready to give
a defense to everyone
who asks you a reason
for the hope that is in you,
with meekness and fear.

First Peter 3:15
The New Testament

15

Using Christian Evidences

Proving that God is, or that the Bible is the Word of God, or that Jesus is the Savior, does not—by itself—lead anyone to salvation. However, when a nonbeliever has serious and sincere questions about the validity of the Bible, the reality of Christ's resurrection, His deity, or other important questions challenging the truthfulness of things found in the Bible, evidences can be invaluable in causing such a one to become convinced that they can trust what they find in Scripture.

There are some great books on Christian evidences and apolgetics and I heartily recommend you read some of them. For my part, I keep the presentation of evidences very simple and I've found that the vast majority of the time *simple* is better and more effective. One other observation: if I can demonstrate that the Bible must be from God then the other questions are much easier to deal with because the *source* of such things as Christ's resurrection, His deity, life after death, etc., is now seen as being from a *reliable* source. So, let's talk about—

Why I Believe the Bible is the Word of God

First, the Bible *Claims* to Be from God.

Consider **Second Timothy 3:16, 17:** *All Scripture is given by inspiration of God, and is profitable for doctrine, for reproof, for correction, for instruction in righteousness, that the man of God may be complete, thoroughly equipped for every good work.*

Remember that in **Psalm 119:160** we find that all of Scripture is inspired, including every word: *The entirety of Your word is truth, and every one of Your righteous judgments* *endures forever.*

Another way the Bible claims inspiration is the fact that over 2,000 times the Bible says, *"Thus says the LORD"* or its equivalent. Of course, any author may claim his or her writings were given to them directly from God. Mary Baker Eddy claimed inspiration for her book *Science and Health with Key to the Scriptures* (the foundation of Christian Science), Joseph Smith, Jr. claimed God gave him inspired writings through an angel (*The Book of Mormon*), Islam claims that the *Koran* was given from God to Muhammed. Claiming it is one thing; demonstrating it is something else. We move on.

Secondly, The Bible *Seems* to Be from God

Consider the fact that the Bible speaks *with authority* on every conceivable subject: from man's origin, to angels, from heaven to hell, from Satan and demons, to God, and even speaks dogmatically about future events on earth .

Another trait that points to the fact that the Bible may be from God is the peace that it promises is experienced *when* people believe it and live by it. I realize that there are other writings that produce peace in one, so this is not a proof that the Bible is from God. However, if one who believes and practices the precepts found in the Bible does not experience inner peace, that would be good grounds for questioning its divine origin—especially since such peace is promised (see John 14:27; Psalm 119:165).

Thirdly, when believers pray *as the Bible describes* they receive consistent answers to their prayers, even answers that may well be described as nothing short of miraculous. A mere human production could not empower the one reading and applying its principles to receive supernatural results. Prayer is an integral part of the relationship that exists between the believer in Christ and God. What God promises He delivers on, and that indicates the Bible is of divine origin.

Finally, the Bible *Proves* to Be from God

If the Bible is God's Word there *ought* to be things about it that cannot be explained in any other way other than that God is the Author of it. That is exactly the case in at least four areas.

The First Form of Proof of the Bible's Inspiration is Fulfilled Prophecy

Isaiah 48:3-5 is my favorite passage to use in demonstrating how fulfilled prophecy proves God has to be the Author of Scripture. Let its powerful message sink in as you read: *I have declared the former things from the beginning; they went forth from My mouth, and I caused them to hear it. Suddenly I did them, and they came to pass. Because I knew that you were obstinate, and your neck was an iron sinew, and your brow bronze, even from the beginning I have declared it to you;* **before it came to pass I proclaimed it to you,** *lest you should say, "My idol has done them, and my carved image and my molded image have commanded them."* The fulfilled prophecies of the Bible often contain such minute details given hundreds of years before the events happened, that there is only one logical conclusion: God, who knows the end from the beginning, gave those prophecies through chosen prophets.

Here are some examples of just a few of the prophecies regarding Christ which were fulfilled during His earthly life. There are many more, but these are some that I use over and over again.

His Virgin Birth.

Isaiah 7:14 gives the prophecy: *Therefore the LORD Himself will give you a sign: Behold the virgin shall conceive and bear a Son, and shall call His name Immanuel.*

Matthew 1:18, 22-23 records the fulfillment: *Now the birth of Jesus Christ was as follows: After His mother Mary was betrothed to Joseph, before they came together, she was found with child of the Holy Spirit....Now all this was done that it might be fulfilled which was spoken by the Lord through the prophet, saying, "Behold, the virgin shall be with child, and bear a Son, and they shall call His name Immanuel," which is translated, "God with us."*

His Birth Place.

Micah 5:2 gives the prophecy: *But you, Bethlehem Ephrathah, though you are little among the thousands of Judah, yet out of you shall come forth to Me the One to be ruler in Israel, whose goings forth have been from old, from everlasting.*

This prophecy gives the birth town/city (Bethlehem), the

"county" (Ephrathah), the state (Judah), and the country (Israel). There were at least two Bethlehems when this prophecy was given and Bethlehem of Judea was the smaller of the two. The prophecy pinpoints the exact town so there would be no mistake. Unlike other so-called prophecies such as those from Nostradamus, Edgar Cayce or Jean Dixon, Biblical prophecies are often minute in their details.

Luke 2:4-7 records the fulfillment: *And Joseph also went up from Galilee, out of the city of Nazareth, into Judea, to the city of David, which is called Bethlehem, because he was of the house and lineage of David, to be registered with Mary, his bethrothed wife, who was with child. So it was, that while they were there, the days were completed for her to be delivered. And she brought forth her firstborn Son, and wrapped Him in swaddling cloths, and laid Him in a manger, because there was no room for them in the inn.*

Matthew 2:1 also records the fulfillment: *Now after Jesus was born in Bethlehem of Judea in the days of Herod the king, behold, wise men from the east came to Jerusalem.*

His Crucifixion.

Psalm 22:16–18 is the prophecy: *For dogs have surrounded Me; the assembly of the wicked has enclosed Me. They pierced My hands and My feet; I can count all My bones. They look and stare at Me. They divide My garments among them, and for My clothing they cast lots.*

In **John 19:23-24** we have the fulfillment: *Then the soldiers, when they had crucified Jesus, took His garments and made four parts, to each soldier a part, and also the tunic. Now the tunic was without seam, woven from the top in one piece. They said therefore among themselves, "Let us not tear it, but cast lots for it, whose it shall be," that the Scripture might be fulfilled which says, "They divided My garments among them, and for My clothing they cast lots."*

The Second Form of Proof of the Bible's Inspiration is the Scientific Truths Found in the Bible.

Here are some examples of scientific statements in Scripture which were not known or believed by men that long ago.

Leviticus 17:11 states: *For the life of the flesh is in the* *blood...* Until fairly recently blood letting was commonly practiced in this country. In fact, it is believed by some that the real cause of the death of George Washington was the blood letting they used to bring down his fever.

Now how did Moses know so many thousands of years ago that the life of the flesh is in the blood? I'm not at all sure he did know because, you see, verse one of this seventeenth chapter of Leviticus says, *"And the LORD spoke to Moses, saying..."* The rest of the chapter is what *the Lord* said to Moses, and He certainly knows where the life of the flesh is since He is the One who created us to begin with.

First Corinthians 15:39 makes this phenominal statement regarding types of flesh. *All flesh is not the same flesh, but there is one kind of flesh of men, another flesh of beasts, another of fish, and another of birds.* Did the apostle Paul *know* all flesh was not the same, or was it revealed to him? It's pretty clear that what he wrote was "Scripture"—that is, given to him by God (compare Second Peter 3:14–16 where the apostle Peter put Paul's writings in with "the other Scriptures"). Today, when police are looking for a hit-and-run driver who killed a pedestrian, they can check the blood, or skin, or hair on your bumper and tell what kind of creature it came from—a human being, a deer, or a dog. The apostle Paul, however, did not have that scientific capability in his day, yet he was exactly and scientifically right.

Consider further, **Acts 17:24-26:** *God, who made the world and everything in it, since He is the Lord of heaven and earth, does not dwell in temples made with hands. Nor is He worshipped with men's hands, as though He needed anything, since He gives to all life, breath, and all things. And He has made from one blood every nation of men to dwell on all the face of the earth....* Scripture is clear that God has made "from one blood every nation of men." If you needed a blood transfusion, your doctor would not request white blood, or black blood, or yellow blood; he would request your blood type but it would have nothing to do with your race or the color of your skin. The Bible is an amazing book, isn't it?

In **Job 26:7** Job gives a very good laymen's description of what is involved in gravity insofar as it relates to earth's revolving in space. He said this about God: *He stretches out the north over the empty space; He hangs the earth on nothing.* Now

Job is not using technical or scientific language here, but he certainly gave an apt description of what we would call the influence of The Law of Gravity. Try hanging something on nothing and see how well it works! This must have seemed utterly foolish in his day, yet Job was led by the Lord to record it, and it's just another evidence that the book we call the Bible is anything but your "normal" human production.

A Third Evidence of the Bible's Inspiration is Seen in What the Bible Does *Not* Contain.

Speaking of Job, there have been various theories about the earth over the centuries. The Egyptians held the view that the earth was on the back of a giant elephant which was standing on the back of a turtle, and the turtle was swimming in the cosmic sea. The Romans believed that the earth is on five pillars, but no one seemed to speculate about what the pillars were on. The Greeks had it figured out that a giant of a man named Atlas had the earth on his back. What a back ache he must have had! These were all commonly believed in the ancient world—from Job's time on, and none of them came anywhere near being accurate.

High school and college text books have been changed so many times over the past fifty years that it's hard to keep up, and that's exactly how the Bible would be if written by mere men. There would be hundreds, and maybe even thousands, of statements in it that would have been believed true at the time, but would have been proven false later on. Second Peter 1:21 tells us how Scripture came to us. It says, *"For prophecy never came by the will of man, but holy men of God spoke as they were moved by the Holy Spirit."* What is NOT found in the Bible is, in my mind, the greatest proof of its Divine origin. But there is yet another evidence of the Bible's divine inspiration.

Logically the Bible must be from God.

Think this through: Approximately forty different human authors, writing about every conceivable subject, over a period of about 1,600 years, many of whom never met (they were not contemporaries), from various levels of culture and education, and yet they agree perfectly. Consider the possibility of having forty contemporaries writing about a single subject, such as "How to Catch the Most Fish in the Least Amount of Time," and having them be in one hundred percent agreement.

John Wesley taught that the Bible must be from 1) good men or angels, 2) bad men or demons, or 3) God. He said:

- Good men or angels *could not* have been the authors because over 2,000 times the Bible says that the *Lord* was speaking. That would make the good men or angels habitual liars; so they wouldn't be good.
- Bad men or demons *would not* have written it because the Bible condemns them to an eternal hell.
- That only leaves God as the possible Author.

What I've described in these pages on Christian evidences is utter simplicity—purposely so. I have not given the evidences in great detail because you will not normally need minute detail to convince the average person of Scripture's divine origin. For those times when you may need an elaborate defense of your Christian faith, I recommend a few books at the end of this book. Avail yourself of them, but remember that usually the more direct and simple you are with the person you are trying to win, the more effective you will be in winning them.

Following are two lists—one of Bible prophecies regarding Christ and their fulfillment; the other is a list of scientific statements found in Scripture. Neither list is exhaustive, but is intended to give you ample information from which to draw in defending your own faith. Why not narrow the lists down to a few you can easily remember, and then use them in witnessing when you need to.

Biblical Prophecies about Jesus Christ.

* The virgin birth of Christ: Isaiah 7:14.
Fulfilled in Matthew 1:18, 24, 25.

The Messiah to come through Abraham's Seed: Genesis 22:18.
Fulfilled in Matthew 1:1; Galatians 3:16.

The Messiah to come through the Tribe of Judah:
Micah 5:2; Genesis 49:10.
Fulfilled in Luke 3:23-33.

The Messiah would come through the family line of Jesse:
Isaiah 11:1, 10.
Fulfilled in Luke 3:23-32; Matthew 1:6.

* Messiah's place of birth: Micah 5:2.
Fulfilled in Matthew 2:1

Christ's preexistence: Micah 5:2.
Fulfilled in John 1:1-3; Colossians 1:17

* Jesus would be Emmanuel—God with us: Isaiah 7:14.
Fulfilled in Matthew 1:23; John 1:1, 2, 14.

The Messiah would be preceded by a special messenger:
Isaiah 40:3.
Fulfilled in Matthew 3:1, 2

Christ would have a ministry of miracles: Isaiah 35:5-6a.
Fulfillment seen in Matthew 9:35.

Messiah would enter Jerusalem riding upon a donkey:
Zechariah 9:9.
Fulfilled in Luke 19:35-37a

Messiah would be forsaken by His disciples (friends):
Zechariah 13:7.
Fulfilled in Mark 14:50.

Messiah would be silent before His accusers: Isaiah 53:7.
Fulfilled in Matthew 27:12-19.

Messiah would be bruised and wounded: Isaiah 53:5.
Fulfilled in Matthew 27:26.

Messiah would be smitten and spit upon: Isaiah 50:6.
Fulfilled inMatthew 26:67.

Messiah would be mocked: Psalm 22:7, 8.
Fulfilled in Matthew 27:31.

* Messiah's hands and feet would be pierced: Psalm 22:16.
Fulfilled in Luke 23:33.

Messiah would be rejected by His own people: Isaiah 53:3.
Fulfilled in John 1:10, 11; 7:5, 48.

* Messiah's garments would be parted and
lots would be cast for them: Psalm 22:18.
Fulfilled in John 19:23, 24.

* Messiah's side would be pierced: Zechariah 12:10.
Fulfilled in John 19:34.

* Messiah would be buried in a rich man's tomb: Isaiah 53:9.
Fulfilled in Matthew 27:57-60.

Scientific Truths Found in the Bible

* The earth is spherical: Isaiah 40:22.

There is an empty place in the north: Job 26:7.

* The earth is suspended in space: Job 26:7.

There are four "corners" or pivots of earth: Isaiah 11:12.

Air has weight: Job 28:25.

The wind travels in currents: Ecclesiastes 1:6.

Light can be parted: Job 38:24.

* The life of the flesh is in the blood: Leviticus 17:11.

* All animal flesh is not the same: First Corinthians 15:39.

* All nations of men are of one blood: Acts 17:24-26.

Every star is different from all others: First Corinthians 15:41.

* The stars are numberless: Jeremiah 33:22.

These are the prophecies and scientific statements I use most often when I am sharing the Gospel and am using evidences.

For Personal Reflection and Application

❖ Though God didn't have to do it, aren't you glad He has given us abundant evidences of His existence and of the truthfulness of His Word?

❖ What we call *Christian evidences* may be intended more for the benefit of God's children than for the unbelieving world, for when we are undergirded by the certainty of His Word, we are more bold and confident as we reach out to lost humanity. Have you discovered the deep–seated confidence and assurance that God's Word can give you?

There is only one gospel—
only one true message
of good news from
Heaven. But there are
many substitutes offered
in place of the gospel.
It was so in the beginning.
It is so now. It is a
fearfully wicked thing
to trifle with the sacred
heaven-sent message
that has come to a
needy world declaring
the grace of God to
poor lost sinners.

Harry A. Ironside

16

False Messages and Crucial Issues

False Messages and Unclear Ones

When I refer to a message being a *false* one I am referring to so-called "gospels" that in some way detract from the Person and Work of Christ, usually by adding works as additional conditions to faith. Such things as keeping the Ten Commandments, being baptized in water, lifelong faithful obedience, and surrendering one's total life to Christ's Lordship, are a few of the false gospels that are commonly proclaimed.

An *unclear* Gospel, on the other hand, is not false in the sense that the speaker or writer is deliberately adding conditions to faith alone in Christ alone. A message might be considered unclear if the messenger believes the Bible's teaching about salvation through faith in Christ alone, but does not clearly communicate what the Bible says about how to be saved. Remember the pastor in Missouri who I mentioned earlier who told me he always told the unsaved to give their heart or life to Christ. He was giving an unclear message as seen by the fact that what he was really trying to get the unsaved to do was to "trust in Christ to save them."

So, one can be true to the Gospel of Scripture and yet not convey that truth clearly. Such an one needs encouragement to be more Biblical in his or her presentation. They should not be condemned for preaching a false gospel since they really believe in salvation by faith alone. They are often doing the best they can with what they have been exposed to. They do not need condemnation. We should, instead, come along side to help.

Now let's consider some false messages—messages that do not save—messages that lead people away from the truth of the Gospel of Christ rather than leading them to Him, plus some vital issues that need clarification if our witness is to be the most effective.

1. Commandment Keeping

When you ask someone what they think they must do to go to Heaven and they reply, "Live by the Ten Commandments," you have a number of Scriptures at your disposal to clarify the purpose of the Commandments, as well as to refute salvation by commandment keeping.

Here are a few of those powerful verses.

We begin with **Romans 3:19, 20, 28:** *Now we know that whatever the law says, it says to those who are under the law, that every mouth may be stopped, and all the world may become guilty before God. Therefore by the deeds* (the doing) *of the law no flesh will be justified in His sight, for by the law is the knowledge of sin....Therefore we conclude that a man is justified by faith apart from the deeds of the law.*

Notice what this passage reveals about *the purpose of the Law.* It was given "that every mouth may be stopped, and all the world may become guilty before God." When the Mosaic Law says, "You shall not lie" and we do lie, we are guilty before God now and when we stand before Him, our mouths will be "stopped." The Law reveals our sinfulness and a proper use of the Law is to bring conviction so that we might see our need for salvation. The Law of Moses was never given as a means of salvation—never.

Also note how this passage makes it unmistakably clear that by obeying the Law, *"no flesh will be justified* (declared righteous) *before God"*(vs. 20). And the conclusion of the entire line of logic in this portion of Romans is in verse twenty eight where it states *"that a man is justified by faith apart from* (without) *the deeds of the Law."*

Now let's turn to the book of Galatians. This small book is really big in clarifying and defending the true Gospel. The apostle Paul denounced Peter because his behavior was "not straightforward about the truth of the gospel" (2:14), and in revealing Peter's hypocrisy God led Paul to pen **Galatians 2:16:** *Knowing that a man is not justified by the works of the law but by faith in Jesus Christ, even we have believed in Christ Jesus, that we might be justified by faith in Christ and not by the works of the law; for by the works of the law no flesh shall be justified.* "No flesh" means no one can be saved or justified by keeping the law.

There are no exceptions.

This thought is continued in **Galatians 3:10–13:** *For as many as are of the works of the law are under the curse; for it is written, "Cursed is everyone who does not continue in all things which are written in the book of the law, to do them." But that no one is justified by the law in the sight of God it is evident, for "The just shall live by faith." Yet the law is not of faith, but "The man who does them shall live by them." Christ has redeemed us from the curse of the law, having become a curse for us....* Among other things, this passage is literally saying that those who desire to be saved by law keeping must *continually* keep *every* part of it; not just the Ten Commandments—there are over six hundred commandments in the Mosaic Law. Failure to continually *do* "all things" contained in the Law leads to certain judgment and spiritual death.

When someone tells me that they think they'll get to Heaven by keeping the Ten Commandments, I often ask, "Well, tell me, do you keep them perfectly?" The usual response to that question is, "Well, probably no one does, but I do the best I can to keep them."

Then I ask, "Do you always do the *best* you can?" This is normally answered with, "Well, I try." In light of the verses I just quoted, *trying the best you can*, is not good enough and leads to condemnation, not salvation.

James 2:10 also addresses the necessity of keeping the entire law if one is expecting to be saved by obeying it. It says, *For whoever shall keep the whole law, and yet stumble in one point, he is guilty of all.*

Is the Law, then, a bad thing? Not at all. Notice what God says in **Galatians 3:21, 22**: *Is the law then against the promises of God? Certainly not. For if there had been a law given which could have given life* (eternal), *truly righteousness would have been by the law. But the Scripture has confined all under sin, that the promise by faith in Jesus Christ might be given to those who believe.* There is no law—neither that of Moses, or Mohammed, or the Mormon Church, or anyone else—that can bring salvation to the keeper of such laws. That's why God had to send His Son. Had there been any other possibility for salvation to come to man through something he could do, God certainly would have spared His own Son.

So remember, that to be a fruitful soul winner, you must have verses like these at your finger tips. Memorize them so that in those situations when you do not have a Bible with you, you may still quote it to the one to whom you are speaking. God's promise is, *Faith comes by hearing, and hearing by the Word of God* (Romans 10:17).

2. Baptismal Regeneration

All this term means is that water baptism is essential if one expects to be saved; it is an absolute necessity. It is true that there are some verses in the Bible that seem to demand water baptism for salvation, but when carefully studied in context, none of these verses actually teach baptismal regeneration.

There are three major passages upon which baptismal regeneration people stake their position: John 3:3-7, Acts 2:38, and Mark 16:16. We'll now look at all three of these.

First, there is John 3:3–7.

Jesus answered and said to him, "Most assuredly I say to you, unless one is born again he cannot see the kingdom of God." Nicodemus said to Him, "How can a man be born when he is old? Can he enter the second time into his mother's womb and be born?" Jesus answered, "Most assuredly I say to you, unless one is born of water and the Spirit, he cannot enter the kingdom of God. That which is born of the flesh is flesh, and that which is born of the Spirit is spirit. Do not marvel that I said to you, 'You must be born again.'"

Once I know one's position on this issue, I may ask, "Is there anywhere in the Bible that says we absolutely MUST be baptized in order to enter kingdom of God?" This question is the Set–Up Technique in action. I emphasize the word *MUST* in my question because I want it to trigger a certain passage in their minds. The same is true with my use of the phrase "to enter the kingdom of God." The question, when phrased in this way, will usually cause them to refer me to John 3:3–7, and that's the passage I want them to turn to.

The most important statement of this passage that baptismal regeneration people emphasize is: *"Unless one is born of water...he cannot enter the kingdom of God."* Knowing that they think "born of water" means to be baptized in water, I usually ask, "Where does it say in this passage that we must be baptized in order to be saved?"

They will normally just say, "Born of water means baptized in water." If that is so, then we ought to be able to work our way through the entire passage replacing the word "born" with "baptized" and have it make sense. So let's do it.

Verse three: *unless one is **baptized** again he cannot see the kingdom of God.* Are two or more baptisms necessary for salvation?

Verse four: *Nicodemus said to Him, "How can a man be **baptized** when he is old? Can he enter the second time into his mother's womb and be **baptized**?"* Is there a special dispensation for older folks who want to be baptized? And does water baptism spring from a mother's womb? Obviously there is a vast difference between birth and baptism.

Verse five: *Jesus answered, "Most assuredly, I say to you, unless one is **baptized** of water and the Spirit, he cannot enter the kingdom of God.* This is the verse that *seems* to fit the doctrinal position of the baptismal regeneration people. However, it decidedly does not fit in the context.

Verse six: *That which is **baptized** of the flesh is flesh, and that which is **baptized** of the Spirit is spirit.*

Verse seven: *Do not marvel that I said to you, "You must be **baptized** again."*

I believe it is as clear as can be that substituting "baptized" for "born" just does not work. Therefore, "born of water" refers to physical birth—which all of us have experienced—and "born of the Spirit" refers to the new birth which becomes ours when we place our faith in Christ. This is confirmed further in the context of verses nine through eighteen.

Once I have explored John 3:3–7 with someone who believes one must be water baptized to be saved, I usually move on and ask about the thief on the cross as recorded in **Luke 23:42, 43**. *Then he* (the thief) *said to Jesus, "Lord, remember me when You come into Your kingdom." And Jesus said to him, "I say to you, today you will be with Me in paradise."*

The thief died shortly after that. He had just become a believer in Christ because when he and his fellow criminal were crucified on either side of Jesus, both of them were unbelievers. Mark 15:27 says, *With Him they also crucified two robbers, one on His right hand and the other on His left.* Then in the last part of verse thirty–two it says, *And those who were crucified with Him reviled Him.*

In the hours that the three of them hung on their crosses something obviously impressed this one thief so much that he recognized Christ as the Messiah and called upon Him for salvation. He was not baptized; he could not have been, and yet Jesus guaranteed him that he would be with Him that very day in paradise.

So what do the baptismal regeneration folks say about the thief on the cross? There are usually three lines of thought concerning this man. First, they say, he would have been baptized if he could have been. Beyond the fact that this is pure speculation, there is not a hint anywhere in the Bible that one can be saved by good intentions.

Secondly, we are told that God knew his heart and therefore would not condemn him for something that he couldn't help— meaning that he couldn't help it if he was nailed to a cross and couldn't come down to be baptized. Again, this is strictly speculation. There is no Scriptural support for it.

Thirdly, and the most frequent reply, is that he lived in a different age or dispensation than we do. Water baptism was not required of him in the age in which he lived, but it is required of us today. There is one major flaw with this response. Nicodemus and the thief lived in the same dispensation—that of the Law— and these dear folks use Jesus' conversation with Nicodemus to try to prove their point that water baptism is essential for salvation *today.* If Nicodemus had to be baptized, then certainly the thief had to be, and if the thief did *not* have to be baptized in order to be saved, then neither did Nicodemus have to be. Therefore—using *their* logic—it is not permissible to use what Jesus said to Nicodemus and to attempt to apply that to our situation today.

Another powerful Scripture passage to share with those who depend on water baptism for their salvation is **First Corinthians 1:14–17.** The apostle Paul, writing to the Corinthian church said, *I thank God that I bapitzed none of you except Crispus and Gaius, lest anyone should say that I had baptized in my own name. Yes, and I also baptized the household of Stephanas. Besides, I do not know whether I baptized any other. For Christ did not send me to* *baptize, but to preach the gospel, not with wisdom of words, lest the cross of Christ should be made of no effect.*

There are several important points to note in the above verses. First, Paul could count on one hand the number of people he baptized, yet we know that multitudes came to a saving knowledge of Christ through Paul's ministry (compare Acts 13:38-44; 14:1, 21; 16:4, 5, 14, 15, 30, 31; 17:1-4, 10–12; 18:4; 19:8-10). He could not recall if he baptized any others than he named in this passage. If water baptism is absolutely essential for one's salvation, does it stand to reason that it would appear to be so unimportant to Paul in this area of salvation?

And what of Paul's strange statement—if water baptism is necessary for salvation—when he said, *"Christ did not send me to baptize, but to preach the Gospel?"* Surely there is something amiss here. If water baptism is necessary for salvation, then God certainly *did* send Paul to baptize. But he says God did not do that. Not only so, but the apostle makes it very clear that baptism is *not* part of the Gospel. Paul contrasts the two—he was not sent to baptize but he was sent to preach the Gospel. Strange wording indeed, if water baptism is a part of God's saving message!

Secondly, there is Acts 2:38.

Then Peter said to them, "Repent, and let every one of you be baptized in the name of Jesus Christ for the remission of sins; and you shall receive the gift of the Holy Spirit."

Usually the interpretation goes something like this: in order to be saved you must repent (turn from your sins) and be baptized in water. When you meet these conditions (and usually a few others as well) you will receive "remission of sins." On the surface this may seem to be a reasonable interpretation—*until* you begin doing some *biblically* guided thinking. For instance, it is most striking that nothing is said in the verse about *believing* in Christ, and *belief* in Him is the key Gospel word throughout the New Testament (over 160 times). Would Peter—particularly after emphasizing the person of Christ, His death and His resurrection—now tell these concerned Jews to quit sinning and be baptized in water to be saved, and not even mention the absolute need to believe in Him? Not hardly, especially in light of the fact that the record of his message is divinely inspired by the Holy Spirit.

Here are some key observations on this verse.

263

If the interpretation described above is correct then we have a major problem of the Bible contradicting itself because elsewhere Scripture is clear that salvation is not by man's works or merit, it is the gift of God, and it is received by faith alone in Christ. What then must we conclude? Either the Bible is contradictory or those who see baptismal regeneration in Acts 2:38 are mistaken as to its meaning. I, of course, take the latter approach. Let's examine a few things in the passage.

What had Peter been telling them? He reminded these men that they *knew* that God had confirmed Jesus' true identity by "miracles, wonders, and signs" (v. 22); he made it plain that though God had predetermined that His Son would die as prophesied, *they* had *"taken by lawless hands,* (and had) *crucified"* Him and put Him to death (v. 23); but *God* had raised Him up (v. 23). Peter's powerful conclusion was: *Therefore let all the house of Israel know assuredly that God has made this Jesus, whom you crucified, both Lord and Christ,* or Messiah (v.36).

Note carefully the reaction to these now convicted Jewish men: *Now when they heard this, they were cut to the heart, and said to Peter and the rest of the apostles, "Men and brethren, what shall we do?"* (v. 37). Peter's answer to their question is the verse we are considering.

The first thing Peter tells his listeners to do in response to their question of desperation is that they must *repent.* Is he telling them to turn from the sin of crucifying the Messiah? What good would that do? He's already been put to death. Was he urging them to quit their other sins? That's not the issue, either here in this setting or in other New Testament salvation passages.

The literal meaning of the Greek words translated repent or repentance is *to reconsider, to change your mind or attitude,* and that is exactly what Peter is telling these distraught men to do. His preaching had convincingly demonstrated that this Jesus is both Lord and Messiah—something they had not previously known (see First Corinthians 2:7, 8). So now he urges them to *change their minds about Christ, the One whom they had a hand in crucifying.* He's telling them to see Him for who and what He really is, their promised Messiah, the Lord Himself. The Jewish *leaders* as a whole had rejected Jesus as their Messiah, but now Peter is inviting these *individual* Jews to receive Him.

Later, the apostle Paul described the message he preached in these telling words recorded in **Acts 20:20, 21**: . . . *I kept back nothing that was helpful, but proclaimed it to you, and taught you publicly and from house to house, testifying to Jews, and also to Greeks, repentance toward God and faith toward our Lord Jesus Christ.* Repentance *may* involve changing one's mind concerning sin or even concerning something good, but in salvation the change of mind (true repentance) that is absolutely *necessary* is a change of attitude toward God Himself.

Secondly, Peter tells these convicted Jewish men to "be baptized." As with repentance, we have read into baptism what essentially is not there. For instance, there are at least eleven baptisms in Scripture and water was by no means the element employed in many of these instances. The word *baptize* is not really a translation of the Greek word *baptizo*. It is a transliteration. If it had been translated consistently throughout the New Testament it would have been translated—depending upon the context in which it was used—as *to dip, to immerse, to submerge, to cleanse, to wash, to make clean, to wash one's self, bathe, or to overwhelm* (Thayer, and Arndt & Gingrich).

I understand the primary meaning of the phrase *"let everyone of you be baptized in the name of Jesus Christ for the remission of sins"* to mean, "let everyone of you be *cleansed* in the name of Jesus Christ for the remission of sins." Here's why I take this position.

First, a legitimate meaning of *baptized* is *to be cleansed.* Consider one example as an illustration: Mark 7:4 states, *When they come from the marketplace, they do not eat unless they **wash** (baptizo). And there are many other things which they have received and hold, like the **washing** (baptismos) of cups, pitchers, copper vessels, and couches.*

Secondly, is the consideration that they were told to be baptized "in the name of Jesus Christ." This is not the baptismal formula given by Christ in the Great Commission. There He commanded the eleven to *make disciples of all nations, baptizing them in the name (singular) of the Father and of the Son and of the Holy Spirit* (Matthew 28:19).

In Acts 2:38 the admonition is to be *cleansed in Jesus' name*—not in a pool of water. This is consistent with all other New Testament passages on this subject: **John 3:18**. *He who* *believes in Him is not condemned; but he who does not believe is condemned already, because he has not believed* **in the name** *of the only begotten Son of God.* **Acts 4:12**: *Nor is there salvation in any other, for there is* **no other name** *under heaven given among men by which we must be saved.*

Thirdly, the apostles and the multitude were in the Temple area. If these Jews were being told to be *water* baptized (which would have been by immersion) where could a minimum of 3,000 new converts have been immersed? Certainly not in the area of the Temple (check any map of that area—you probably have one in the back of your Bible).

A parallel situation was brought to light when Paul shared his testimony in Acts 22. It is commonly taught that he was saved on the Road to Damascus, but what of his own testimony? He was blinded by the bright light and the Lord told him to go to Damascus where Ananias came and explained how God had revealed to him things which Paul would have to suffer. Then Ananias said, *And now why are you waiting? Arise and be baptized* (cleansed)*, and wash away your sins,* **calling on the name of the Lord** (v. 16). Ananias and Paul were in a house. Paul was to arise and be cleansed of his sins right then and there. How? By calling on the name of the Lord, not by water from a pool which wasn't even present.

There is a fourth reason to question that the baptism in Acts 2:38 is water baptism: A two-fold promise was given: (1) these men would have their sins forgiven, and (2) they would receive the gift of the Holy Spirit. Neither forgiveness nor the Holy Spirit is ever given on the basis of one being baptized in water. Rather, forgiveness comes to us as Peter preached in **Acts 10:43**: *To Him all the prophets witness that,* **through His name**, *whoever* **believes** *in Him will receive remission of sins.* Paul preached the same message in Antioch when he said, *Therefore let it be known to you, brethren, that through this Man is preached the* **forgiveness** *of sins; and by Him every one who* **believes** *is justified* (declared righteous) *from all things from which you could not be justified by the law of Moses* (13:38, 39).

As for the Holy Spirit, he is also received by believing in Christ: *In Him you also* **trusted**, *after you heard the word of truth, the gospel of your salvation; in whom also,* **having believed**, *you were sealed with the Holy Spirit of promise* (Ephesians 1:13).

There is no Scripture anywhere that offers forgiveness, the Holy Spirit, or eternal life through water baptism, but there are abundant Scriptures which promise God's salvation through faith in Christ alone. Here are some by way of reminder:

Romans 4:4,5: *Now to him who works, the wages are not counted as grace but as debt. But to him who does not work but **believes** on Him who justifies the ungodly, his **faith** is accounted for righteousness.*

Ephesians 2:8, 9: *For by grace you have been saved through **faith**, and that not of yourselves; it is the gift of God, not of works, lest anyone should boast.*

One other thought before we move on: the portion of Acts 2:38 which mentions baptism may also be translated: *let everyone of you be baptized in the name of Jesus Christ **because of** the remission of sins*....In other words, be baptized—if it is speaking of water—because sins are forgiven, not in order to receive forgiveness.

It is an unalterable rule to never interpret clear, literal statements of Scripture by the vague or unclear; instead *always* interpret the ambiguous or unclear by what is crystal clear. This is especially true when an interpretation seems contradictory to *many* other verses. It's not the Bible that is wrong in such instances, but one's understanding.

Thirdly, Mark 16:16 is also used.

It says: *He who believes and is baptized will be saved; but he who does not believe will be condemned.* What can this mean? I'll ask a few questions that may help in our understanding.

Who is speaking? Answer: Jesus.

What kind of believing is in view here—the lower form, such as, *"demons believe in one God";* or the higher more spiritual form, such as, *"Believe on the Lord Jesus Christ, and you will be saved"* (Acts 16:31)? Answer: the higher form.

What is the level of salvation mentioned here—the lower form, such as, *"Unless these men stay in the ship, you cannot be saved"* (Acts 27:31); or the higher more spiritual form, such as, *"Believe on the Lord Jesus Christ, and you will be saved"* (Acts 16:31)? Answer: the higher form.

Which kind of baptism is in view here—the lower form by water, such as, *"And both Philip and the eunuch went down into the water, and he baptized him"* (Acts 8:38); or the higher more spiritual form, such as, *"For by one Spirit we were all baptized into one body...."* (First Corinthians 12:3)? Answer: the more spiritual.

Now on this last point, you may be wondering, "What convinces you that the baptism in Mark 16:16 is speaking of Spirit baptism rather than water baptism?" There are four reasons why I've come to this conclusion.

First, is the logic of the above questions. If all of the other components of the statement in Mark 16:16 are on the higher spiritual plane, it stands to reason that the baptism would also be on that same plane. But this is not the most convincing reason.

Secondly, the absence of baptism in the last part of Jesus' statement is vitally important and gives evidence to the fact that baptism here is not a work or duty that one performs. Jesus said, *"...but he who does not believe will be condemned."* If the baptism in the first part of His statement is referring to water, then it would be something that the individual would have to do—a work. It would be a condition for salvation in addition to faith. So, then, the last phrase would have to say, *"...but he who does not believe and is not baptized will be condemned."* It is unbelief alone that condemns, as clearly stated in John 3:18: *He who believes in Him is not condemned; but he who does not believe is condemned already,* **because** *he has not believed the only begotten Son of God.*

You can look at the entire statement in a more personal light and ask yourself, "If I believe in Jesus as my Savior, but I am not baptized, can I be saved?" The Biblical answer—at least one hundred and sixty times in the New Testament—is a resounding, "YES!"

A third reason I do not believe the baptism in Mark 16:16 is water baptism is found in Mark 1:8. John the Baptizer is speaking and here is what he said, *"I indeed baptized you with water, but He (Jesus) will baptize with the Holy Spirit."* My first question earlier was, "Who is speaking?" The answer is Jesus. And how does He baptize—by water or by the Spirit? John the Baptizer said He would baptize with the Holy Spirit. Not only that but when Jesus was on earth—during the same era in which Nicodemus and the thief on the cross lived—He did not baptize anyone.

Note carefully these two verses in **John 4:1,2:** *Therefore,* *when the Lord knew that the Pharisees had heard that Jesus made and baptized more disciples than John (though **Jesus Himself did not baptize, but His disciples** did).* Is it even conceivable that Christ would insist that Nicodemus (and all others) be baptized in water and then refuse to baptize anyone? I contend that such a possibility is unthinkable.

A fourth reason for rejecting the interpretation that baptism in Mark 16:16 is referring to water baptism is the fact that whatever condition or conditions God insists that one must fulfill in order to be saved, must be possible for anyone, anywhere in the world to meet. Believing in Christ—trusting in Him to save—meets such a criterion. Water baptism does not.

Let's say, for instance, that you are an Eskimo living near the frozen Artic. You hear the Gospel over a shortwave radio and you place your faith in Christ to save you. Later, you come to understand that as a believer you should be baptized in order to publicly identify yourself with Christ, but you can't fulfill that privilege until months later when the ice begins to melt a little. Would you not be saved during those months before you could be baptized, even though you are trusting in Christ alone to save you? You absolutely would be saved according to Scriptures such as John 3:18, 36; 5:24; 6:28,29; Romans 4:5; Ephesians 2:8, 9, and many more. Salvation comes immediately upon believing in Christ. Jesus guaranteed it in **John 6:47**: *Most assuredly, I say to you, "He who believes in Me has* (present tense) *everlasting life."*

I mentioned earlier that there are a number of baptisms in Scripture in addition to water baptism. So that you will know where these baptisms are mentioned in Scripture, I thought I would share those references with you. You might want to jot them down somewhere—perhaps in your Bible—so that they will be at your finger tips when you need to refer to them.

Baptisms in Scripture:

1. John's baptism: Luke 7:29; Acts 19:3,4 (water).
2. Christ's baptism: Matthew 3:13 (water).
3. Baptism of fire: Matthew 3:11 (judgment on unbelievers).
4. Baptism with the Holy Spirit: Matthew 3:11; Mark 1:8.
5. Baptism of death: Luke 12:50.
6. Baptism for the dead: First Corinthians 15:29 (water).
7. Baptism of water: Mark 1:8.

8. Baptism of repentance: Mark 1:4.
9. Traditional Jewish baptisms: Hebrews 6:2; 9:10 (water).
10. Baptism by Moses in the cloud: First Corinthians 10:2.
11. Baptisms of household items and utensils: Mark 7:4, 8 (water).

Of these eleven, five refer to people being baptized in water; one speaks of washing household items and utensils in water—nothing to do with salvation; and five refer to other elements in which one may be baptized other than water, such as fire, a cloud, and the Holy Spirit. It is important to recognize that when baptism is spoken of in Scripture *without* identifying the element—as in Romans 6:3,4 and Ephesians 4:5—you should not automatically conclude that it is referring to water. Let the context determine that for you.

3. Faith Without Works

"Can a person be saved by faith, without any works at all?" How often this question arises and how important it is to know the Biblical answer. Let me be blunt. *Not only is it true that a person can be saved by faith without any works of any kind, but it is the only way that anyone can ever be saved at all.* The many verses we've already studied should demonstrate this fact without question. But someone will ask, "What about the second chapter of James which says that faith without works is dead?"

As soon as salvation by faith alone in Christ alone is brought up by a Christian who is clear on the issues of grace and works, someone invariably mentions this passage in the second chapter of James Verse seventeen of the chapter says, *"Thus also, faith by itself, if it does not have works, is dead."* And verse twenty one adds, *"Was not Abraham our father justified* (declared righteous) *by works when he offered Isaac his son on the altar?"*

To whom is James writing, and what point is he attempting to make? The answer to these two questions opens up the passage so that there need not be any confusion as to its true meaning.

The passage covers verses fourteen through verse twenty-six, and verses fourteen to seventeen are the key to the passage. James—under the Holy Spirit's direction—asks a question in verses fourteen and sixteen which is the foundation for understanding the entire passage. Here's the question: *"**What** *does it profit, my brethren, if someone says he has faith but does not have works? Can faith save him? If a brother or sister is naked and destitute of daily food, and one of you says to them, 'Depart in peace, be warmed and filled,' but you do not give them the things which are needed for the body,* **what does it profit?** *Thus also faith by itself, if it does not have works, is dead."*

It's important to notice several key points here. First, James is addressing fellow believers. He calls them "my brethren" in verse fourteen. He goes on to speak of "a brother or sister" who comes for help; a clear indication that he is speaking of a relational matter between believers.

Secondly, the issue of the entire passage is "what does it profit?" (vs. 14 and 16). What does *what* profit? What profit is there in doing nothing for needy believers but offering pious platitudes when one could do something concrete to relieve those needs? Such an illustration is analogous of faith without works. Such faith is dead.

The question then is, "What is meant by faith being dead?" The word "dead" in this passage comes from a Greek word meaning unfruitful, barren or nonproductive. Some assume "faith without works" means that true faith is not present. However, "dead" here does not mean nonexistent. The discussion centers around the fruitfulness (or lack of fruitfulness) of a faith that does not produce works. *The passage does not define saving faith; instead it describes the condition of a faith that is not accompanied by good works; in other words, an unfruitful, nonproductive faith.*

For instance, if I told you that the battery in my minivan is dead, I wouldn't mean that I didn't have a battery—that it was nonexistent; I would mean that it was not producing juice; there would be no power coming from it. The battery would be there under the hood where it is supposed to be. It would just be in a temporary condition of being useless insofar as it being effective in turning over the motor when I turn the key in the ignition. So it is in James. The "dead" faith is a nonproducing faith, a barren, an unfruitful faith—but faith, nonetheless.

Abraham Offering Isaac: What Does It Demonstrate?

James uses Abraham as an illustration of faith and works being joined together to produce the perfected, complete, mature faith. *Was not Abraham our father justified* (considered or

271

declared righteous) *when he offered Isaac his son on the altar? Do you see that faith was working together with his works, and by works faith was made perfect* (complete or full grown)*?* (vs. 21, 22).

Was James speaking of Abraham *having* faith or of *displaying* his mature, grown up faith? How can we tell? Well, first of all, we consider the immediate context. Verse twenty-two clearly states that *"by works his faith was made perfect"* or that it was perfected or matured. Nothing in the passage suggests that when Abraham offered up Issac that his faith was initiated at that moment in his life.

We also consider the testimony of the rest of Scripture on the same topic. The twenty-third verse of this second chapter of James quotes Genesis 15:6 which says, Abraham *"believed in the LORD, and He accounted it to him for righteousness."* Now when God accounted Abraham's faith as righteousness Isaac was not even born! Yet, James 2:21 states that Abraham was *"justified by works when he offered his son Isaac on the altar"*— perhaps as much as fifteen years after God declared Abraham righteous by faith alone. Do we have a contradiction here? Not when we consider all of the Scripture's testimony on this.

Was James illustrating Abraham's faith before men or before God?

Again we ask, "How can we tell?" We discover the answer to this question in the same way we discovered the answer to the previous question, by considering the context and other verses which touch on the same subject.

First, a reminder: the point of the passage is the proper relationship between believers who are in need and those who could help alleviate that need (vss. 14-16—*What does it profit?*) Secondly, "dead faith" speaks of the barren, nonproducing faith of a believer, not whether or not the "brother" has faith in the first place.

Turning to other Scripture, it is clear that Abraham's justification before God was by faith alone, and his justification before men was by faith demonstrated by good works.

Romans 4:1-5 is the key. *What then shall we say that Abraham our father has found according to the flesh? For if Abraham was justified by works, he has something of which to boast, but not before God. For what does the Scripture say?*

"Abraham believed God, and it was accounted to him for righteousness." Now to him who works, the wages are not counted as grace but as debt. But to him who does not work but believes in Him who justifies the ungodly, his faith is accounted for righteousness.

Before God we are justified by faith alone; before men we are justified by faith and works. James makes a key point: *But someone will say, "You have faith, and I have works." Show me your faith without your works, and I will show you my faith by my works* (v. 18). Is it possible to show one's faith before others without works? Of course not. And that is the point. The "brother" in verse 14 did not show faith by works, but Abraham and Rahab did demonstrate their faith by their works. (vss. 21, 25) But before they demonstrated their faith before men they already had faith before God, and God—who knows all things— knew the true condition of their hearts. The passage does not teach that the faith of Abraham and Rahab came into existence by their works. No, their faith was present and recognized by God before it was ever demonstrated by their works. This is the way it always is with those who believe in or trust in the Lord. The facts of the Gospel come first, then faith in the facts; finally, evidence of the faith should result though such evidence is not always present.

Scripturally speaking, works should follow saving faith. **Ephesians 2:10** is clear on this: *For we are His workmanship, created in Christ Jesus for good works, which God prepared beforehand that we should walk in them.* **Titus 3:8** also bears this out. *This is a faithful saying, and these things I want you to affirm constantly, that those who have believed in God should be careful to maintain good works. These things are **good and profitable to men***. Then there is **Titus 3:14** which says, *And let our people also learn to maintain good works, **to meet urgent needs, that they may not be unfruitful***. Sounds just like James, chapter two, doesn't it? The Biblical pattern, then, is faith in Christ for justification before God (eternal salvation), and a working faith before men for effective fruitfulness and testimony.

4. Lordship (or Discipleship) Salvation

Ever since the First Church Council was held in Jerusalem

(Acts 15) there has been an ongoing, constant turmoil brewing among Bible believing people concerning what is required for a person to be saved. Then the issue boiled down to this equation: *Unless you are circumcised according to the custom of Moses, you **cannot** be saved* (v.1) and *it is **necessary** to circumcise them* (Gentile believers)*, and to command them to keep the law of Moses* (v.5). In the dispute that followed among the apostles and elders, Peter brought everything into sharp focus when he described his ministry to the uncircumcised Gentiles and concluded with: *Now therefore why do you test God by putting a yoke on the neck of the disciples which neither our fathers nor we were able to bear? But we believe that through the grace of the Lord Jesus Christ we shall be saved in the same manner as they* (the Gentile believers).

Law keeping is still a big issue in many church circles, but another escalating area of debate today—especially among evangelicals—is the Easy Believism versus Lordship Salvation debate.

Easy Believism

The attack against easy believism usually takes one of two forms. First, there is the attack against those who say they "believe in Jesus" but there is *no outward evidence* that they do. Of course, no one is ever saved by simply *saying* they believe anything. Of equal importance is to concede that the "evidence" which may convince others that one is a true Christian may be very subjective at the very best. Obviously, many *appear* to be believers in Christ when, in fact, they are not believers at all in the Biblical sense of that word (Matthew 7:22, 23; Second Corinthians 11:13-15). And the converse is also true, that one may *appear* to *not* be a child of God when they truly are. Any believer who is not presently walking close to the Lord would be an example of such a person.

The second line of attack against easy believism will normally agree that salvation is by faith in *Christ* alone, but not admit that salvation is by *faith alone* in Christ alone. You will often hear statements like this one: "You can't tell me that all you have to do is to believe. The demons believe in Jesus and they're not saved."

The proof text for such a pronouncement is James 2:19: *You believe there is one God. You do well. Even the demons believe— and tremble!* What is it that the demons believe? That there is one God. A good devout Jew or Muslim, or pew warming Protestant, may believe that. Does the verse say anything at all about demons believing in Jesus Christ? Not a word. If the kind of easy believism described in this verse were the Gospel, then any sincere Jew, Muslim, or Jehovah's Witness would be saved;—so would all the demons of hell! The kind of belief described in James 2:19 does not save anyone, nor is it descriptive of the kind of faith that does save.

In light of this, we *should* condemn as unbiblical any message that teaches or implies that a person can be saved by either simply *saying* they believe in Christ, or who contends one is saved by a belief in a monotheistic God, whatever god that may be. However, the Biblical doctrine of justification by faith alone in Christ alone does save, and is the only message that saves!

Lordship Salvation

The gist of most Lordship Salvation teaching is that one must surrender every facet of one's life to the complete control of Jesus Christ or such an one cannot be saved. To make it more personal, you must yield absolutely to Him as total Lord and Master over every area of life and over all you do—*for salvation!*

There are three verses commonly used to support this idea that Christ must be Lord and Master of your life for you to be saved.

The first verse is Acts 9:6.

Saul (Paul) was temporarily blinded by a bright light and he fell to the ground and heard a voice speaking to him. This verse records that Saul *trembling and astonished, said, "Lord, what do You want me to do?"* The advocates of Lordship Salvation point out that Saul did not call Jesus *Savior*; he called him *Lord*, indicating (we are told) that Saul then and there surrendered to the Lordship of Christ over his life and, therefore, was saved on the basis of that complete surrender.

Is all of that in this one little word, *Lord?* As evidenced by the immediate context, I hardly think so. Though *Lord* is used in the Bible in addressing God, it is also often a designation of respect, similar to our word *Sir*, and that is how it is used in this context. Note, for instance, that even before Saul knew it was Jesus speaking, he said, *"Who are You, Lord?"* He would hardly be surrendering the control of his life over to a voice about which he knew nothing, not even so much as the identity of the one speaking.

Saying, therefore, that Saul was saved in verse six by making Jesus Lord of his life is a pretty weak statement upon which to pin such an important doctrine. In fact, Scripture indicates Saul was *not* saved while on the Road to Damascus. *The Lord said to him, "Arise and go into the city, and you will be told what you must do"* (v. 6b). He was instructed to go to a specific house. Later, Paul related how Ananias came into the house, healed him of his blindness, and said, *And now why are you waiting? Arise and be baptized, and wash away your sins, calling on the name of the Lord* (Acts 22:16). That's the same message as in Romans 10:13: *Whoever shall call upon the name of the Lord shall be saved.*

The second verse is Acts 16:31.

The Philippian jailer, who was on the verge of suicide, asked Paul and Silas, *What must I do to be saved?* Their reply was, *Believe on the Lord Jesus Christ and you will be saved, you and your household.* As in Acts 9:6, the same connotation is given to the word *Lord* in this verse by those who advocate Lordship Salvation; that is, that the jailer had to surrender to the Lordship of Christ over his life in order to be saved. But the use of *Lord* here is showing that this man, Jesus, who is the Christ (Messiah), is also Lord (deity), and you must believe in Him as such—as the *Lord* Jesus Christ. Surrendering your life is not the issue; *admitting His true identity and trusting in Him to save you, is the issue.*

The third commonly used verse is Romans 10:9.

That if you confess with your mouth the Lord Jesus (or, Jesus as Lord) *and believe in your heart that God has raised Him from the dead, you will be saved.* In reading the context from 9:30 to 10:13, there is no hint that God's emphasis here is upon the unbeliever's *life*. The emphasis is that Israel had missed the message and had been going about to establish their own righteousness before God, and in doing so, had not realized that *Christ is the end of the Law for righteousness to everyone who believes* (10:1-4). *Lord* in this instance is used to give us the true identity of Jesus as God Himself—*the* Lord. *Believing in* this One is the need.

While Easy Believism (as described earlier) is decidedly *too easy*, so making Christ Lord over one's life is just as certainly too hard *(impossible*, in fact) for the unbeliever who does not possess the empowering of the Holy Spirit within. When followed to its logical conclusion, it becomes salvation by works, for Jesus plainly said, *"Why do you call Me, "Lord, Lord", and do not **do** the things I say?* (Luke 6:46). If He must be Lord of your life in order for you to be saved, then you must be totally obedient to Him for **obedience** is what His Lordship over you is all about; and obedience is just another name for *good works* which is required of believers, but never of the unsaved! Scripture is crystal clear that salvation is not, nor can it be, of works: John 6:28, 29; Romans 3:28; 4:5; 10:1–4; Ephesians 2:8,9; Second Timothy 1:9; Titus 3:5.

Regarding this issue of works, the works of believers are going to be judged at *The Judgment Seat of Christ* to determine the degree of their rewards or loss of rewards, never to determine their salvation. That was settled when they believed in Christ (Second Corinthians 5:10). Similarly, the works of unbelievers will be judged at *The Great White Throne Judgment* to determine their degree of punishment in hell, never to determine their destination. That was settled when they died in unbelief (Revelation 20:11-15).

Salvation and Discipleship

At the heart of the Lordship Salvation position is the mistaken view that salvation and discipleship are the same; that all the verses calling *believers* to be *disciples* are really invitations to nonbelievers to be saved. For this reason and others, I do not think the label *Lordship Salvation* is as accurate as it could be in describing this theological position. *Discipleship Salvation* is a much more accurate term for this view. Let's see what the Bible actually teaches concerning salvation and discipleship.

Consider these *contrasting* facts about salvation and discipleship:

- By definition the Greek word translated *salvation* or *saved* means *deliverance, protection, safety* or

277

salvation. By contrast *disciple* means *learner*; so discipleship involves a process of willingness to learn, to one degree or another.

- *Salvation* was costly to God—He gave His only begotten Son: John 3:16; Romans 8:32. *Discipleship*, on the other hand, is very costly to the believer—he or she must forsake *all* that they have. Luke 14:28-33.
- There is *one* condition for salvation—faith in Christ. John 3:18; 6:28, 29, 47; Romans 4:5. There are *numerous* conditions for discipleship, summarized by the word *obedience.* Matthew 16:24-27; Luke 6:46.
- Salvation is *a gift received,* not a reward for good works or obedience. John 4:10, 14; Romans 4:5; 6:23; Ephsians 2:8, 9; Second Timothy 1:9; Titus 3:5. Discipleship *involves work done* for which there is reward. Luke 14:25–35; First Corinthians 3:11-15.
- Our salvation depends solely on *God's ability* to keep us. John 10:28–30; Romans 8:31–39; Hebrews 13:5, 6; Jude 24. Discipleship—to be maintained—depends upon the *believer's submissive obedience.* Romans 6:16; 8:5; 12:1-2.
- Salvation *cannot be lost;* it is Eternal. John 3:16, 18, 36; 5:24; 10:28-30; First John 5:9-13. Discipleship can be lost or forsaken; one may give up at any time. John 6:59-71.
- The Gospel invitation can be summed up with words such as *come, receive, believe.* Matthew 11:28–30; John 1:12; 3:18. The invitation to discipleship is seen in the use of such admonitions as *go, tell, follow, forsake, deny self.* Mark 16:15; Matthew 28:18-20; Lk. 9:23, 24; Jn 21:19, 22
- Salvation involves *sonship.* John 1:12,13; Romans 8:16, 17; Galatians 3:26. True discipleship involves *sacrifcial service.* Mark 9:23, 24; First Corinthians 4:1-2; 9:19, 24–27.
- Salvation is found in *the Person of Christ.* Ephesians 1:7; Philippians 3:9; Colossians 1:13, 14. Discipleship is found in *the person of the believer.* First Corinthians 9:19–27.
- In salvation one recognizes *Christ the Lord as one's*

Savior. Luke 2:11; Titus 1:4; 2:13; 3:6—believing in Him. In discipleship one recognizes *Christ as Lord over all of one's Life.*—obeying Him as Lord and Master. Romans 12:1, 2; Luke 6:46.

Broadly speaking, New Testament disciples were those who were willing to be taught by the Lord and to embrace at least *some* of what He taught. These were not necessarily believers, such as Judas Iscariot. (John 2:11; 6:63-71). In a more narrow sense, disciples were true believers who willingly learned from Him and obediently followed Him (John 8:30-32; 15:8—cp. vss.1–5, 16).

Finally, no matter what position one takes on this issue, I do not believe that any sincere person can honestly say that "whoever *believes* in Him" (John 3:16, plus many other verses) *is the same as* "hate father, mother, wife, children, brothers and sisters…bear your cross daily, forsake all that you have" (Luke 9:23, 24; 14:26–33; Matthew 10:34–39). The demands of discipleship are only meant for those who are already in God's family, who have the inner power to be the kind of disciple Christ expects (John 8:30, 31; 15:8, 16—*disciples indeed*).

Here is a solemn reminder: most people to whom you witness will not be Gospel hardened; they will be *Gospel ignorant* because even in this spiritually enlightened nation, few have ever heard or understood the true Gospel of the grace of God. If we fail to distinguish between salvation and discipleship we only add to their confusion and contribute to their continued ignorance! God help us to be clear.

5. Head Belief versus Heart Belief

You will often hear someone express the thought that it is not enough to believe in Christ with your head; you must believe in Him with your heart. In fact, I have in my files a gospel tract entitled *"Missing Heaven By Eighteen Inches."* The thought of the tract is that if you only believe in Christ with your head and not with your heart you will miss Heaven, and the average distance between the head and the heart is eighteen inches! I'm sure the writer of the tract meant well but failed to communicate his point accurately.

You see, belief of any kind comes from the head. The heart

pumps blood; it does not do any believing. What, then, does the Scripture mean when it says we must believe "with the heart?" It means the same thing you and I do when we say such things as, "I love you with all my heart." What do *we* mean when we make such a statement? Do we not mean something like, "I really love you?"—or "I love only you?"—or "I love you with my entire being?"

The "heart" in Scripture often refers to the deepest recesses of man's being—his deepest and truest feelings or beliefs. Take, for instance, the statement in **Proverbs 3:5:** *Trust in the Lord with all you heart, and lean not on your own understanding.* What does it mean to trust in the Lord *with all your heart?* Does it not mean to really and truly trust in Him; that is, to trust Him completely? This contrast to *"leaning upon your own understanding"* seems to indicate that trusting the Lord with all your heart is to trust in Him alone—not upon your understanding at all.

The same can be said of the familiar passage of **Romans 10:9:** *that if you confess with your mouth* (acknowledge) *the Lord Jesus and believe in your heart that God has raised Him from the dead, you will be saved.* What is meant by "believe in your heart?" Again, I remind you, that it means to really and truly believe. It is describing a genuine belief in Christ—a sincere trust in Him, rather than simply believing certain facts about Him. This is the point that so many think they are making when they warn others of the danger of only believing in Christ with the head and not with the heart.

I recall one summer I was manning the book table at a youth conference in Boca Raton, Florida. The table was located on the upper level of the auditorium overlooking the main floor. It was break time and I was chatting with the camp's director, when a very well known Gospel singer walked up. The director greeted him enthusiastically. After introducing me to the singer, the camp director and he began speaking of the things of the Lord. My friend asked the singer, "How are things going for you?" His reply went something like this: "Well, everything had been going well until recently when I heard an evangelist say that if we only believe in Christ with our heads and not with our hearts, we're not really saved. I know I believe in Christ but this "head-heart" thing has thrown me for a loop, and I've been having doubts about my own salvation."

My friend wisely asked, "Well, tell me, who or what are you depending upon to get you to Heaven? Where is your trust?" The singer responded by saying, "In Christ." "Only in Christ?" my friend asked. "Yes," came the immediate reply, "*only* in Christ." The camp director then reassured him that when one truly believes in—trusts, relies upon, depends on—Christ *alone* for salvation, that is believing with the heart. He then explained, as I have in these pages, that all of us believe whatever we believe with our heads, but we do not necessarily trust in all that we are intellectually convinced of. *Trusting in* Christ is heart belief; simply believing certain things about Him—even correct things—might be called mere head belief.

Our job, then, is to be certain that we are making it clear to nonbelievers that the need is to *trust in* Christ alone for their salvation. Do not be satisfied with getting the unbeliever to agree with correct doctrinal truths about Christ, for they can do that while still depending upon themselves for salvation. In such a case they would still be lost.

6. Repentance

Repentance is not, nor can it be, another step or condition for obtaining salvation. It is, however, something that happens with every unbeliever who becomes a believer in Christ. "How," you might ask, "can repentance be a necessity and yet not be a step one must take in order to obtain God's salvation?"

The answer to the above question is best answered by observing the Bible's definition of repentance in contrast to man's view of it.

The Greek word translated "repentance" is *metanoia* and always means a change of mind or attitude. For instance, the apostle Paul described the Gospel message he preached as *"repentance toward God and faith toward our Lord Jesus Christ"* (Acts 20:21). I believe it is safe to say that every nonbeliever has some misconception concerning God and how to be in right relationship with Him through Christ. It is impossible, therefore, for an unbeliever to become a believer in Christ without having a change of mind or attitude concerning God and His offer of salvation. As you share the Gospel and the person to whom you are witnessing trusts in Christ, that one has repented—he has progressed from an attitude of unbelief to a heart attitude of trusting in Christ alone. That's Biblical repentance.

Why Biblical repentance is not a work,
but man's idea of repentance is a work

To become a Christian one must change his mind from any misconception he has about God or His way of salvation. And God's way of salvation is always by grace through faith in Jesus Christ without the addition of any human merit or works of any kind (Ephesians 2:8, 9; Romans 4:5). Therefore, if man must repent to be saved, repentance cannot be something the unsaved can point to as having some human worth or merit by which to commend themselves to God.

The way a man thinks about God is the real issue, not what sins he may or may not have committed. This is demonstrated so beautifully in **Second Corinthians 4:3-6:** *But even if our gospel is veiled, it is veiled to those who are perishing, whose minds the god of this world* (that's Satan) *has blinded, who do not believe, lest the light of the gospel of the glory of Christ, who is the image of God, should shine on them.... For it is the God who commanded light to shine out of darkness who has shone in our hearts to give the light of the knowledge of the glory of God in the face of Jesus Christ.*

In contrast to God's Word, man defines repentance as turning from sin, being sorry for sin or quitting certain more obvious sins or bad habits. By this definition repentance, and therefore salvation, would be by man's works or efforts instead of by God's matchless and undeserving grace.

The issue is not turning from sin; it is changing one's attitude toward Christ and trusting in Him for salvation. Turning from sin would involve service, which is only demanded of one who is already saved. Salvation, on the other hand, is always a gift, never the result of what we do concerning our sins. It is trusting in Christ and what He has done about our sins that saves. The issue is not what one will do concerning his sins, but rather what he will do concerning the Son.

An unsaved person cannot really please God even if he does "good works." **Romans 8:8** is pretty clear on this point: *So then, those who are in the flesh* (the natural man) *cannot please God.* And **Isaiah 64:6** removes any hope of man relying on his goodness when it declares that *"all our righteousnesses* (that's the best we can do) *are as filthy rags. . . "*

It is only after one has come to Christ by faith that he, as a member of God's family, is commanded to change his life. Such changes undoubtedly involve turning from or leaving certain sinful habits. In fact, the Bible makes that very clear. For instance, **Titus 2:11, 12:** *For the grace of God that brings salvation has appeared to all men, teaching us that, denying* (renouncing, rejecting) *ungodliness and worldly lusts, we should live soberly, righteously, and godly in the present age.* You might want to also look up Romans 12:1,2; 13:14; Ephesians 2:10; and 4:27-32.

Rediscoving the Correct Emphasis

It is due largely to the wrong emphasis on this matter of repentance that so many unsaved folks feel they can't be saved until they give up their beer, or cigarettes, or swearing or whatever. The confusion has come from the Christian professionals who have themselves been mistaught in Bible school or seminary. But, thank God, not all have just followed the theological crowd. Here, for instance, are some of my favorite quotes from spiritual giants of the past.

Lewis Sperry Chafer, D.D., Litt.D, ThD, founder of Dallas Theological Seminary, in his *Systematic Theology*, Volumn III on Soteriology, page 372, writes: "The word *Metanoia* is in every instance translated repentance. The word means a change of mind. The common practice of reading into this word the thought of sorrow and heart-anguish is responsible for much confusion in the field of Soteriology."

Harry A. Ironside, Litt.D, *Except Ye Repent*, pages 12-15: "But in order to clarify the subject, it may be well to observe carefully what repentance is not, and then to notice what it is.

First, then, repentance is not to be confounded with penitence.

. . penitence is simply sorrow for sin. . . . Nowhere is man exhorted to feel a certain amount of sorrow for his sins in order to come to Christ.

Second, penance is not repentance. Penance is an effort in some way to atone for the wrong done.

In the third place, let us remember that reformation is not repentance.

Need I add that repentance then is not to be considered synonymous with joining a church, or taking up one's religious duties, as people say. It is not doing anything.

The Greek word, *metanoia*, which is translated "repentance" in our English Bibles, literally means a change of mind."

William L. Pettingill, D.D., *Bible Questions Answered*, pages 215-216: "What place has repentance in salvation? Should we tell people to repent of their sins to be saved?" The Gospel of John is the Holy Spirit's Gospel Tract, written that men might believe that Jesus is the Christ the Son of God; and that believing they might have life through His name (20:31). And it does not mention the word "repentance." But that is only because repentance is a necessary part of saving faith. Strictly speaking, the word repentance means a "change of mind." It is by no means the same as sorrow (II Corinthians 7:10). Since it is not possible for an unbeliever to become a believer without changing his mind, it is therefore unnecessary to say anything about it. The only thing for a man to do in order to be saved is to believe on the Lord Jesus Christ: and to believe on Him is the same thing as receiving Him (John 1:11-13).

An Urgent Reminder

If you are to be effective in making God's saving Gospel clear to the unsaved world you must become convinced that any teaching that demands a change of conduct on the part of the unbeliever before God will accept him and give him salvation, is adding works or human effort to faith and it contradicts all clear Scriptures on salvation. It is, in fact, an accursed message that cannot save. See Galatians 1:8, 9 and Deuteronomy 27:18.

Please realize that these comments on repentance are not meant to be an attempt to split some theological hair; they are a sincere effort on my part to help God's people who desire to reach the unbelieving world with the Gospel to share that Gospel in a clear, understandable and Biblical way.

7. Public Confession

Romans 10:9: *That if you confess with your mouth the Lord Jesus and believe in your heart that God has rasised Him from the dead, you will be saved.*

I have come to the conclusion that the key word in verse nine is the word "and." It is a translation of the Greek word *kai*, and depending on the context and the author's purpose, kai may be variously translated. It has more than one use and more than one meaning in the New Testament.

- *Kai* is usually translated "and" *when it is used as a simple connective.* For instance, Matthew 2:11: *And when they* (the Wise Men) *had come into the house, they saw the young Child, with Mary his mother, and fell down and worshipped Him. And when they had opened their treaures, they presented gifts to Him: gold, frankincense, and myrrh.* All four occurrences of *kai* in this verse are used to connect each thought. This is the common way we use *and* in English.

- *Kai* is also used *to indicate contrast.* We see it used this way in John 16:13: *However, when He, the Spirit of Truth, has come, He will guide you into all truth; for He will not speak of His own authority, but* (kai) *whatever He hears He will speak; and will tell you things to come.*

- A third use is seen *when the intention of a passage is to emphasize something.* This emphatic use is clear in Second Corinthians 11:1: *Oh, that you would bear with me in a little folly—and indeed* (kai) *you do bear with me.*

- Finally, it is important to note that *kai* is used at times *when the Holy Spirit wants to give some additional explanation to what has just been said.* When used in this way *kai* is generally translated *even*, as in First Corinthians 2:10: *For the Spirit searches all things, even* (kai) *the deep things of God.* In this instance "all things" particularly includes "the deep things of God."

Now, how does all of this apply to our verse? Simply this: I believe *kai* in Romans 10:9 should be translated *even*, so that it would read, *That if you confess with your mouth the Lord Jesus, even believe in your heart that God has raised Him from the dead, you will be saved.* Applying this useage, "confess with your mouth" is further explained to mean "even believe in your heart."

What has brought me to this conclusion? Two things primarily (other than the actual contents of the verse): context and the testimony of all other Scripture on the same subject of salvation. I'll illustrate.

The emphasis in Romans 10 is twofold: righteousness by faith in contrast to righteousness by works (especially the works of the Law), and the recognition of Jesus as Lord, that is, His deity.

- Righteousness by faith: *Brethren, my heart's desire and prayer to God for Israel is that they may be saved. For I bear them witness that they have a zeal for God, but not according to knowledge. For they being ignorant of God's righteousness, and seeking to establish their own righteousness, have not submitted to the righteousness of God. For Christ is the end of the law for righteousness to everyone who believes* (vs. 1-4).

- The Lordship (deity) of Christ: *That if you confess with your mouth the Lord Jesus (literally, Jesus as Lord)...* (v. 9). *For there is no distinction between Jew and Greek, for the same Lord over all is rich to all who call upon Him. "For whoever calls upon the name of the LORD* (Jehovah, quoted from Joel 2:32) *shall be saved* (vs. 12, 13).

These were the very two things the Jews refused to do: yield to a by-faith righteousness provided by God through the Messiah, Jesus (see 9:30-33), and recognize the full deity of the Lord Jesus Christ.

Also, in the context it is essential to notice that in verse nine Paul places confession with the mouth before believing in the heart, following the order of the just quoted statement from Moses found in **Deuteronomy 30:14:** *"The word is near you, even in your mouth and in your heart"* (that is, the word of faith *which we preach* (v.8). But in verses ten and following he gives the order of actual experience, and we see that believing comes before confession. This is verified in verses 13–15: *For whoever calls upon the name of the LORD shall be saved. How then shall they call on Him in whom they have not believed? And how shall they believe in Him of whom they have not heard? And how shall they hear without a preacher? And how shall they preach unless they are sent?* The "confession" of verses nine and ten is the "calling" of verses thirteen and fourteen. See the order as we work our way *backwards* from verse fifteen to to verse thirteen:

How shall they preach unless they are sent? Which comes first, the preaching or the sending? The sending.

How shall they hear without a preacher? Which comes first, the hearing or the preaching? The preaching; otherwise, there is nothing to hear.

And how shall they believe in Him of whom they have not heard? Which comes first, the believing or the hearing? The hearing, as stated in verse seventeen. Without the hearing there is nothing to believe.

How shall they call on him in whom they have not believed? Which comes first, the calling or the believing? The believing. Someone once said, *"The mouth confesses what the heart has already believed."* So, the *call* of verse thirteen is a call to the Lord (not necessarily to men) springing from a heart that already believes.

The Testimony of All Scripture

The united testimony of Scripture on salvation is that God offers salvation to the lost on one condition and one condition only—belief in Christ. To be justified we must have God's righteousness credited to our account: *But to him who does not work but believes on Him who justifies the ungodly, his faith is accounted for righteousness* (Romans 4:5). In the first five chapters of Romans God carefully explains that salvation is by faith in Christ, plus nothing else. This agrees with 160 New Testament verses. After giving the most detailed explanation of salvation by faith found in the Bible, Paul would not then teach there is something more that must be done for one to be saved, namely, verbal confession.

There is also the further testimony of those who were genuinely saved but who did not publicly declare their faith.

287

They were, at least for a time, secret believers. There are three I want to draw your attention to:

Nicodemus. In all references to him he is described as he who "came to Jesus by night" (John 3:1,2; 7:50; 19:39), and he did not demonstrate that he had already believed in Christ until after His crucifixion when he brought spices for Jesus' burial.

Joseph of Arimathea. John 19:38 describes him as *"being a disciple of Jesus, but secretly, for fear of the Jews."* We must accept this testimony of God's Word as being valid.

The Many in John 12:42: *Nevertheless even among the rulers many believed in Him, but because of the Pharisees they did not confess Him, lest they should be put out of the synagogue.* Some declare these were not genuine believers, but who shall we believe, men or God? It says they "believed in Him" and throughout his Gospel that is what John says the unbeliever must do (look up these verses: 1:12; 3:15, 16, 18, 36; 4:39, 41, 42; 5:24; 6:29, 35, 47; 7:38, 39; 8:30; 11:27, 45; and the key verse—20:31). The testimony is overwhelming that *believing in Him* brings eternal life to the believer, with or without publicly declaring that belief.

So, public confession of Christ, though expected by God and normal for the believer, is not a condition for receiving eternal life, nor is it really the subject of Romans 10:9, 10.

For Personal Reflection and Application

❖ Do you grieve over the "many" (Matthew 7:22, 23) throughout the world who say and do all the proper "Christian" things, but who do not truly *know* the Lord Jesus Christ personally? What a shock it will be to them to awaken in eternity totally lost and eternally separated from God when they thought all along that they would make it to Heaven based on their performance.

❖ Have you ever caught yourself using "in Jesus name" as a magic formula through which miracles may be performed. False prophets use His name freely but they are lost and will suffer forever for their lying, deceiving ways. Check out Deuteronomy 13:1–5; 18:18–22; Isaiah 8:19, 20; Jeremiah 14:13–15; 27:14, 15; Ezekiel 22:28; Matthew 7:22, 23; and Second Corinthians 11:13–15.

❖ Do you ever find yourself wanting to endorse, cooperate with, or fellowship with those who preach an accursed message?— see Galatians 1:6–9; 2:4, 5. Don't—under any circumstances!

With the many pious
substitutes for the one
Gospel of Grace today,
and the ecclesiastical
influence and blind
enthusiasm of their
promoters, evangelism
has new enemies to face,
and her glorious work
can never be accomplished
by waving the white
flag of tolerance
before these foes.

Lewis Sperry Chafer, Founder of
Dallas Theological Seminary

17

Contending for the Faith
Without Being Contentious

Whenever you witness to someone there are usually going to be differences of opinions, especially on the issue of what a person must do to be saved. Other times you will find yourself at odds with fellow believers about what issues or doctrines are important enough to discontinue fellowshipping with one another. Then, of course, there are the seemingly never-ending stream of false teachers flooding the television, radio and literature media, who must be opposed and exposed for what they are.

Contending for the faith is a clear Biblical mandate few of us enjoy obeying. We would rather acquiesce and not confront anyone. It is much easier to "love" everyone so much that we never ruffle anyone's feathers or cause any divisions or severe disturbances with others. However, the Scripture does not allow us to get off so easily.

Consider **Jude 3, 4:** *Beloved, while I was very diligent to write to you concerning our common salvation, I found it necessary to write to you exhorting you to contend earnestly for the faith which was once for all delivered to the saints. For certain men have crept in unnoticed, who long ago were marked out for this condemnation, ungodly men, who turn the grace of our God into licentiousness and deny* (contradict) *the only Lord God and our Lord Jesus Christ.*

The phrase "contend earnestly" portrays a wrestling match. We are to earnestly *wrestle* for the faith. Wrestling can be a sweaty business. It is not easy work. It is not always pleasant. It sometimes leads to bruises, sore muscles and defeat. In spiritual wrestling (contending) we may be misunderstood, wrongly judged, ostracized, even lied about. But contend we must, if we are to be loyal to our Savior.

Unfortunately contending for the faith has sometimes received bad press from poor examples, like those who go about looking for a fight. You know the kind I mean: if you don't dot your theological "i's" and cross your theological "t's" in exactly the same way they do, you become their newest target for a full frontal attack. While I am totally committed to contending for the faith, I am, at the same time, convinced we can do so without being contentious.

In the first chapter of Philippians the apostle Paul made it clear that he was *"appointed for the defense of the gospel"* (vs. 17). Earlier he reminded his Philippian readers: *I have you in my heart, inasmuch as both in my chains* (imprisonment) *and in the defense and confirmation of the gospel, you all are partakers with me of grace* (vs. 7). But perhaps the most revealing comment Paul made in this regard may be found in these two verses:

Philippians 1:9, 10: *And this I pray, that your love may abound still more and more in knowledge and in all discernment, that you may approve the things that are excellent, that you may be sincere and without offense till the day of Christ.*

In this matter of contending for the faith without being contentious, there may be no quality more important than that which Paul described in these two verses—*having a sincere, informed, discerning love toward others.* If our love is sincere, we won't be playing hypocritical religious games. If our love is based upon solid and correct information, we won't hastily judge others. If our love is discerning, we won't be led astray ourselves, nor will we lead others astray. This a great passage to read over and over again in reminding yourself that there is a Christlike way to confront, expose and even oppose others.

To understand how to contend for the faith properly, I'd like to share just a few practical suggestions. When confronted with someone or some teaching that you may question, do the following:

- *Investigate.* Don't take someone else's word or opinion about a questionable situation. Look into it firsthand. Let's say a friend comes to you and says, "Did you know that the Reverend Twiddle, D. D. believes that there is no salvation outside of the church?" Now with this bit of information coming from a friend, your first reaction would be to believe what you are hearing. After all, would your friend lie to you? Probably not, but he or she may be mistaken; they may have done nothing more than repeat to you what someone else has told them without attempting to verify it for themselves. Don't you make the same mistake.

Suppose you do feel it necessary to investigate Rev. Twiddle's doctrine, what should you do then?

- *Evaluate in the light of Scripture.* If others are questioning him and even attacking him, but you find that his doctrinal views are Biblical, say so. Don't allow false accusations to continue in your presence. On the other hand, if you discover that his views on salvation, and that which is taught in Scripture are at variance, don't hesitate to point that out as well; just do so in as loving a manner as possible.

- *Take a firm stand on the side of Scripture.* Always make the Word of God your sole authority whether or not anyone else stands with you. As long as you stand where God's Word leads, He will stand with you— you'll not be alone in the struggle.
  Psalm 119:126–128 reminds us: *It is time for You to work, O LORD, for they have regarded Your law as void. Therefore I love Your commandments more than gold, yes, more than fine gold! Therefore all Your precepts concerning all things I consider to be right; I hate every false way.*

- *Be Loving and Compassionate at All Times.* Recall *The Winning Attitude*—speaking the truth in love. As long as your compassion is Biblically based (Philippians 1:9, 10) it is never wrong to love even the most unlovable. In fact, it pays rich dividends.

- *Avoid Compromise.* Human sympathy and empathy will sometimes lead us to compromise truth because our warm caring feelings toward someone tends to override the truth of God. **First Thessalonians 5:21, 22** is good to remember: *Test all things; hold fast what is good. Abstain from every form of evil.* **Ephesians 5:11** adds, *And have no fellowship with the unfruitful works of darkness, but rather expose them.*

There may even be times when you must be very firm, as Christ was upon occasion—see Matthew 15:1-14; 23:1–36, where His words were absolutley scathing). The apostle Paul's admonishments are ones you may have to heed as well, though it will not be easy to do.

In **Titus 1:13** he told Titus what to do regarding deceivers who were leading others astray: *Therefore rebuke them sharply, that they may be sound in the faith.*

In **Second Thessalonians 3:6 and 14, 15**, Paul gives clear instructions on how to handle disorderly or disobedient believers: *But we command you, brethren, in the name of our Lord Jesus Christ, that you withdraw from every brother who walks disorderly and not according to the tradition which he received from us....And if anyone does not obey our word in this epistle, note that person and do not keep company with him, that he may be ashamed. Yet do not count him as an enemy, but admonish him as a brother.*

He also recorded his public confrontation with a rebuke of Peter when Peter's hypocritical conduct was not "straightforward about the truth of the gospel" (Galatians 2:11-21). So there are times when we must allow the Holy Spirit to strengthen our backbones as we firmly stand our ground based upon the unchanging Word of God.

- *You should live a life totally surrendered to Christ.* Exemplify Him in all you do, being genuine through and through, and when you must confront others they will know that the confrontation is borne out of love rather than lesser motives.
- *Faithfully proclaim the Gospel of God's grace.* Know the Gospel thoroughly. Present it clearly and with simplicity. Make it the goal of your life to obey the last command Christ gave His disciples before returning to Heaven.
- *Practice the golden rule of contending for the faith:*
  In MAJOR things, let there by *UNITY!*
  In MINOR things, let there be *LIBERTY!*
  In ALL things, let there be *CHARITY!*

For Personal Reflection and Application

❖ You may be—as I naturally am—somewhat timid. Perhaps you would do everything in your power to avoid arguments and confrontations of any kind. However, we are commanded to "earnestly contend for the faith." If you *are* hesitant about confronting others over doctrinal error, how could you apply Philippians 4:6, 7 and Second Timothy 1:7,8 to that natural hesitancy? Could you trust the Lord for *His* boldness and strength?

❖ Have you observed situations where contending for the faith was done in a contentious way? What were the results? What lessons can be learned from such instances?

THE

GOSPEL

MESSENGER

Too often Christians are freezing in intellectualism or frying in emotionalism and have no concern for others. The soul winner is marked by compassion for the lost. . . . No candle on the altar will substitute for a flame in the heart.

C. Sumner Wemp

18

Your Mission

Who you are is determined by *Whose* you are. In the case of all who know Christ, we know that we *belong* to Him. We are not our own, for we have been bought with a price (First Corinthians 6:19, 20). We are eternally, immutably joined to Him by spiritual birth. We are God's children by faith.

Ephesians 5:30 states: *For we are members of His body, of His flesh and of His bones.* We are here on earth in His place, representing Him, testifying of Him, living for Him. We are, as the song says, *A Child of the King*! As such, He has a purpose for each of us; He has a position in His Body—the Church—for each of us. He has a divine mission for each of us. He has a divine mission for *you*! Let's consider what it might be, as indicated by various Bible terms.

Your Mission as an Ambassador

The Biblical basis for you being an ambassador is found in **Second Corinthians 5:20:** *Therefore we are ambassadors for Christ, as though God were pleading through us: we implore you on Christ's behalf, be reconciled to God.* An earthly ambassador represents one country to another. As a heavenly ambassador you are to represent one country (Heaven) to another (the world), you are to do this "on Christ's behalf"—that is, in His place. If you were an ambassador for the United States of America you would go to a foreign country *in place of* the President as an official representative of your country.

As an ambassador for Christ you are to properly represent Him to the unbelieving world. How faithfully you fulfill your ambassadorship will determine whether or not you will receive His, *"Well done, good and faithful servant."* To be unfaithful or disloyal in this position will mean loss of rewards and shame before Him at His coming. In other words, you may be a good or poor ambassador. How you fulfill your lofty position as Christ's ambassador will bring its own reward; what you sow, you *will* reap.

The apostle John warned us of this when he wrote this in **First John 2:28:** *And now little children, abide in Him, that when He appears we may have confidence and not be ashamed before Him at His coming.*

Be His ambassador!

Your Mission as a Witness

Not only are you an ambassador for Christ, you are also to be His witness. A witness is one who tells what he knows—usually about someone else or an event. In promising the coming of the Holy Spirit, Jesus spoke to the eleven disciples and said, *"But when the Helper comes, whom I shall send to you from the Father, the Spirit of truth who proceeds from the Father, He will testify of Me. And you also will bear witness, because you have been with Me from the beginning"*—**John 15:26, 27.**

In the same conversation with these men in the upper room, He went on to say this about the Holy Spirit in **John 16:14:** *He will glorify Me, for He will take of what is Mine and declare it to you.*

Acts 1:8 gives further testimony as to the purpose of the Holy Spirit being given to believers today. Jesus said, *"But you shall receive power when the Holy Spirit has come upon you; and you shall be witnesses to Me in Jerusalem, and in all Judea and Samaria, and to the end of the earth."*

I gather from these and other Scriptures that a major reason the Holy Spirit was given to us—if not *the* major reason—was to empower us or to enable us to be witnesses for Christ. Therefore, if in any way or for any reason, you stifle that purpose, you are sinning for the Bible commands: *Do not grieve the Holy Spirit of God, by whom you were sealed for the day of redemption*—**Ephesians 4:30.**

Be His witness!

Your Mission as a Missionary

Though the word missionary does not appear in the Bible, the concept does. Take, for instance, the Great Commission as recorded in **Mark 16:15**: *And He said to them, "Go into all the world and preach the Gospel to every creature."* That's what a missionary is supposed to do. "But," you say, "I'm not called to be a missionary." Oh, yes you are!

You see, the word "call" as used in "a missionary call" simply means an invitation. Jesus gave a parable in **Matthew 22:1-14**. The gist of the parable was that a certain king arranged a marriage for his son and *sent out his servants to call those who were invited to come to the wedding.* But they refused to come and made light of it, even going so far as to kill the king's servants. The king then sent out other servants and told them to *"go out into the highways"* and to *invite all whom they found, both bad and good.* Then the wedding hall was filled with guests, and Jesus gave the lesson: *For many are called but few are chosen.*

Who were the *called*? Those who were invited. And who were the *chosen*? Those who responded to the invitation. It is the same today. You are invited by way of Christ's command to preach the Gospel wherever you go, for you see, the command could literally read, "*As* you go, be preaching the Gospel to every creature." So, the command is not to go; it is to preach the Gospel *as* you go—and we are all called to that.

Biblically speaking, a missionary is not one who goes some place to preach the Gospel; rather, a Bible missionary is one who preaches the Gospel as they go anywhere and everywhere.

Be His missionary!

Your Mission as a Soul Winner

I discussed earlier whether or not Christians are to *win* souls and concluded that we are definitely to do all we can to win as many as we can. By winning, you might recall, I mean to *persuade*, to *lead*, to *influence* unbelievers to place their faith in the Lord Jesus Christ as their Savior.

To be a soul winner, therefore, requires the giving of the Gospel, not just living a good life in front of unbelievers. As an effective soul winner you must *explain* the Gospel, you must *lead* them into the Word, you must *persuade* from Scripture concerning Christ and what He has done for them. Finally, you must be a positive *influence* on them for good—the ultimate good being to trust in Christ to save them.

The apostle Paul is probably the best example we have in the Bible as to what a soul winner's heart and life should be like.

Romans 9:1-4a reveals the depth of his burden for the lost, especially for his own Jewish brothers. He wrote: *I tell the truth in Christ, I am not lying, my conscience also bearing me witness in the Holy Spirit, that I have great sorrow and continual grief in my heart. For I could wish that I myself were accursed from Christ, for my brethren, my kinsmen according to the flesh, who are Israelites....*

One chapter later in **Romans 10:1, 2**, he writes further: *Brethren, my heart's desire and prayer to God for Israel is that they may be saved. For I bear them record that they have a zeal for God, but not according to knowledge.*

What exactly did Paul do to win others? How did he conduct his life so that he might reach the lost? He tells us in **First Corinthians 9:19–23**: *For though I am free from all men, I have made myself a servant to all, that I might win the more: and to the Jews I became as a Jew, that I might win Jews; to those who are under the law, as under the law, that I might win those who are under the law; to those who are without law, as without law (not being without law toward God, but under law toward Christ), that I might win those who are without law; to the weak I became as weak, that I might win the weak. I have become all things to all men, that I might by all means save some. Now this I do for the gospel's sake, that I may be partaker of it with you.*

Five times in these verses Paul uses the word "win" in describing what he was attempting to do in reaching the unsaved world. He adapted himself to the ones he was trying to win. You, my friend, could do no better.

Be His soul winner!

Your Mission as a Discipler

Only one of the four Gospels in the New Testament mentions

disciple-making as part of the Great Commission. **Matthew 28:18-20:** *Then Jesus came and spoke to them, saying, "All authority has been given to Me in heaven and on earth. Go therefore and make disciples of all the nations, baptizing them in the name of the Father and of the Son and of the Holy Spirit, teaching them to observe all things that I have commanded you; and lo, I am with you always, even to the end of the age."*

The fact that only Matthew's account of the Great Commission contains the element of disciple-making does not mean that the making of disciples is not important. After all, how many times does God have to command something for it to be important enough to obey? Having said that, however, it is puzzling to me how much current emphasis is placed upon making disciples while evangelizing the lost seems to have been put on the back burner of Christian thinking and action.

What's involved in proper discipling? To answer this question we need to understand the three words—*disciple, discipleship,* and *discipling.* A *disciple* is a learner. In ancient times men were disciples of various thinkers, philosophers and religious zealots, such as Plato and Aristotle. Jesus had multitudes of disciples, though the New Testament focuses on the eleven. *Discipleship,* in its fullest conotation, refers to the dedicated, sacrificial life of a true disciple—Jesus called such a one "a disciple *indeed*" (John 8:31). It involves a difficult choice to follow Christ no matter how or where He may lead. One is told to count the cost before making such a choice (Luke 14:26-33). The life of a Biblical disciple is a very difficult life. It is costly. It may cost the presence and companionship of those you love the most. It may lead to an austere lifestyle with few of this world's goods. It is not a life that the majority of Christians seem to choose. *Discipling* refers to the process of one disciple leading another believer into the choice to live the life of Christ's disciple.

Paul laid out this process of discipling in **Second Timothy 2:1–7,** especially in the first two verses: *You therefore, my son, be strong in the grace that is in Christ Jesus. And the things that you have heard from me among many witnesses, commit these to faithful men who will be able to teach others also.*

Discipling others is an ongoing process. It involves pouring your life into the lives of others, who will pour their lives into others, who will pour their lives into others, and on and on. Notice in the above verses the four generations of believers mentioned. There was Paul, the writer (*"the things that you have heard from me"); * there was Timothy (*"the things that* **you** *have heard from me");* there were those whom Timothy was to disciple (*"commit these to* **faithful men** *");* and there were those whom these faithful men would disciple (*"who will be able to teach* **others** *also").*

Some common misconceptions of disciple-making.

Scenario Number One.
Here is an all-too-common concept of disciple-making that goes on repeatedly in our churches. Pastor Jones asks brother Dogood if he would like to be discipled. Brother Dogood is delighted at the prospect, and so Pastor Jones assigns deacon Smith to take brother Dogood through the church's discipleship program. Smith and Dogood meet once a week every Tuesday evening and work their way through the Discipleship Manual. There are twelve convenient chapters in the Manual, corresponding with the Sunday School's quarterly lessons. Upon completion of the DM and upon meeting all the requirements laid out by the church (such as water baptism), brother Dogood receives his certificate designating that he is now a full-fledged Disciple of Jesus Christ. Once he has completed the discipleship program, brother Dogood can sink comfortably down into his pew and resume his usual level of Christian living.

Obviously I'm guilty of a little tongue-in-cheek here, but the description above is not too far off the mark of what does actually happen in many local congregations. Their intentions may be well–meaning, but the results of such an approach to discipleship can be devastating.

You see, New Testament discipleship is absolutely radical. There is nothing convenient or comfortable about it, except for the inner comfort that comes by knowing your entire life is totally given over to the Lord Jesus Christ to do with as He sees fit.

Scenario Number Two.
One of my students comes to me and asks, "Mr. Seymour, would you disciple me?" I may have this student in three of my classes each week, for a total of six or more hours of instruction

in God's Word; I may have him in my prayer group of seven other male students, meeting once a week for prayer; I may eat several meals with him during the week; I may play volleyball or softball with him weekly; I may take him with me for witnessing opportunities several weekends a month—and he's asking me to *disciple* him? He would already be in the process of being discipled in such a setting, whether he knew it or not.

Much of Christ's teaching and discipling took place before multitudes, and much of it took place with a hand full of believers. In both instances discipling would only be taking place *with those who were taking in the teaching and applying it to themselves.* And that is the key. You cannot disciple someone who will not be discipled. You may take them through a course of study, you may pray with them, and you may live the example before them of what a true disciple should be, but if they are not assimilating God's Word into their hearts and personally applying it to themselves they are not being discipled!

Teaching the Bible and related topics is not a profession with me; it is not simply a Christian occupation. I teach to change lives, and I believe any teacher of God's Word who does not have that as his or her aim should get out of the teaching field. Because of my driving aim to change people by the Word of God, I am discipling every time I teach or preach from the Bible. Meeting with someone one-on-one does not make the discipling process any more real or permanent. The heart attitudes of the discipler and the ones being discipled is of utmost importance. When the heart attitude of all involved is what it should be, discipling is taking place as it was intended.

The apostle John wrote in **Third John verse two,** *I have no greater joy than to hear that my children walk in truth.* You may find that to be true of your efforts as well. To lead someone to Christ and then to see them go on with the Lord in their lives, brings a joy that cannot be properly expressed in words.

Sometimes we confuse follow-up of a new believer with making disciples. Follow-up is often a much simpler process than disciple making. Follow-up may involve nothing more than giving the new believer a book on how to live the Christian life. It may entail obtaining his phone number or email address so as to stay in touch, especially if he doesn't live near you. As much as is possible, we should follow-up each person we lead to Christ, and the best time to do that is right after they have become a Christian.

Making a disciple out of a believer, however, will usually require much more of your own time, energy, efforts, money and sacrifice. But disciple-making is well worth whatever the cost may be to you. Making disciples out of believers continues the divine plan of producing "fruit that remains" through your life. Jesus spoke of it in **John 15:16**: *You did not choose Me, but I chose you and appointed you that you should go and bear fruit, and that your fruit should remain, that whatever you ask the Father in My name He may give you.*

Be His discipler!

Before I close this chapter, I want to briefly discuss two other issues that relate somewhat to your mission. The first involves the place of the Great Commission in the Church today, and the second concerens itself with the concept of Gospel multiplication and why it does not work.

Is the Great Commission for today?

The question may surprise you. You may be thinking, "Don't all Christians take the Great Commission seriously? Isn't it the Marching Orders for the Church?" No, all Christians do not see the Great Commission as binding upon the Church today. And, yes, it does contain our Marching Orders.

There are some who feel that the Great Commission was only for the original disciples and the early believers before Paul's conversion. The Church, we are told, did not begin until Paul's conversion.These dear folks are usually very clear on the Gospel—after all, they take only what Paul says about it, so they are bound to be clear! They usually believe that water baptism is not for today, even though Paul himself did baptize as he said in **First Corinthians 1:14–16**: *...I baptized none of you except Crispus and Gaius, lest anyone should say that I had baptized in my own name. Yes, I also baptized the household of Stephanas. Besides I do not know whether I baptized any other.*

When he ministered in Corinth he not only baptized Crispus and his household but he must have also approved of many others being baptized, for in the middle of the passage describing his ministry there, the followng is recorded in **Acts 18:8:** *Then Crispus, the ruler of the synagogue, believed on the Lord with all his household. And many of the Corithians, hearing, believed and were baptized.* Surely, if baptism was not for today, Paul would have put a stop to the practice in his ministry.

I bring this up only to reassure the reader that you are doing the right and proper thing when you attempt to obey the Great Commission—preaching the Gospel wherever you go, baptizing believers, and teaching them to observe all that Christ taught. If you are involved in fulfilling Christ's last command, by all means, keep it up.

The second issue upon which I want to comment involves examining why—with all of our high technological advancements and our rapid means of travel and communication—the world is not being reached with the Gospel, or to word it a little differently—

Why Gospel multiplication does not work.

What is Gospel multiplication? It is a mathematical equation that, on paper, should work but that in reality never does. It goes like this: Pretend there is only one Christian in the entire world of roughly seven billion people. In the first year of his Christian life he wins one other person to Christ—no more. There would then be two believers in the world. In his second year, he wins one more to Christ and the person he led to the Lord in the first year leads one person to Christ, and no more. Now there would be four Christians.

If that doubling process continued unabated where each Christian—beginning with only one—won only one other to Christ each year, in a little less than forty years the entire world would be saved. Change the equation to winning one per month, and the entire world could be won—not just reached—in a little over three years!

It sounds good on paper, but why isn't it happening? The answer to that question comes back to this matter of fulfilling our individual mission. The first century church reached (not won) the entire world. Check out **Colossians 1:5, 6, 23** where Paul said the Gospel had been preached *"to every creature under heaven."*

We are not coming close to doing that, even though we have every imaginable high tech tool at our disposal with which to accomplish it.

But the answer to our failure does not lie in technology. The root problem is in our wills. Despite all of our impressive and high-sounding rhetoric, we are not willing to let go of our comforts, our security, our loved ones, for the sake of spreading the Gospel worldwide; until we are, the Church will continue to languish or even to march backwards while the false religions and cults of the world march steadily forward.

Therefore recognizing and fulfilling our personal divine mission in life is of paramount importance. By God's grace, be all God wants you to be in this matter of getting the Gospel to the lost.

For Personal Reflection and Application

❖ Of the various ways God describes your mission on earth, which one appeals to you the most? Which one has the least appeal to you? Why do you think this is so?

❖ If you are a believer in Chrst, do you also see yourself as His disciple as described in Scripture? Why or why not?

❖ Have you ever discipled another believer? Can you think of someone whom you might disciple? If you have a definite person in mind, what do you think it would take on your part to lead him or her into a life totally dedicated to Christ?

The work of individual
soul-winning is the
greatest work that God
permits men to do.

It was Christ's own
preferred method of
work, as it is his
preferred method for
us today. For it is
always the most effective
way of working.

It is the hardest work in
the world to do, and it
always will be the hardest.

Charles Gallaudet Trumbull
in *Taking Men Alive*

19

Your Philosophy of Evangelism

There is much discussion today concerning which is the best mode of evangelism. There are numerous articles and volumes supporting various forms of evangelistic styles. Some advocate Spirit-led evangelism while others promote the confrontational approach. Some are convinced that friendship evangelism is the only effective way to go while others are sold on opportunity evangelism, or lifestyle evangelism. But whatever approach to evangelism one may choose, certain truths are not open for debate. Lost folks must hear the way of salvation explained, whether the "hearing" is via the ear-gate or the eye-gate doesn't matter. What matters is that God's saving message to individuals must be properly understood by the unbeliever.

Romans 10:14, 17 makes the point convincingly: *How shall they call upon Him in whom they have not believed? And how shall they believe in Him of whom they have not heard? And how shall they hear without a preacher* (one to proclaim)*?...So then faith comes by hearing, and hearing by the Word of God.*

We'll consider the pros and cons of various evangelistic styles that are currently being promoted to see how they measure up to Scripture.

Aggressive Evangelism

By aggressive evangelism I refer to the fact that the individual believer in Christ is to be aggressively reaching out with the Gospel to those who are lost. This form of evangelism is also called *confrontational evangelism*—the believer initiating the introduction of the Gospel into a situation. I don't care for the term *confrontational* because it carries the conotation of confronting someone in an argumentative way, while confronting someone *may* be nothing more than clearly bringing a truth to the other person's attention. In this latter sense of the word, there is no doubt that this is definitely a Biblical approach to evangelism. We know this for at least two reasons.

First, we are commanded to *"go...preach...teach...baptize... make disciples"* of all nations. The commands of our Lord make it abundantly clear that we are not to wait for the world to come to us; we are to go to it. We are to initiate contacts, opportunities and conversations. Consider these verses:

Matthew 9:37, 38. *Then He said to His disciples, "The harvest truly is plentiful, but the laborers are few. Therefore pray the Lord of the harvest to send out laborers into His harvest.*

Notice the Lord of the harvest "sends out" laborers. A field full of ripened corn or wheat does not come to the laborer, the laborer goes to it. That's what aggressive evangelism is all about. So if you do not actually and deliberately approach folks about their spiritual condition, you are not being Biblical in your approach.

Matthew 28:19, 20 is another key verse on being aggressive in reaching out to others. *Go therefore and make disciples of all the nations, baptizing them in the name of the Father and of the Son and of the Holy Spirit, teaching them to observe all things that I have commanded you; and, lo, I am with you, even to the end of the age.*

Mark 16:15 adds: *And He said to them, "Go into all the world and preach the Gospel to every creature."*

Another passage depicting Christ's last command to His disciples is **Luke 24:46-48.** *Then He said to them, "Thus it is written, and thus it was necessary for the Christ to suffer and to rise from the dead the third day, and that repentance and remission of sin should be preached in His name to all nations, beginning at Jerusalem. And you are witnesses of these things."*

The command to witness to all the world is powerfully expressed in **Acts 1:8.** *But you shall receive power when the Holy Spirit has come upon you; and you shall be witnesses to Me in Jerusalem, and in all Judea and Samaria, and to the end of the earth.*

In these four accounts of the Great Commission we have

several strong indications that the apostles were to be aggressive in reaching the world with the Gospel.

In the Matthew passage we have the words *"go to all the nations...make* disciples...*baptizing* them...*teaching* them. These are all action words—things they were to *do.*

In Mark's account Jesus' command was literally, "As you go *be preaching* (proclaiming) the Gospel to every creature." Again, something definite was expected of them wherever they may travel—to be proclaiming the Gospel.

In Luke it is equally clear that these men were expected to preach *"repentance and remission of sin to all nations."* They were to *do* it, not just sit around for a special impression, or calling or moving of the Spirit. Failure to do what Christ commanded would have been naked disobedience and unfaithfulness to Him and to His message.

Acts is emphatic: *You **shall** be witnesses to Me...to the end of the earth.*

In all of these instances the proclamation of the Gospel was to be pursued *till all heard:* "*all* the nations" (Matthew), "*every* creature" (Mark), "to *all* nations" (Luke), and "to the *end* of the earth" (Acts). Obeying the Great Commission demands that we be aggressive.

Secondly, we see the example of our Lord Jesus Christ. In the third chapter of the Gospel of John, Nicodemus came to Jesus by night and the first words out of his mouth were complimentary: *"Rabbi, we know that You are a teacher come from God; for no one can do these signs that You do unless God is with him."* Jesus could have easily thanked Nicodemus for his kind words and proceeded to have a nice little religious chat with such a learned Jewish scholar. But instead He went straight to the need and told Nicodemus, *"Unless one is born again he cannot see the kingdom of God."* That's being aggressive.

One chapter later, **John 4:3,4** records, *He left Judea and departed again for Galilee. But He needed to go through Samaria.* The Jewish way was to go around Samaria, not ever through it. The Jews despised the Samaritans for they were Jews who intermarried with the Gentiles. Why did Jesus need to go *through* Samaria? The rest of the chapter explains why. He *needed* to talk to that sinful Samaritan woman who turned out to be so ready for the "water of life." That's aggressive evangelsim at its best. It is the Biblical way.

319

Opportunity Evangelism

This is where the Chistian is open to opportunities to share the Gospel and takes advantage of those opportunities as they come along. This differs slightly from aggressive evangelism in that the aggressive witness is *seeking to make* opportunites, not to just take advantage of opportunities as they fall into his lap. Opportunity evangelism is good as long as you do not totally rely on opportunities coming your way. If you do just rely on the presence of opportunites, you may find that even though opportunities to share Christ may come your way, your ability to recognize them may become dull. Remember, we are to go to the world, not wait for the world to come to us.

Responsive Evangelism

This is where the witness waits for the unbeliever to introduce something into the conversation that is either spiritual in nature, or that reveals a willingness to talk about his or her hurts or needs. As with opportunity evangelism, it is good to be readily responsive to situations as they open up. However, this is also an inadequate approach to your usual evangelistic practice. If all you do is respond to unbelievers, your outreach is going to be very limited. Such an approach to witnessing takes away the urgency of evangelizing the world for Christ while there is still time; it dampens the drive toward reaching out to the lost.

Availability Evangelism

This is very similar to responsive evangelism except that it is even less agressive than that. The mentality of such a witness is: "I'm available. All God has to do is make it crystal clear to me that I should do something concrete to reach a lost person, and I'm willing to do it." You see this type of attitude so often when folks—usually young people—dedicate themselves to go to the mission field. Thousands upon thousands have publicly declared their willingness to go; a mere trickle end up going. It makes one wonder about the sincerity of their "willingness." You must guard against a false sense of dedication to the Lord based on your declared willingness to reach out to others. What often happens is that all of these *willing* Christians do very little of a tangible nature to actually win others to Christ. I'm afraid that many believers are in reality unfaithful stewards of the Gospel and yet do not see themselves as unfaithful because of constantly affirming their willingness. Willingness, you see, without consistent action, is hypocrisy. Be careful of the possibility of deceiving yourself in this regard.

Friendship Evangelism

This is where the witness builds friendships with the unsaved before encountering the unbeliever in a conversation about his or her salvation. This approach to evangelism has become very popular over the last fifteen years with the introduction of a couple of very popular books on the subject.

Friendship evangelism can be a very effective means of reaching the lost because you get personally involved in other people's lives, you meet them where they are—on their turf; and that's *very* good. But there are a few warnings I'd like to give you:

First, do not allow friendship evangelism to be your *only* approach to witnessing. You'll be very limited in your outreach if you do.

Secondly, do not let it become an excuse for convincing yourself that the time is never ripe for sharing the Gospel. **Ecclesiastes 11:1, 4, and 6** remind us: *Cast your bread upon the waters, for you will find it after many days....He who observes the wind will not sow, and he who regards the clouds will not reap....In the morning sow your seed, and in the evening do not withhold your hand; for you do not know which will prosper, either this or that, or whether both alike will be good.*

I've observed that the friendship approach to witnessing has led some to constantly postpone actually confronting the lost person with the Gospel because the situation didn't ever seem right. Satan is delighted with this kind of spiritually sounding procrastination.

Thirdly, while every witnessing opportunity should be done in a friendly manner; that is, you should *be a friend* to whomever you witness, you do not have to develop a personal friendship with every person with whom you share the Gospel. If you limit yourself to where you only witness to those with whom you have built a lasting friendship, think how few there will be with whom you will ever share the Gospel.

Finally, even if your major approach to witnessing is the friendship approach, you need to be constantly reminding yourself that it doesn't always take years to build up a friendship to the point where you are free to share Christ. The friendship approach may actually become a hindrance because some Christians convince themselves that they never gain their friend's confidence enough where they feel free to approach the subject of their friend's eternal destiny. An attitude may develop where the believer is so concerned about offending his friend that the Gospel is never shared. Do not let this happen to you.

Lifestyle Evangelism

There are two common approaches to this style of evangelism. The first is that you live the Christian life before nonbelievers; then, when they ask you why you are different, you introduce them to the Gospel. We should all *live the life*, but one is not really *living* the life that pleases God if he is not faithfully *speaking* of Christ. **First Thessalonians 2:4** says: *As we have been approved by God to be entrusted with the gospel, even so we speak, not as pleasing men, but God who tests our hearts.* We are further reminded of the need to be loyal to our trust in **First Corinthians 4:2:** *Moreover it is required in stewards that one be found faithful.*

If we convince ourselves we are living the proper Christian life but we're silent regarding the Gospel, no one will be won to Christ, for *"faith comes by **hearing**, and hearing by the word of God"* (Romans 10:17). It doesn't say that faith comes by *watching* someone's life. No one is ever won to Christ solely by your good life, as important as that is. They must be told what they must do to be saved.

The other approach to lifestyle evangelism is that you live your life in such a way that witnessing of Christ is at the center of it; it becomes your main focus. Evangelism *is* your lifestyle. This is as it should be. Paul wrote of his view of lifestyle evangelism in **First Corinthians 9:16, 17:** *For if I preach the* *gospel, I have nothing to boast of, for necessity is laid upon me; yes, woe is me if I do not preach the gospel! For if I do this willingly, I have a reward; but if against my will, I have* (still) *been entrusted with a stewardship.* We are to share the Gospel whether we are willing to or not. The stewardship of the Gospel has still be entrusted to us.

Spirit-Led Evangelism

Those who advocate Spirit-led witnessing usually depend on a special *indication* or *impression* from God that this one or that one should be witnessed to. God can certainly give such impressions to His children; He has done it in the past. He gave a special leading to *Philip* to leave his successful outreach in Samaria and to go to the desert to witness to a lone Ethiopian of great authority (Acts 8:26–35). God also led *Ananias* to the house of one Judas where he led Saul of Tarsus to Christ (Acts 9:10–12; 22:12–16). And the Lord granted *Peter* a special vision, making it clear that he was to go to the house of Cornelius to bring the Gospel to him (Acts 10:1–20; 11:12–18).

In each of these examples, however, God *named* either the person to whom His servant was to preach the Gospel, or He *named* the exact location where the servant was to go—all *before* the servant went and before he encountered the unbeliever. This approach was not the norm then, nor is it now. I have been impressed at times to definitely witness to certain ones, but I realize that those times were the exceptions, not the normal ways God has used me in witnessing situations.

On the surface, Spirit-led witnessing seems to be the most spiritual, the most Biblical, the most God-directed, and the safest way to go in the matter of giving the Gospel to another person. In the earlier days of my Christian journey I briefly advocated and practiced this approach. I finally gave up on it for these simple reasons: 1) I ended up wintessing less than before, which means I led fewer to Christ. It didn't seem very logical that the more I was led by God's Spirit, the fewer people I would witness to and the fewer I would win. 2) I could never be certain when I was being led by God's Spirit to witness or to refrain from doing so. I discovered that not all feel-good impressions were necessarly from the Lord. 3) The whole approach—because it does depend on impressions or feelings—is much too subjective and, therefore, unreliable. 4) It finally dawned upon me that it didn't work and that it wasn't really taught in the Scriptures. Being led or controlled by God's Spirit is definitely taught in the Bible, but the Bible does not teach that a believer should never witness unless he *knows* he is being directly led by the Holy Spirit to do so.

Every creature evangelism

When the apostle Paul would enter a town he would repeatedly go first to the Jewish synagogue and witness to them out of their own Scriptures, but he was primarily the apostle to the Gentiles; Peter, James and John were apostles to the Jews (Galatians 2:7–9). Once, when Paul was in Athens, he was greatly disturbed by the idolatry in that city, and while he waited for Silas and Timothy to join him, he did his usual thing: *he reasoned in the synagogue with the Jews and with the Gentile worshipers, and in the marketplace daily with those who happened to be there* (Acts 17:16, 17).

Please note that Paul was aggressive in his witnessing. He initiated sharing the Gospel in the synagogue by *going* there where he knew he would be able to share Christ. Similarly, he *went* daily to the marketplace where he knew there would be multitudes of shoppers. And how did he know to whom he should witness? It was simple. He was under the same divine command as we are to "preach the Gospel to every creature." So what did he do? He witnessed *"in the marketplace daily **with those who happened to be there**."* What a revelation! How practical and sensible! Nothing mysterious about it. Paul didn't look for some kind of spiritual-feeling impressions. He was burdened over their idolatry and felt certain that they were all lost. The only God-honoring thing to do was to obey His command and to preach the Gospel to any and all of those lost folks who would listen.

You, dear reader, *will be led of the Spirit in your witnessing as you obey what He has already revealed in His Word concerning His will for you in this matter of getting the Gospel to everyone.* In one sense of the word, there are no wrong people to witness to. There may be wrong times to bring up the Gospel (but probably fewer times than most would tend to think); there are wrong ways in which to present the salvation message; but rarely will there be a person with whom you should not attempt to share the Gospel. That's something we convince ourselves of because of our own natural cowardice. It is not a truth you will find in Scripture.

There is one other approach to evangelism that I heard a speaker refer to: he called it the Nike Approach—*Just Do It!* Not bad advice. Be aggressive, be responsive, be willing, be friendly, be Spirit led, be burdened for every soul, and then *do it!*

For Personal Reflection and Application

❖ How would you describe your own witnessing style or philosophy?

❖ Do you see ways in which you might incorporate some elements of other evangelistic philosophies to strengthen your own?

❖ Would you say you have a true burden for the lost—so much so that you gladly and eagerly use any Christ–honoring means to reach them?

❖ In what kind of settings would you think it might be unwise to share the Gospel? Why do you think so?

❖ I've noticed over the years that there have been times when I was "waiting" for God to open doors to witness, but as a result I often did very little witnessing while I was in this "waiting" mode. Isn't it strange how seldom God opens doors for us who are so "willing" to walk through them? Or is it that our *willingness* is sometimes only surface, only a facade to hide our stubborn and rebellious heart that refuses to obey God?

We admire a man who was
firm in the faith, say
four hundred years ago…
but such a man today is
a nuisance, and must be
put down. Call him a
narrow-minded bigot,
or give him a worse name
if you can think of one….
It is today as it was in the
Reformer's days. Decision
is needed. Here is the day
for the man, where is the
man for the day? We who
have had the gospel passed
to us by martyr hands dare
not trifle with it, nor sit by
and hear it denied by
traitors, who pretend to
love it, but inwardly
abhor every line of it.

Charles H. Spurgeon

20

Your Oppostion

Whether we recognize it or not, there is a constant warfare going on in the spiritual realm in the area of getting the Gospel to the lost world. The attempts to hinder the Gospel come in various forms, some of which seem quite innocent. Dedicated powers are at work to either keep the unsaved from hearing the Gospel, or to hinder believers from spreading God's only saving message.

If you are determined to be the ambassador, the witness, the soul winner God wants you to be, you must settle it in your mind that you *will* be opposed. And the opposition will come to you in many and various ways, some very subtle and undetected, to get you to fail in your God-appointed task. Unless you are extremely alert to the devious shenanigans of the enemy of your soul, you will fall back into being the typical, well respected, *average* Christian who faithfully attends church, reads the Bible daily, prays for the missionaries overseas, gives faithfully to your church, but refuses to enter into the real battle over the souls of men.

By being educated as to the opposition you will face when you are out-and-out for Christ, it's my prayer you will be better equipped to defeat the enemy on every hand. Here, then, are common ways in which we are opposed in our efforts to get the Gospel to all nations.

Satan

Our chief enemy, and the one who is behind every kind of opposition we will ever face, is the devil himself. He is the arch enemy of God and of Christians worldwide. He opposes and hinders us in every way he possibly can—all to the end of keeping *his* unsaved children from being snatched out of his kingdom and born into God's. He opposes us in the following ways:

First, Satan's opposition is seen in *his direct attacks* upon God's children, especially upon those who are most earnest in their zeal for the Lord. **First Peter 5:8** warns: *Be sober, be vigilant; because your adversary the devil, walks about like a roaring lion, seeking whom he may devour.* Notice, he is called "your" adversary. It is personal. Just as he forcefully attempted to get Job to curse God, he is after you. He wants to demolish you, to completely destroy you!

But there is victory. In **First Peter 5:9** God adds: *Resist him, steadfast in the faith, knowing that the same sufferings are experienced by your brotherhood in the world.* Our ability to resist him comes from being "steadfast in the faith," not by engaging him in battle in our own strength or cunning.

Another comforting passage is **Luke 22:31, 32:** *And the Lord said, "Simon, Simon! Indeed, Satan has asked for you, that he might sift you as wheat. But I have prayed for you, that your faith should not fail; and when you have returned to Me, strenghten your brethren."* That was spoken directly to Peter, but **Hebrews 7:25** applies to all of us who have placed our faith in Christ. Its promise is: *Therefore He is able to save to the uttermost* (completely) *those who come to God through Him, since He ever lives to make intercession for them.* While our major enemy is strong, our God and Savior is stronger—and always prevails! We should be strengthened and greatly encouraged to know that twenty-four hours a day He "ever lives" to pray for us.

One of the most revealing passages depicting Satan's prime objective is found in **Second Corinthians 4:3, 4:** *But even if our gospel is veiled, it is veiled to those who are perishing, whose minds the god of this age* (Satan) *has blinded, who do not believe, lest the light of the gospel of the glory of Christ, who is the image of God, should shine on them.* The battle ground is the mind, and he works overtime to keep the minds of unbelievers blinded. We should do all we can to counter his maneuvers, especially in two ways: 1) give the Gospel faithfully, and 2) present it clearly as revealed in Scripture.

As we read on in this same passage, we see God's provision for turning the unbelievers blindness into sight. **Verses 5, 6** give the rest of the story: *For we do not preach ourselves, but Christ Jesus the Lord, and ourselves your servants for Jesus' sake. For* *it is the God who commanded light to shine out of darkness who has shone in our hearts to give the light of the knowledge of the glory of God in the face of Jesus Christ.* Why has God given us the Light of the Gospel? "To give the light" to those in spiritual darkness and bondage.

Satan may be more powerful than any of us, but he is no match for the Lord Jesus Christ. Nor can he overcome the power that is resident within the Gospel. I love Paul's statement in **Romans 1:16:** *For I am not ashamed of the gospel of Christ, for it is the power of God to salvation for everyone who believes, for the Jew first and also for the Greek.* The Gospel is God's power to bring salvation to those who believe it. The power is in the Message, not necessarily in the messenger. Live and proclaim it!

The World

The world is defined for us in **First John 2:15, 16**: *Do not love the world or the things in the world. If anyone loves the world, the love of the Father is not in him. For all that is in the world—the lust of the flesh, the lust of the eyes, and the pride of life—is not of the Father but is of the world.* This three-fold description of the world system is pretty apt. It tells it like it is, doesn't it? And the world hates Christ and everything He stands for. Jesus said so in **John 15:18-21:** *If the world hates you, you know it hated Me before it hated you. If you were of the world, the world would love its own. Yet because you are not of the world, but I chose you out of the world, therefore the world hates you. Remember the word that I said to you, "A servant is not greater than his master." If they persecuted Me, they will also persecute you. If they kept My word, they will keep yours also. But all these things they will do to you for My name's sake, because they do not know Him who sent Me.*

Don't be surprised, therefore, if those whom you work with, or go to school with, or your relatives or neighbors, despise your attempts at winning them to Christ. **First Peter 4:12** reminds us: *Beloved, do not think it strange concerning the fiery trial which is to try you, as though some strange thing happened to you.* Opposition from those of the world should be expected. It is the norm, but thank God there are always some in the harvest field who are ready and ripe for the picking.

The *flesh* often speaks of the nature we have that craves things to satisfy it—our lower sinful nature. That's the meaning I have in mind here when I speak of the flesh as being opposed to what God wants to do in your life and mine.

Christ gave a parable that we often call The Parable of the Sower. It is recorded in Matthew, Mark and Luke. All three Gospels give the parable and Christ's interpretation of the parable. In a nutshell, Christ used various types of ground as analogies of how different types of people respond to the Word of God as it is sown in their hearts. He speaks of the seed of the Word being sown *by the wayside, on stony ground, among thorns*, and *on good ground.*

In light of the flesh being opposed to the spread of the Gospel, I want to focus on the seed sown "among thorns." Here's the Lord's interpretation of what that means, taken from **Mark 4:18, 19:** *Now these are the ones sown among thorns; they are the ones who hear the word, and the cares of this world, the deceitfulness of riches, and the desires for other things entering in choke the word, and it becomes unfruitful.* Do you see the tragic story here?

Here is a believer who apparently starts off well. But something begins to slowly eat away at his devotion to the Lord. The *"cares of this world"* enter in. What could they be? Perhaps nothing more than paying bills, establishing a stable career, taking care of the family. Not bad things at all, just normal cares. Then there is *"the deceitfulness of riches."* "If only I had more, I would be set for life," we reason. We look around and notice that the Joneses drive a nicer car than we do; they live in a fancier house than we do. Oh, if only we had what they have, how much better we would be. Perhaps we are spending too much of our time and effort doing "church" work, and not enough thought and effort in getting ahead in life. So, being a witness for Christ begins to fade in the shadows while "making it big" becomes the focus.

Then there are *"the desires for other things."* These may not be connected to the desire for riches at all. These desires may be for more acceptable pursuits, such as, more education, more time to relax and enjoy your hobbies, or maybe sightseeing, or traveling (a nice cruise sounds exciting). As with the cares of this life, these are not in and of themselves bad things. They are simply things that have a tendency to "choke the word." No wonder the writer of Hebrews admonishes us to *"lay aside every* **weight**, *and the sin which* **so easily** *ensnares us"* (12:1).

The flesh does not like to be inconvenienced, does not like sacrifice, does not enjoy interruptions (especially in the middle of your favorite television program or football game), and is not partial to being thought of as a weird person who is too religious. So, the natural tendency of man—the Christian man included—is to shy away from what may be viewed as fanaticism and to settle for what is more normal. The flesh loves "normal" and "average." Stop and think, though, that *average* is the best of the bad and the worse of the good. Do you really want to be *that*?

Well Meaning Fellow Believers

These are fellow Christians who may advise you not to be so heavenly minded that you are of no earthly use. They are concerned for you. They don't want you to be too fanatical. These may be very loving family members. They mean well and they think they are right in giving such advice.

Of course, there are believers whom I consider fanatical in an unhealthy way. They can't hold a job. They offend unbelievers and believers alike by their crude mannerisms. They are often very disorganized in their personal lives, and jump from one "urgent" thing to another. In a word, they are often undependable, irrational and closed-minded to any counsel at all.

I do not put dedicated Bible disciples in that same category, but many others do—dumping all zealous religious people into one pile and labeling it "fanatics." That's unfortunate, but to be expected. It was true in Bible times and it is true today. I find, however, that the problem is not that committed Christians are "too heavenly minded that they are of no earthly use." I believe the much greater—and therefore, the more serious— problem is that far too many Christians (perhaps as many as ninety percent) are too earthly minded that they are of little heavenly use!

Listen to the caring advice of these well meaning fellow believers; consider what they say, but take your final direction from the Word of God, not from the natural wordly advice of those who may not be as committed as they should be themselves.

333

Unsaved Religious People

Few people are more difficult to reach and to win to Christ than religious folks—especially those who are certain that they are right with God. For them to believe the Gospel— which dispels any and all merit attached to one's good deeds—they must admit they've been wrong. That is a hard pill to swallow, especially if such an one is a parent or grandparent who has taught you wrongly "for all those years."

Some of the most ardent persecutors of soul winners who are clear on the Gospel are faithful church attenders who are steeped in their own self-righteousness. Expect their opposition, but do not retaliate with anything but loving concern.

Unsaved Anti-Religious People

These are the ones from whom you most expect severe criticism and persecution. The pages of the New Testament are full of such militant, antagonistic persecution. Don't let it deter you in faithfully following Christ and proclaiming His Gospel. Some of the most memorable experiences I've ever had in witnessing have been with those who were blasphemous and cursing at the beginning of our conversations, but who melted under the sound of the wonderful news of salvation by grace. So don't assume that folks like this cannot be reached. They certainly can be, and God may bring them across your path to be the instrument of winning them, or of at least planting the Gospel seed in their hearts.

Believers who are Convicted by Your Commitment to Christ

This is the most bewildering opposition of all. You would think that other believers who are challenged by your committed life would long to have what you have, but often the opposite is true. They may envy your peace and joy, and your upbeat attitude, but they will also realize that to have what you have would cost them too much. So, instead of joining you in your great adventure, they try to drag you down to their level. If they can get you to compromise your principles then your frailty will be obvious to all and they will feel more comfortable in their own low-level Christian existence. Someone pointed out that there are two kinds of Christians. There's *the thermometer Christian* who adapts to the spiritual temperature around him. Then there is *the thermostat Christian* who sets the spiritual temperature. Be a thermostat Christian and don't allow carnal, fleshly Christians to bring you down to their levels.

Flawed Theologies

One of the most subtle forms of "opposition" to the true Gospel of God's amazing grace will enter your life through what I call *flawed theologies*. I'll mention just a few.

First, there is the school of theology known as *Arminianism*, named after James Arminius. Most Arminians are not even aware that they are such. They belong to churches that may teach that salvation is by grace, but it can be lost if one falls into sin or doesn't produce sufficient good works. Such teaching is really a salvation by works that comes in by the back door rather than upfront. Some of these dear folks have never even heard of Arminius, yet their doctrinal beliefs stem from him.

On the positive side of Arminianism is the frequent emphasis on the need to get the "gospel" to the ends of the earth, but the gospel they proclaim is too often a mixture of grace plus works, which is not the Gospel at all. Their zeal sometimes springs from their belief that if they do not fervently serve the Lord they may end up being lost in the end.

There is no certainty of salvation in such churches. The best they can do is to "hope" they will be saved when their lives come to an end. This theology would rob you of your assurance of salvation, would kill any joy spinging from a know-so salvation, and would pervert your message severely. Stay clear of it.

Secondly, there is *extreme Calvinism*, named after John Calvin, though Calvin himself did not believe all that those who bear his name adhere to. By *extreme* Calvinism I refer to those who rigidly hold to what is usually called *The Five Points of Calvinism*. One of those points teaches that Christ did not die for the whole world, but only for the elect (the group whom God has chosen without any consideration at all of man's response). We've already shown from Scripture that Christ *"tasted death for every man"* (Hebrews 2:9), that His death was the propitiation (satisfaction) for our sins, *"and not for ours only but also for the whole world"* (First John 2:2), and that God gave His only begotten Son because He loved **the world**, not just a few out of the world (John 3:16).

There are other problems with some of the remaining *Five Points*, but this belief in "limited atonement" can be deadly as far as your serious involvement in world evangelization is concerned. If Christ did not die for all, then there is no reason to go to all. The extreme Calvinist says, "Oh, yes, there is a reason to go. He commanded us to do it." What an odd command if God's heart of love only extends to a relative few.

The Bible's Gospel invitations would be misleading and hypocritical if Jesus did not provide salvation for all. The last invitation of Scripture, found in **Revelation 22:17**, is: *And the Spirit and the bride say, "Come!" And let him who thirsts come. And whoever desires, let him take the water of life freely.* Are we to believe that the only spiritually thirsty people in the world are the elect, and that they are the only ones who desire salvation? Some say, yes, that is true. What then are we to make of Jesus' own invitation: *Come to Me all you who labor and are heavy laden, and I will give you rest* (Matthew 11:28). Surely there are millions who "labor and are heavy laden" who would respond to the Gospel invitation if they only heard and understood it. *Anyone* who fits the description of one who labors and is heavy laden, is invited to come. That surely involves *most* of humanity.

There is also the view (imbedded in this extreme view of things) that whomever God wants to save He will save, and nothing anyone does is going to change it. Taking the Gospel to the lost, praying for them, reasoning with them, persuading them (as Paul the apostle and others did repeatedly) does not change a thing. One of the most popular contemporary proponents of this extreme view even preached a sermon in which he emphasized that prayer does not really change anything.

I think you can see that such a theological position can be a major hindrance to the spread of the Gospel. If you embraced such a doctrine and were consistent in following it through to its logical end (and not many do), it would be deadening to your personal zeal for the Lord. It may appeal to the intellect, but do not allow yourself to be sucked into it. It could take years before you would recover, if you ever would recover.

Here's an extremely valuable principle to remember when weighing the pros and cons of any theological view. Mark it well and never forget it: If in order to embrace a theological system you must ignore or twist certain portions of Scripture to make them "fit" your adopted position, you had better drop that position in a hurry. It doesn't matter if you are investigating Arminianism, Calvinism, or any other isms, *you don't have to manipulate Scripture if you are letting the Scripture **alone** be your guide!*

For Personal Reflection and Application

❖ Look carefully at the context—verses 17–32—of Acts 20:24: *"But none of these things move me; nor do I count my life dear to myself, so that I may finish my race with joy, and the ministry which I received from the Lord Jesus, to testify to the gospel of the grace of God."* Ask yourself, "Would I have been moved by similar hardships, conflicts, tribulations or afflictions? How much would it take to stop me in my quest to obey Christ's command to preach the Gospel to every creature?"

❖ What do you think would be the most difficult type of opposition for you to deal with as you witness for Christ?

❖ What can you do to properly handle obstacles that come into your life to hinder the spread of the Gospel through you?

The deepest of all convictions settled upon the heart of Lance Latham within a year after his conversion to Christ. He knew with unshakeable faith that he had now discovered the message that could answer every need of a thirsty and lost world. The message was grace – grace for salvation, and grace for living.

Lance: a Testimony of Grace
by Dave Breese

In God's school, the teachers must be masters of the art of holiness.... An unholy ministry would be the derision of the world and a dishonor to God. *Be ye clean, who bear the vessels of the Lord!*

Charles H. Spurgeon

21

Your Power

Fortunately for us, the task of reaching and winning the lost to Christ does not depend on us alone. If it were true that the eternal salvation of the lost depended upon me, I'm afraid I would have ended up in a mental ward a long time ago. The thought of the destiny of eternal souls resting solely in my fickle hands would be too great of a burden to bear. But some maintain that the salvation of souls does not depend on any human involvement at all. If that is so, then we should remove much of what we find in Scripture.

A few Bible examples should make it clear that world evangelization is a partnership between God and His willing child. Both are necessary. Paul, for instance, refers to such a partnership in **First Corinthians 3:6–9:** *I planted, Apollos watered, but God gave the increase. Now he who plants and he who waters are one* (equal)*, and each one will receive his own reward according to his own labor. For we are God's fellow workers; you are God's field, you are God's building.*

Please note that the one who plants the Gospel seed and the one who waters are seen as equals before God. Perhaps you have spread the seed of the Gospel far and wide and have seen little or no results. Someone comes behind you and wins people to the Lord regularly. Do not get discouraged if you see little results. Keep in mind that very few people trust in Christ the first time they hear the Gospel. It normally takes several or many exposures to the message before they place their faith in Him. So the seed sower and the one watering the seed are equally essential.

More than that, though, is the fact that we are *"fellow workers with God"* in this matter of sowing and reaping. He alone is capable of producing the new birth in one who believes in Christ. We are God's instruments to make the message known—to plant and water the seed, but He is the Producer of Spiritual Life.

God, in His goodness, has provided means by which we may be empowered to perform the task of world evangelization, reaching folks one-by-one. No child of God can ever say, "I didn't have the proper tools to witness or to win others to Christ." God has seen to it that everyone of us can be enabled if we are *willing* to be.

First, He has Provided the Holy Spirit

I want to draw your attention to the Spirit's ministry to the lost world, and then to the believer.

To the lost world His primary ministry is that of conviction. **John 16:7–11** describes it: *Neverthless I tell you the truth. It is to your advantage that I go away; for if I do not go away, the Helper will not come to you; but if I depart, I will send Him to you. And when He has come, He will convict* (persuade) *the world of sin, and of righteousness, and of judgment: of sin, because they do no believe in Me; of righteousness, because I go to My Father and you see Me no more; of judgment, because the ruler of this world is judged.*

Notice three areas in which the Holy Spirit convicts mankind. First, He convicts the unbelieving world of its sin of unbelief in Him. Secondly, He persuades the unbelievers that they need His righteousness. Thirdly, He convinces them that judgment is certain to come.

If we are going to be in step with the Holy Spirit in our witnessing endeavors, we need to emphasize the very same truths about which He is convicting the world. He is not primarily convicting the unbelievers of the world of their sins (plural), such as, cursing, adultery, lying, or stealing. He convicts of THE sin which condemns them—unbelief (John 3:18). Yet, how often I've heard speakers (mostly so-called evangelists) hammer away on sins instead of the one and only sin that leads to hell.

By the same token—as I have previously emphasized, we need to press home the unbeliever's need for God's righteousness which only comes through belief in Christ.

Finally, it is our responsibility to remind unbelievers that if they die in their unbelief they will be judged by God, and be separated from Him forever.

Another practical and encouraging lesson to be learned from the Holy Spirit's convicting work is that when we do witness, He has already been busy doing *His* job; we are not in this alone. He has been our forerunner to prepare the way. Isn't that good to know?

Then there is the Holy Spirit's ministry in and through the believer. Christ promised that when the Holy Spirit would come *"He will testify of Me....and He will glorify Me"* (John 15:26; 16:14). When Jesus left His final marching orders to the disciples, as recorded in **Luke 24:48, 49**, He said, *You are witnesses of these things. Behold, I send the Promise of My Father upon you; but tarry in the city of Jerusalem until you are endued with power from on high.*

That promise was the Holy Spirit Himself. Why were they to be endued with His power? What did He expect them to accomplish? We go to **Acts 1:8** to find out: *But you shall receive power when the Holy Spirit has come upon you; and you shall be witnesses to Me in Jerusalem, and in all Judea and Samaria, and to the end of the earth.*

Empowered to witness! That's it. Not empowered to show off so-called spiritual gifts; not empowered to impress others. Empowered to take the Gospel "to the end of the earth." Child of God, you are in this awesome business of soul winning with God's power working in and through you. You are an important key in reaching the world for Christ. Trust Him to work in and through you.

Secondly, God has Given us His Word

The Word of God is "the sword of the Spirit" (Ephesians 6:17). God's Word is the Spirit's weapon, and we are to "take" it, Ephesians says. There is real power in the Bible. **Hebrews 4:12** states: *For the Word of God is living and powerful, and sharper than any two–edged sword, piercing even to the division of soul and spirit, and of joints and marrow, and is a discerner of the thoughts and intents of the heart.* I would say that's pretty powerful, and certainly sharp enough to pierce through a man's hardered heart. Notice these further Scriptures on the power and effectiveness of God's Word.

Jeremiah 23:28, 29: *"The prophet who has a dream, let him* *tell a dream; and he who has My word, let him speak My word faithfully. What is the chaff to the wheat?" says the Lord. "Is not My word like a fire?" says the Lord, "and like a hammer that breaks the rock in pieces."*

Romans 10:17: *So then faith comes by hearing and hearing by the word of God.*

First Peter 1:23–25: *Having been born again, not of corruptible seed but of incorruptible, through the word of God which lives and abides forever, because "all flesh is as grass, and all the glory of man as the flower of the grass. The grass withers, and its flower falls away, but the word of the Lord endures forever." Now this is the word which by the gospel was preached to you.*

In R. A. Torrey's classic little book, *How to Bring Men to Christ*, he said this about using God's Word in our witnessing endeavors: *We must know how to use the Bible to show men their need of a Savior, to show them Jesus as the Savior they need, to show them how to make this Savior their own Savior, and to meet difficulties that stand in the way of their accepting Christ.*

But there is still more God has done to enable us to reach others for Christ. Consider, thirdly—

Thirdly, God has Given Us the Privilege of Prayer

God commands us to pray for all men with the intent that they would be saved. **First Timothy 2:1-6** is a powerful passage that directs us to do so: *Therefore I exhort first of all that supplication, prayers, intercessions, and giving of thanks be made for all men, for kings and for all who are in authority, that we may live a quiet and peaceable life in all godliness and reverence. For this is good and acceptable in the sight of God our Savior, who desires all men to be saved and to come to the knowledge of the truth. For there is one God and one Mediator between God and men, the Man Christ Jesus, who gave Himself a ransom for all, to be testified in due time* (at the right time).

Please note that we are to pray for *all* men for God desires that *all* men be saved, because Christ is the ransom for *all!*

Not only are we to pray for all men, but *we are to pray specifically for God's servants.* **Colossains 4:2-4** says, *Continue earnestly in prayer, being vigilant in it with thanksgiving;*

meanwhile praying also for us, that God would open for us a door for the word, to speak the mystery of Christ, for which I (Paul) *am also in chains.* Then **Ephesians 6:18–20** gives a similar admonition: *Praying always with all prayer and supplication in the Spirit, being watchful to this end with all perseverence and supplication for all the saints—and for me, that utterance may be given to me, that I may open my mouth boldly to make known the mystery of the gospel, for which I am an ambassador in chains; that in it I may speak boldly, as I ought to speak.*

We are also to pray for the lost. Paul the apostle is a great example to follow in this matter of praying for the lost. **Romans 10:1** expresses the longings of his heart for his own people, Israel. *Brethren, my heart's desire and prayer to God for Israel is that they may be saved.* In **Romans 9:1–3** he is even more explicit in saying, *I tell the truth in Christ, I am not lying, my conscience also bearing me witness in the Holy Spirit, that I have great sorrow and continual grief in my heart. For I could wish that I myself were accursed from Christ for my brethren, my kinsmen according to the flesh, who are Israelites....*

I should insert a word of warning here that we should only pray for the lost in a way that is in keeping with the revealed Word of God. For instance, it would be unscriptural to pray, "Lord, *make* so-and-so believe in Christ." God does not *make* anyone believe. We are not robots. We can pray for their situation, for God to send other messengers, but not that God would *force* them to believe in Christ.

We are commanded to be in a constant attitude of prayer, which would certainly include praying for witnessing opportunities, for wisdom, for conviction upon those to whom we witness, for clarity, for boldness, and for glory to come to God through our efforts. **First Thessalonians 5:17** tells us to, *Pray without ceasing.* And in **Luke 10:2** Christ instructed His disciples to pray for more laborers. *Then He said to them, "The harvest truly is great, but the laborers are few; therefore pray the Lord of the harvest to send out laborers into His harvest."*

I strongly urge you to read the following passages on prayer. As you do, realize how tremendous God's prayer promises are. We take them so lightly and act upon them so infrequently! Luke 11:5–13, 18:1–8, John 15:7, and First John 5:14,15.

Fourthly, Faith is Essential in Soul Winning

If you do not believe God can use you to influence others for Christ, then He more than likely won't. If you cannot trust Him to work through your stammering lips to make the Gospel clear to others, then you will always be on the sidelines while others are blessed by Him to win the lost—simply because they rely upon His power and wisdom to get the job done.

There is a striking passage in **Matthew 13:53–58** that records Jesus returning to His own country and not being received by the locals because they reasoned, *"Is not this the carpenter's son? Is not His mother called Mary? And His brothers James, Joses, Simon, and Judas? And His sisters, are they not all with us? Where then did this Man get all these things? So they were offended at Him.* (vss.55–57a). Jesus followed their comments with His now famous statement that *"a prophet is not without honor except in his own country and in his own house"* (vs. 57).

The concluding statement of the passage is the shocker: *And He did not do many mighty works there because of their unbelief.* Notice the cause and effect principle in operation here. You can trace this principle occurring all throughout the Scriptures. Imagine, the creature's lack of faith hindering the Creator's actions, but that's exactly what happened. Those who believe that God never does anything in reponse to man's faith or actions should read this verse every day for at least a year!

Perhaps the clearest verse on the importance of faith in our Christian lives is **Hebrews 11:6:** *But without faith it is impossible to please Him, for he who comes to God must believe that He is, and that He is a rewarder of those who diligently seek Him.*

The following quote from pastor Jim Cymbala ties in beautifully with the thought expressed in the above verse. He said, *If we do not yearn and pray and expect God to stretch out His hand and do the supernatural, it will not happen. We must give Him room to operate.* So as you go your way to share the Gospel, make sure your dependence—for that's what faith is—is in the Lord: His strength, His wisdom, His everything.

Fifthly, Obedience Brings Added Blessing and Fruit

I don't know why we think we can casually float through our

lives day by day with little or no thought of the condition of the unsaved, and then seriously wonder why God doesn't use us more than He does.

There is another strong Biblical principle that has a direct bearing on how much God uses us, especially in this area of soul winning. This principle is the first cousin to the cause and effect principle. It is the sowing and reaping principle. What you sow is what you reap; how much you sow determines the degree to which you reap.

Consider these verses.

Second Corinthians 9:6: *But this I say: He who sows sparingly will also reap sparingly, and he who sows bountifully will also reap bountifully.* In its context, the verse is speaking of giving and receiving, but the principle applies to any and all areas of the Christian's life. If you only proclaim the Gospel on rare occasions, you will rarely win anyone to Christ. If you only pass out one or two Gospel tracts a year, you shouldn't expect any responses from such a feeble effort. On the other hand, if you are consistently sharing the Gospel then you can expect results. Sometimes those results will be when someone else draws in the net and reaps what you sowed, but the reaping will come—that's the important thing, not who gets credit for it. You do the sowing; God guarantees the crop.

Here's another verse.

Galatians 6:7: *Do not be decieved, God is not mocked; for whatever a man sows, that he will also reap.* You always reap the *kind* of crop you plant. If you sow sin, you reap the results of sin. If you sow the spiritual seed of the Gospel, you reap in the spiritual salvation of souls. But it is also true that you also reap more than you sow. In the natural realm, a farmer plants seeds, but when harvest time comes, he will reap far more than just the seeds he planted. So it is in sowing the Gospel. The harvest is always of the same kind, but more than was sown—whether you are in on the reaping or someone else is, the harvest will come.

Finally, there is **Psalm 126:5, 6** where it says: *Those who sow in tears shall reap in joy. He who continually goes forth weeping, bearing seed for sowing, shall doubtless come again with rejoicing, bringing his sheaves with him.* I love the word "doubtless" in the verse. It is certain that if we sow God's way, with a broken heart over the lost, we will *doubtless* come again bringing our *sheaves* (not seeds) with us. Praise the Lord. One fruitful soul winner said about this verse, "Winners of souls are first weepers for souls!"

Finally, It's Helpful to Surround Yourself with Other Praying, Witnessing Christians

They will provide the encouragement, the renewal you will often need from the toils of spiritual battle. Two passages bear this out. **First Corinthians 15:33, 34** states: *Do not be deceived: Evil company corrupts good habits. Awake to righteousness, and do not sin: for some do not have the knowledge of God. I speak this to your shame.* Do you sense the connection between having the wrong kind of companions and some not having a knowledge of the Lord? The opposite is also true: surround yourself with godly, soul winning believers and, guess what? You will also be strengthened in your walk to be like them.

The other verse is **Proverbs 12:26** where it says, *The righteous should choose his friends carefully, for the way of the wicked leads them astray.* Love all people, be friendly to everyone you meet, but make sure your closest friends are Christlike in every way. Spend time with those with a godly burden for the lost; go witnessing with them; learn from them; emulate their lifestyle. If you do not have those kind of friends to choose from, ask God to bring them into your life. Meanwhile you be the godly person from whom others may draw strength and encouragement. There is real power in that kind of companionship.

For Personal Reflection and Application

❖ What can you do to be assured that you are being empowered by the Holy Spirit as you witness?

❖ God has said that His Word will not return to Him void, but shall accomplish what He pleases (Isaiah 55:11). How do you think such a promise might apply to your witnessing?

❖ Does it matter to you whether you *feel* God has someone "prepared" for your witness? Why or why not?

❖ Is prayer a vital part of your daily life? Do you consistently spend uninterrupted time praying to the Lord, especially about your influence on a lost world?

The Gospel is not a
secret to be hoarded
but a story to be
heralded. Too many
Christians are stuffing
themselves with
Gospel blessings,
while millions have
never had a taste.

Vance Havner

I have but one passion—
it is He, it is He alone.
The world is the field,
and the field is the world;
and henceforth that country
shall be my home where
I can be most used in
winning souls for Christ.

Count Nicholas Ludwig von Zinzendorf
Moravian Leader (1700-1760)

22

A Final Challenge

Fishing for Men as a Lifelong Priority

There are several worthwhile things to live and die for such as family, freedom, lifting up the destitute, caring for the infirm, teaching the next generation proper values and morals—these are certainly commendable ways in which to invest one's life. However, according to the Bible there are only two things on earth that are eternal in nature: the Word of God (Matthew 24:35) and people—everyone is going to live forever somewhere. So if you, as God's child, want to invest your own life in that which has eternal value, you cannot do better than to saturate yourself with God's Word and then pass it on to people.

Paul the apostle displayed his excellent 20/20 spiritual vision when God inspired him to write **Second Corinthians 4:16–18**: *Therefore we do not lose heart. Even though our outward man is perishing, yet the inward man is being renewed day by day. For our light affliction, which is but for a moment, is working for us a far more exceeding and eternal weight of glory, while we do not look at the things which are seen, but at the things which are not seen. For the things which are seen are temporary, but the things which are not seen are eternal.*

If you devote your life to the Lord Jesus Christ and the spreading of the Good News concerning Him, you will be doing exactly what God wants you to do. Nothing could ever possibly be more fulfilling or rewarding than that.

But in light of all that you now know about the Gospel and the importance of reaching the world with its message, if you decide to live for yourself—*your* dreams and plans, *your* ambitions, *your* own goals—I want to leave you with one more passage of Scripture. I hope you will take it to heart.

Deliver those who are drawn toward death, and hold back those stumbling to the slaughter. If you say, "Surely we did not know this." Does not He who weighs the hearts consider it? He who keeps your soul, does He not know it? And will He not render to each man according to His deeds? (Proverbs 24:11, 12).

Christians sometime tell unbelievers that "the road to hell is paved with good intentions." The point they are making is that no one is ever saved because they *intended* to be. Salvation is determined by what one *does* with Christ, not by what they might do one day.

The same principle applies to how a Christian lives his or her life. Good intentions do not get the job done. When we *all* stand before the Judgment Seat of Christ where *each one* of us will give an account of himself to God, we will be judged "according to our deeds"—not our intentions (Romans 14:10–12; First Corinthians 3:11–15; Second Corinthians 5:10). Too many believers plan to really get serious about serving the Lord *when* they get through college, *when* they know enough to adequately defend their faith, *when* they are financially secure, *when* the kids are grown and gone, *when* they retire, and on and on it goes.

Meanwhile people all around us are lost and being *"drawn toward death and...stumbling to the slaughter."* What good are future intentions in view of the present condition and destiny of those without Christ. What real, lasting value is there in being proficient in some area of endeavor if God's revealed purpose for you is shoved to the background of your life?

God's urgent reminder in **First Corinthians 15:34** should serve as a constant wakeup call for all of us: *Awake to righteousness, and do not sin for some do not have the knowledge of God. I speak this to your shame.*

Would you consider making the following your sincere, heartfelt prayer of commitment?

Dear Lord, I belong to You. You have saved me from an eternal hell, and I thank You with all of my heart. I know You have left me here to be Your ambassador—a witness for the Lord Jesus Christ. I want to be the best witness I can possibly be. And so I surrender all that I am and all that I ever hope to be to You, for You to do with me whatever You please. I do not care how or where You may lead me, or what sacrifices I may be called upon to make for Your sake; only let me be the best fisher of men possible through Your power and grace. My surrender to You and Your will is absolute and without any reservations of any kind. I make this surrender for Jesus' sake.

Signed _____   Date _____

God's Kind of Burden

Burdened enough to pray...for hours on end if need be;
Burdened enough to speak to any and all around me;
Burdened enough to speak until the light
breaks through upon one's soul;

Burdened enough to study until the answers are
found and the Scriptures are memorized
that will answer the *heart* needs of people;

Burdened enough to go out of my way in time,
effort, transportation, and money
to reach someone for Christ;

Burdened enough to listen to the burdens
of others and to lift those burdens to
the Lord for supply;

Burdened enough to count my life
as nothing in order that Christ
might be my all-in-all;

Burdened enough to accept the drudgery,
misery and disappointments of life as it is,
in order to gain the joy of communion
with Christ as He is!

I do not care where I live or what
hardships I must go through,
just so I can win souls for Christ.

When I sleep, I dream of it; as soon
as I awake I think of the great
needs and the ripened harvest.

All my desire is for the salvation of souls.
There is so much to do and so few to do it.

"Lord, make me first, last, and always
a soul winner."

RAS

For Personal Reflection and Application

❖ If you have accepted this Final Challenge, what changes can or should you make in your life to make you an effective witness for the Lord? Don't overlook such things as analyzing those habits or interests that eat up a lot of your time even though they may not be "bad" things—hobbies, television, video games, computers, magazines, motor vehicles, sports, career, or just "hanging out" with friends. **Hebrews 12:1** tells us to *"lay aside every <u>weight</u> and the <u>sin</u> which so <u>easily</u> ensnares us, and let us run with endurance the race that is set before us"*—a race that has been set before us *by God.*

❖ If you did *not* accept this Final Challenge, and you have not made such a commitment aleady to the Lord, what excuses do you expect to give to Jesus Christ when you face Him? Do you think they will stand up under His piercing gaze?

Recommendations

Here are some recommended books that will help you in understanding the Gospel and challenge you to share it with others far and wide. Please realize that my recommendation of a book does not mean that I necessarily agree with all that's in it, especially the books dealing with evangelism and soul winning. I may recommend a book because of its challenging nature; its ability to motivate the reader to action. I may not approve whole–heartedly with all of the methods used or even all the doctrine that may be advanced.

Books on the Doctrines of Salvation and the Gospel

What Happened to the Word Believe? Donald H. Bunge
    Self-Published. Omaha, NE.

The Gospel Under Siege. Zane C. Hodges. Redencion Viva.
    Dallas, TX.

Salvation—Crystal Clear, and *Salvation—Crystal Clear, II.*
    Curtis Hutson. Sword of the Lord. Publishers.
    Murfreesboro, TN.

The Two Gospels. Lance B. Latham. AWANA.
    Rolling Meadows, IL.

Salvation by Grace, and *Studies on the Doctrine of Redemption.*
    J. Irvin Overholtzer. Child Evangelism Fellowship.
    Grand Rapids, MI.

So Great Salvation. Charles C. Ryrie. Victor Books.
    Wheaton, IL.

So Great Salvation, and *Shall Never Perish.* J. F. Strombeck.
    Get all five of Strombeck's books if at all possible.
    The others are *Grace and Truth* (on John's Gospel),
    First the Rapture, and *Disciplined By Grace.*
    They are all excellent.

Confident in Christ and *You Can Be Sure.* Robert N. Wilkin.
    The Grace Evangelical Society. Irving, TX.

Books on Evangelism and Soul Winning

Profiles in Evangelism: 46 Biographical Sketches of Great
Men of God. Fred Barlow. Sword of the Lord
Publishers. Murfreesboro, TN.

True Evangelism: Winning Souls Through Prayer.
Lewis Sperry Chafer. Zondervan Publishing House.
Grand Rapids, MI.

The Art of Fishing for Men. Percy B. Crawford. Moody Press.
Chicago, IL.

The Stranger on the Road and *And Beginning at Moses.*
John R. Cross. Good Seed International, Inc.
Alberta, Canada.

Hand-Gathered Fruit. Edward Last. Out of print.

Building on Firm Foundations (3 volumes). Trevor McIlwain.
New Tribes Mission. Sanford, FL.

The Golden Path to Successful Personal Soul Winning, and
Soul Winner's Fire. John R. Rice. Sword of the Lord
Publishers. Murfreesboro, TN.

How–To Book on Personal Evangelism. R. Larry Moyer.
Kregel Publications. Grand Rapids, MI.

The Soul Winner. Charles H. Spurgeon. Zondervan
Publishing House. Grand Rapids, MI.

Handbook of Personal Evangelism. A. Ray Stanford.
Self–Published. Pharr, TX.

How to Work for Christ. R. A. Torrey. Fleming H. Revel.
Westwood, NJ.

Taking Men Alive. Charles Gallaudet Trumbull.
Fleming H. Revel. Westwood, NJ.

Individual Work for Individuals. H. Clay Trumbull.
The International Committe of the YMCA.
New York, NY.

Great Personal Workers. Faris Daniel Whitesell. Moody Press.
Chicago, IL.

Scripture Index

Through Clarity Ministries International Dick frequently publishes
a paper entitled the *Clarity Trumpet,* which is a teaching tool
on various Biblical issues and current trends about
which believers in Christ should be aware.
In fact, some of the material in this book is from past *Trumpets.*
He mails these *Clarity Trumpets* (along with his newsletter) without
charge to those who want it. You may request these items
to be sent to you either via regular mail or email.

Send your request via regular mail to:

CMI
Post Office Box 10
LaGrange, WY 82221

Visit our website at:
www.ClarityMinistries.org

Or email us at:
CMI@ClarityMinistries.org